Henry William Wilberforce

The church and the empires

historical periods

Henry William Wilberforce

The church and the empires
historical periods

ISBN/EAN: 9783743309289

Manufactured in Europe, USA, Canada, Australia, Japa

Cover: Foto ©ninafisch / pixelio.de

Manufactured and distributed by brebook publishing software (www.brebook.com)

Henry William Wilberforce

The church and the empires

THE CHURCH
AND THE EMPIRES

HISTORICAL PERIODS BY

HENRY WILLIAM WILBERFORCE

PRECEDED BY

A MEMOIR OF THE AUTHOR BY J. H. NEWMAN, D.D.

OF THE ORATORY

WITH A PORTRAIT

HENRY S. KING & CO.
65 CORNHILL & 12 PATERNOSTER ROW, LONDON
1874

CONTENTS.

		PAGE
	Memoir of Henry W. Wilberforce	1
I.	*The Formation of Christendom*	17
II.	*Champagny's Roman Empire*	55
III.	*Champagny's Cæsars of the Third Century*	102
IV.	*The Gallican Assembly of 1682*	138
V.	*The Church and Napoleon I.*	184
VI.	*Pius VII. and Napoleon I.*	228
VII.	*Pius VII. at Savona and Fontainebleau*	264

MEMOIR

OF

HENRY W. WILBERFORCE.

HENRY WILLIAM WILBERFORCE, the subject of this Memoir, was the youngest son of William Wilberforce, well known as the friend of Pitt and Member of Parliament for Yorkshire, and still more distinguished for his persevering and successful resistance in Parliament to the Slave Trade and Slavery, and for his high Christian character in a time of general religious declension.

He was born at Clapham on September 22, 1807. When nine years old, he was entrusted to the care of the Reverend John Sargent, the friend and biographer of Henry Martyn, and Rector of Graffham, Sussex, one of whose daughters he eventually married. With Mr. Sargent, who educated him with one of his own sons, he remained till he was fifteen, when he was transferred to the Reverend F. R. Spragge, who took pupils at Little Boundes, near Tunbridge Wells, and had charge of him till the time came for his going to the University. He was entered at Oriel College, Oxford, and came into residence in Michaelmas Term, 1826.

I well recollect my first sight of him, on his presenting himself before the tutors of his college,—when the lectures had to be arranged for the Term, and his place in them, as a Freshman, determined. He was small and timid, shrinking from notice, with a bright face and intelligent eyes. Partly from his name, partly from his appearance, I was at once drawn towards him ; and, as he subsequently told me, he felt a corresponding desire to know me ; and, in a little time, though I was not formally his college tutor, and only had relations with him as with other undergraduates in my lecture room, we became very intimate. He read with me, as his private tutor, during a portion of four long vacations—at Hampstead in 1827, at Nuneham in 1828, at Horsepath in 1829, and in Oriel in 1830. In Michaelmas Term, 1830, he went up for his B.A. examination, and was placed by the examiners in the first class in classics, and in the second in mathematics.

At Oxford he remained after taking his degree of B.A. for several years ; at least to the year 1833, when he gained the Ellerton Theological Prize, and took his Master's degree. His chief associates in his own college during his Oxford residence were, besides his elder brother Robert, and the Reverend R. Hurrell Froude, at that time Fellows and Tutors of Oriel, Mr. Frederic Rogers, now Lord Blachford ; Mr. S. F. Wood, brother to the present Lord Halifax ; Mr. George Ryder, son of the Bishop of Lichfield ; Mr. Robert F. Wilson, at present examining chaplain to the Bishop of Salisbury ; Mr. William Froude, F.R.S. ; and Mr. Thomas Mozley, Rector of Plymptree, Devon. I am not able to name any of his friends outside of his college besides the late Mr. John Rogers, and the present Archbishop Manning, both of Balliol, and Mr., now Sir Thomas, Acland, of Christ Church. He had a large acquaintance in the University, while an undergraduate, in consequence of the interest he took in the University Debating Society, called the Union. Of this Society he was at one time President, and for several years he took a prominent part in its debates. One speech, or rather act, of his, while he occupied the Chair, made a sensation at the time, and remains on the minds of some of his contemporaries even now. In the midst of a debate, a member, I am told, entered under the influence of wine, and began an address to the meeting so incoherent and noisy, and with so ludicrous a mixture of sense and nonsense, as to throw the room into extreme confusion. It seemed hopeless to restore order, when the President rose, and looking round on the members, simply asked, 'Has the noble Lord no friends here?' These words had their effect at once; friends came forward, the offender was removed, and the debate proceeded.

In 1836, after he had left the University, he gained the Deniers Theological Prize by an essay on 'Faith in the Holy Trinity.'

In the same year he took a prominent part in the proceedings at Oxford which followed upon Dr. Hampden's promotion to the Regius Professorship of Divinity.

His talents were of a character to ensure distinction, whether in a University or in a public career. He had a singularly quick apprehension, a clear head, a largeness and sobriety of mind, a readiness in speech, and that sense of humour and power of repartee which makes a man brilliant in conversation and formidable to opponents. But he chose for himself another course. His tastes and habits, his affectionateness, his tenderness of conscience, his love of quiet and the country, his dislike of pomp and display, of routine toil, and of tyrannous obligations, turned him towards a domestic life and the pastoral charge. He liked to be master of his own time and his own movements; and though never idle, whether in mind or body, he had no wish to work under the lash. He used to tell me that it was my doing that he took Orders instead of following the Law. Perhaps it was; we are blind to the future, and are forced to decide, whether for ourselves or for others, according to what seems best at the time being. Certainly he had an oratorical talent so natural and pleasant, so easy, forcible, and persuasive, as to open upon him the prospect of rising to the foremost rank in his profession, had he been a lawyer. On the other hand, the legal disabilities, to which his Anglican Orders subjected him, became a great embarrassment to him when he found himself a Catholic. However, it may reasonably be doubted whether, humanly speaking, he would ever have been a Catholic but for his clerical profession, which, in the studies and enquiries to which it introduced him, served to place his mind and affections in the direction of the Catholic Church. And anyhow, he made an excellent parish minister, with a heart devoted to his Divine Master and to the cure of souls; and his love for his work was ennobled by the prompt obedience with which he gave it up when His Master called upon him for that great sacrifice.

He held successively three parochial cures. First, immediately upon his most happy marriage, which took place on July 24, 1834, he received from the Bishop of Winchester, Dr. Charles Richard Sumner, the perpetual curacy of Bransgore, on the skirts of the New Forest. Here he remained for seven years; then he left it, in the summer of 1841, for the perpetual curacy of Walmer, near Deal, his patron being Archbishop Howley. Lastly, in the autumn of 1843, he was preferred by the Lord Chancellor, at the instance of the Prince Consort, to the well-endowed living of East Farleigh, near Maidstone, which some years previously had been held by his brother Robert.

I have heard various particulars of his earnestness and unweariedness in the discharge of his parochial duties from an intimate friend, who was his partner in them both at Bransgore and Walmer. They are too minute and familiar to put into print; but they are valuable, as coinciding with what I knew of him, and should have expected from him myself. His parsonage itself, in its domestic order, its frugality, its bountiful alms, and its atmosphere of religious reverence and peace, was, as it ought to be, the mainspring and centre of that influence which he exercised upon the people committed to him. To them, and to their needs, temporal and spiritual, he gave himself wholly. He had an almost overpowering sense of the responsibilities which lay upon him as the pastor of a parish; and his habits and ways, his words and deeds, his demeanour, his dress, and his general self-neglect, all in one way or other spoke to my informant of that simplicity of mind and humility which I recognised in him when he was a youth at Oxford.

In all his livings he introduced daily service into his church; at Walmer he had, besides, an evening service for soldiers in hospital; also he addressed himself to the spiritual needs of that fine class of men, the seafaring population of Deal. His activity showed itself in matters ecclesiastical, as well as pastoral. There was no parsonage at Walmer; by an examination of the parish books he was able to ascertain the old glebe which belonged to the living, and he recovered it, together with a house which had been built upon it, for future incumbents. He also took measures for commencing a new church at Lower Walmer, which was built after he left, and, small as were his means, he headed the subscription list with a donation from himself. He had already, when at Bransgore, been instrumental in providing a church for Burley, a neighbouring village; and here too, he succeeded in making a munificent contribution to the building. He had in 1836 gained the prize of two hundred guineas, which had been offered to general competition for an essay on the Parochial System; and he gave this large sum to the fund collected for the new church. At East Farleigh he built a substantial school-house, and here, too, not without taking a part of the cost of it on himself.

A zeal so energetic and vigilant is often met with a jealous resistance on the part of those who are the subjects or witnesses of it, when they belong to the higher or middle classes. At Bransgore, a country district, he was able to act as he thought best, and was rewarded simply by the respect and love of his people. Such a return also followed his pastoral activity both at Walmer and East Farleigh ; but in those places he at certain times had to encounter much opposition in his work ; and then it was found that, gentle and unassuming as he was at first sight and in his ordinary behaviour, and averse to all that was pretentious or overbearing, he had the command of plain words and strong acts when the occasion called for them ; and could (as we all knew he could, who knew him at an earlier date) with fearlessness, directness, and determination speak his own mind and carry out his own views of duty.

It was his confidence, however, in his own ecclesiastical position and claims which alone supported him on such occasions, and the time came when that confidence was shaken. It is not to be supposed that he was an uninterested spectator of the series of events which occurred at Oxford from the year 1841 onwards ; nor was the action of his own mind wanting to bring home those events to himself personally. He had ever accepted the teaching of the standard Anglican divines, strictly confining himself in his conduct within the rules and precedents of the Anglican Church ; but at length he began to have misgivings as to that Church's divine authority and mission, and, as year passed after year, these misgivings increased. At length they became practical difficulties in his course ; and in the autumn of 1849 an accident was the occasion of their ripening into convictions. His parish was visited, year by year, in the hop season by a large influx of Irish from London. The gathering had just commenced in this year, when suddenly there was a fearful outbreak of cholera among these poor people; many were struck down at their work, and lay dead or at death's door in the gardens and barns round about. Being Catholics they could not accept Mr. Wilberforce's services; and the priest who promptly came over to their aid from Tunbridge Wells soon found himself insufficient for the multitude of sick and dying. Several Fathers of the London Oratory came to his assistance, and two nuns of the Good Shepherd from Hammersmith. These, the inmates of the parsonage, regardless of the peril, took into their own house, and supplied to the extent of their power with whatever was needed by their patients. Every act of charity done for our Lord's sake has its reward from Him; and Mr. Wilberforce used to call to mind with deep gratitude that on the day year on which he had received our Lord's servants into his house, he and his, through our Lord's mercy, were received into the everlasting home of the Catholic Church. This event took place on September 15, 1850.

Viewed on its human side, Mr. Wilberforce's conversion may be attributed, on the one hand, to the straightforward logic of a clear mind; on the other, to his intimate profound perception of the unseen world, and of his responsibilities in relation to it. While he was resolute in pursuing his principles to their legitimate issues, he was undaunted in facing those issues, whatever they might be. Religion was to him not knowledge, so much as obedience. The simple question was, as he felt it, not to rid himself of the thousand difficulties speculative and practical, which hem in and confuse our intellect here below, but what was the word and what was the will of Him who gave him a work to do on earth. If that will was plain, it was nothing to the purpose, it was nothing to him, that 'clouds and darkness' closed it in on every side. 'What must I do to be saved?' that was the whole matter with him, as with all serious minds. That there had been a Revelation given from above to man, in order to our eternal salvation, was undeniable; the only point was, what was it? what were its gifts, its promises, its teaching? where were these to be found? how were they to be obtained? His intellect made answer—the more clearly and distinctly the longer he thought upon it—in the Church universally called Catholic, and nowhere else. It, and it alone, carried with it the tokens and notes, the continuity, succession, and claims, of that divine polity which had been founded and formed by the Apostles in the beginning. This, then, was the Fold of Christ, the Ark of Salvation, the Oracle of Truth, and the Anglican communion was no part of it. To this Church he was in consequence bound to betake himself without hesitation or delay, as soon as he had in his intellect a distinct recognition of it. This grave practical conclusion, which ought to be the motive principle of every convert, is signified in the letter which on resigning his living he addressed, with the respectful familiarity due to a friend and relative, to John Bird Sumner, then Archbishop of Canterbury, his diocesan. It ran as follows:—

'Your Grace will not be surprised to learn that I feel myself compelled to request you to accept the resignation of this living. I dare no longer officiate in the Church of England, and feel my individual salvation at stake.

'In taking this step I feel so many heartstrings breaking

that I dare not allow myself to think of the consequences or the cost on earth, either to myself, or to those I love. I have put my hand to the plough, and I must not look back. My own strength is nothing, and I dare not tempt God by presuming He will enable me to stand firm if I subject myself to any temptation which I can avoid. I have, therefore, purposely tried not to think of the pain which I must give to so many who are deservedly dear to me as my own soul.

'There are considerations, which leave me no room to doubt; first, what I should wish a stranger to do were he in my place; secondly, what I should wish to have done were I upon my bed of death; or, thirdly, were I at the judgment-seat of Christ.

'I have, perhaps, said more than I have any right to express to your Grace; but I was going to say, that, among many other bitter remembrances which I am forced to cast aside, the thought of giving pain to yourself, after the many kindnesses which I have received from you, has often forced itself into my mind.

'I can but thank you for your kindness; and yet there is one thing else which I may, and (by God's help) I trust I ever shall continue to do; I mean, to remember you at the Throne of Grace: my prayer must ever be, that He, who has been pleased to call *me*, so deeply unworthy of His grace, may extend the same favour to one so much more meet for it as yourself.

'Believe me, &c., &c.'

There was one among the many severe trials involved in his change of religion, to which time brought no relief.

He had devoted himself, when he became an Anglican clergyman, to the immediate service of God, and had willingly taken upon himself a lifelong ministry; but, while the law of the land refused to regard him, now that he was a Catholic, in any other light, on the other hand in the eyes of Catholics he was a mere layman. He, as many others, in the fulness and maturity of his powers, and with his best years before him, was doomed for life to have no definite place or work in a community which needed such as him so grievously, and to resign himself to the prospect henceforth of running to waste. Henceforth he must look to be a 'pilgrim and stranger' in his own land. He had to give up an honourable post and well-requited services for the almost certainty in time to come of a dull, listless inactivity, or of fitful, precarious employments. However, he was not the man to resign himself without a struggle to a lot as forlorn as it was unnatural. He had counted the cost; his ordination might be invalid, but his self-dedication was his own—hearty, deliberate, irreversible. After a season of retirement and repose, such as became him after the great crisis in his history, he put himself at the disposal of those who seemed likely to make the most use of him. In the spring of 1852 he accepted the office of secretary to the Catholic Defence Association, then lately founded in Dublin, under the auspices, I believe, of the present Cardinal Cullen, on occasion of that notorious 'Ecclesiastical Titles' Act, which has recently been repealed. Though he remained in Ireland only two or three years in this capacity, still he was able, on various occasions, even in that short sojourn, greatly to edify the born Catholics, among whom he found himself, by the singleminded zeal and the devout spirit which he displayed as a convert to their faith.

Indeed, his very presence preached, though he had no ecclesiastical position; for it spoke of a man who, at the call of Christ, had left his nets and fishing, and all his worldly surroundings, to follow Him. As to instances in point, it is scarcely to be expected that, at this distance of time, any record of them should remain. One, however, by a happy accident, I am able to recall, in the words of a good parish priest of County Clare, who, on hearing of his death, thus wrote to one of Mr. Wilberforce's sons:—

'The pecuniary aid I got from your esteemed parents, and from other powerful friends through them, the countenance, advice, and encouragement they gave me about twenty years ago, when four proselytising schools were erected in my parish to pervert my poor people, enabled me, next to God's grace, to succeed in keeping the Faith unbroken and flourishing. We have now entire religious peace. My parishioners all know as well as I do, the benefits your father and mother conferred on the religion of this parish. They sent me a valuable Remonstrance; and, every Festival since, the people have Benediction of the Most Holy Sacrament; and, please God, I will without delay have all my parishioners at a Requiem Mass, offered up for the repose of the soul of their friend and benefactor. The most of them will remember his kindness, and his earnest impressive exhortations to hold fast by their old faith.'

Also, I myself remember a conversation he had with me about one of his charitable acts in a distant part of

Ireland where he had land. He gave a piece of ground for a presbytery, and thereby was the means of gaining for the people a resident priest, whereas hitherto only an occasional Mass was said upon the property.

But these are only accidental records of many good works, forgotten except by Him who inspired them.

From 1854 to 1863 he was the proprietor and editor of the 'Catholic Standard,' afterwards called the 'Weekly Register.' In this, as in all his undertakings, he was actuated by an earnest desire to promote the interests of religion, though at the sacrifice of his own.

In December, 1859, he went with his family to Rome for the winter, and was received with much affection at a private audience by the Holy Father, who had known his brother Robert. On going a second time to the Vatican, after an attack of Roman fever, his Holiness, remarking the traces of illness upon his countenance, gave him his blessing, specially for his recovery. That night the usual access of fever did not take place, and he slept well; and this improvement, which continued for some time, he always attributed to the Apostolic blessing.

He visited Rome again in June, 1862, on occasion of the Canonisations. During that time he sent home many interesting letters, which were published in the 'Weekly Register,' descriptive of the proceedings which accompanied the sacred solemnity.

After his retirement from the management of the 'Weekly Register' he was for the future free from the duties of any formal occupation. Among the employments of these latter years has been the writing of his articles in the 'Dublin Review,' some of which are to follow this Memoir. In 1871 he became sensible of a serious diminution of strength; and, on his proceeding in October to consult his medical friend, a voyage to Jamaica was proposed to him as a means of his recovery. Trying as it was in itself at his age to go so far from home, such advice was not without its recommendations to him. It had been the dream of his life to see the tropics; and now in this unexpected way that dream was to be fulfilled. He set out with a strong hope that his health would receive real benefit both from the voyage and from a climate so genial and so new to him. Yet his hope was tempered by those dominant sentiments which, I believe, never for an instant were absent from his mind. He wrote from Malvern to her who had for so long a spell of years made him so bright a home, 'May God keep His arm over you for good, and unite us hereafter in His kingdom! Coming here, and feeling how much older I am, makes me feel "the time is short." The generations of men are like "the leaves," as the Greek poet says; but our Lord Jesus is the Resurrection and the Life.'

His youngest daughter accompanied him to Jamaica, where, though a stranger, he was received with the warmest hospitality. In his own words, he was received like a brother by the Chief Justice, Sir John Lucie Smith, on his first landing, and, through the winter up in the hills, by Judge Ker. He was amazed and enchanted by the beauty of the island, and for a time he really did gain good by going thither. This improvement, however, did not last; he returned home in July, 1872, to suffer a gradual but visible decay all through the following winter; and, when

Easter came, eternity was close upon him. He had ever lived in the presence of God; and I suppose it was this that specially struck one of his Jamaica friends, who has written, on the news of his death, 'I looked upon him as one of the most holy of men.' Indeed, in these last months his very life was prayer and meditation. No one did I ever know who more intimately realised the awfulness of the dark future than he. His sole trust, hope, and consolation lay in his clear, untroubled faith. All was dark except the great truths of the Catholic religion; but though they did not lighten the darkness, they bridged over for him the abyss. He calmly spoke to me of the solemn, unimaginable wonders which he was soon to see. Now he sees them. Each of us in his own turn will see them soon. May we be as prepared to see them as he was!

With his wife and children round him, and taking their part by turns at his bedside in a perpetual round of prayers, he died, emphatically, in peace on Wednesday morning, April 23, aged 65. He was buried on the 29th in the churchyard, close by his residence, of the Dominican Fathers, who had so carefully attended him during his long illness. Those kind Fathers had said Mass several times a week at an altar in his own house through the winter, by leave obtained from Dr. Clifford, Bishop of Clifton, for whose considerateness his family feel deep gratitude. The two last Masses, when he was in his bed, he heard from his own son of the order of St. Dominic, who also gave him the Viaticum, on his second reception of it, on his last morning. He had received extreme unction three days before; he died in the Dominican habit.

Mr. Wilberforce was not without great family sorrows, from which the happiest homes have no immunity. Of his children four died, in infancy or childhood, between the years 1841 and 1853; but this trial, acute as it was, has been the only trial of his domestic life. To him, a good religious father, has been given the supreme blessing of good children. May they ever recollect how great a name they bear!

J. H. N.

July 14, 1873.

THE CHURCH *and the* EMPIRES.

I.

THE FORMATION OF CHRISTENDOM.[1]

It is somewhat paradoxical, but strictly true, to say that the greatest and most important revolution which ever took place upon earth is that to which least attention has hitherto been paid, and concerning which least is known—the substitution of 'Christendom' for the heathen world. Before our own day no historian, no philosopher of modern times has felt any interest in this vast theme, and whatever information with regard to it is attainable must be sought in the fragmentary remains of ancient writers, or in works very recently published on the Continent. In the volume before me Mr. Allies has taken ground not yet occupied by any English author. He has availed himself of two works—Döllinger's 'Christenthum und Kirche' and Champagny's Histories—and he acknowledges in the most liberal and loyal manner his obligation to them; but, in the main, he has been left to find his way for himself, and no man could well be more highly qualified for the task, whether by the gifts of nature or by the acquirements of many years. I infer

[1] The 'Formation of Christendom,' Part I. By T. W. Allies. London: Longmans.

from the work itself, that his attention was immediately turned to the subject by his appointment as Professor of the 'Philosophy of History' in the Catholic University of Dublin, under the rectorship of Dr. Newman. The duties of his post obliged him to weigh the question, 'What is the philosophy of history?' and the inaugural lecture with which the volume before me commences, although it gives no formal definition of the phrase (which is to be regretted), supplies abundant considerations by the aid of which we may arrive at it. History, in its origin, was far more akin to poetry than to philosophy, and even when it passes into prose it is in the half-legendary form, which makes the narrative of Herodotus and of the annalists of the middle ages so charming to all readers. They are ballads without metre. Next came that style of which Thucydides is the model, and which Mr. Allies calls 'political history.' 'Its limit is the nation, and it deals with all that interests the nation.' 'Great indeed is the charm where the writer can describe with the pencil of a poet and analyse with the mental grasp of a philosopher. Such is the double merit of Thucydides. And so it has happened that the deepest students of human nature have searched for two thousand years the records of a war wherein the territory of the chief belligerents was not larger than a modern English or Irish county. What should we say if a quarrel between Kent and Essex, between Cork and Kerry, had kept the world at gaze ever since? Yet Attica and Laconia were no larger.'

And yet it needed something more than territorial greatness in the states of which he wrote to enable even Thucydides himself to realise the idea of a philosophical history. For the five hundred years which followed the Peloponnesian war brought to maturity the greatest empire which has ever existed among men, and although, at the close of that period, one of the ablest and most thoughtful of writers devoted himself especially to its history, yet, says my author, 'I do not know that in reading the pages of Polybius, of Livy, or even of Tacitus, we are conscious of a wider grasp of thought, a more enlarged experience of political interests, a higher idea of man, and of all that concerns his personal and public life, than in those of Thucydides.' Great indeed was the genius of those ancient historians, magnificent were the two languages which they made their instruments— languages 'very different in their capacity, but both of them superior in originality, beauty, and expressiveness to any which have fallen to the lot of modern nations. It may be that the marbles of Pentelicus and Carrara insure good sculptors.' 'In the narrative—that is the poetic and pictorial part of history —they have equal merit. Their history is a drama in which the actors and the events speak for themselves. What was wanting was the bearing of events on each other, the apprehension of great first principles—the generalisation of facts.' And this no mere lapse of time could give. It is wanting in the works of the greatest ancient masters. It is found in moderns, in all other respects immeasurably their inferiors. 'What, then, had happened in the interval?' Christianity had happened—Christendom had been formed. 'There was a voice in the world greater, more potent, thrilling, and universal, than the last cry of the old society, *Civis sum Romanus*, and this voice was *Sum Christianus*. From the time of the great sacrifice it was impossible to sever the history of man's temporal destiny from that of his eternal; and when the virtue of that sacrifice had thoroughly leavened the nations, history is found to assume a larger basis, to have lost its partial and national cast, to have grown with the growth of man, and to demand for its completeness a perfect alliance with philosophy.'

Thus, then, the 'philosophy of history' is the comparison and arrangement of its great events by one whose mind is stored with the facts which it records, and who at the same time possesses the great first principles which qualify him to judge of it. I may, therefore, lay it down as an absolute rule, that without Christianity no really philosophical history could have been written.

Not unnaturally, then, the first example of the philosophy of history was given by a man whose mind, if not the greatest ever informed by Christianity, was at least among a very few in the first class, was moreover so thoroughly penetrated by Christian principles, that to review the events of the world in any other aspect, or through any other medium, would have been to him as impossible as to examine in detail without the light of the sun the expanse of plains and hills, rivers and forests, which lay under him as he stood on some predominant mountain-peak. God the Almighty Creator—God incarnate, who had once lived and suffered on earth, and now reigned on high until He should put all enemies under His feet, and who was coming again to judge the world which He had redeemed—the Church founded by Him to enlighten and govern all generations throughout all nations, and in which dwelt the infallible guidance of God the Holy Ghost—the evil spirits, powerless against the Divine presence in the Church, but irresistible by mere human power—the saints, no longer seen by man, but whose intercession influenced and moulded all the events of his life—all these were ever before the mind of S. Augustine, not merely as articles of faith which he confessed, but as practical realities. To trace the events of the world without continually referring to all these, would have been to him not merely irreligious, but as unreal, unmeaning, and fallacious as it would be to a natural philosopher of our own day to investigate the phenomena of the material world without taking into consideration the attraction of the earth and the resistance of the air. This should be noticed, because we have all met men who, while professing to believe most, if not all, of these things, would consider it bad taste to introduce such considerations into any practical affair. They are, in short, part of that very remarkable phenomenon, the 'Sunday religion' of a respectable English gentleman, which he holds as an inseparable part of his respectability, but which is well understood to have no bearing at all upon the business of the week. Living as S. Augustine did at the crisis at which the civilisation of the ancient world was finally breaking up, his eye was cast back in review over the whole gorgeous line of ancient history, which swept by him like a Roman triumph. Egypt, Assyria, Greece, Rome, each had its day: the last and greatest of them all he saw tottering to its fall. But far more important than this comprehensive survey, which the circumstances of his times made natural to so great an intellect, was his possession of fixed and certain principles, the truth of which he knew beyond the possibility of doubt, and which were wide enough to solve every question which the history of the world brought before him. Great men there had been before him, but the deeper their thoughts the more had they found that the world itself and their own position in it were but a hopeless enigma without an answer, a cipher without a key. A flood of light had been poured upon the piercing mental eye of S. Augustine when the waters of baptism fell from the hand of the holy Ambrose upon his outward frame. Every part of the Old Testament history glowed before him, as when, from behind a cloud which covers all the earth, the light of the sun falls concentrated upon some mountain-peak; and the man who reverences and ponders as divine that inspired history has learned to read the inner meaning of the whole history of the world as no one else can. In every age, no doubt, Almighty God rules and directs in justice and mercy the world which He has created; but in general He hides Himself behind an impenetrable veil. 'Clouds and darkness are round about Him, justice and judgment the establishment of His throne.' To many an ordinary spectator, the world seems only the theatre of man's labour and suffering. He passes through it as he might through one of the arsenals of ancient Greece or Rome, where indeed great works were wrought, but where the hand of the workman was always as visible as the result produced. A more thoughtful man might see proofs of some unknown power, just as in an arsenal of our day, works, compared to which the fabled labours of giants and cyclops were as child's play, are hourly performed by the stroke of huge hammers welding vast masses of glowing metal, while nothing is seen to cause or explain their motion. All this is understood by one who has once been allowed to see at work the engine itself which sets all in motion. So does the Old Testament history unveil to the eye of faith the hidden causes, not only of the Jewish history, but of the great events of secular history. All that seemed before only results without cause is seen to be fully accounted for; not that we can always understand the ends which the Almighty worker designs to accomplish, or the means by which He is accomplishing them, but everywhere faith sees the operation of Almighty power directed by infinite wisdom and love, and, while able to understand much, it is willing to await in reverent adoration the development of that which as yet is beyond its comprehension. It sees that the history of other nations is distinguished from that of the children of Israel, not so much by the character of the events which it records (for the extraordinary manifestations of Divine power were chiefly confined to a few special periods), as to the principle and spirit in which it has been written, and that secular history viewed by eyes supernaturally enlightened assumes the same appearance.

In fact it is not difficult to write a history of the reigns of David and Solomon and their successors down to the fall of the Hebrew monarchy, which sounds very much like that of any other Oriental kingdom. The thing has been done of late years, both in Germany and in England. It was by this that Dean Milman, many years ago, so greatly shocked the more religious portion of English readers. Nor were they shocked without cause; for his was a history of the Jews, from which, as far as possible, Almighty God was left out, while the characteristic of the inspired narrative is, that it is a record not so much of the doings of men as of the great acts of God by man and among men. Only Dean Milman was more consistent than those who condemned him. He was right in perceiving that the greater part of the history of the Jews is not materially different from that of other nations. But he went on to infer that therefore we may leave God out of sight in judging of Jewish history, as we do in that of other nations, instead of learning from the example of the Jews that in every age God is as certainly working among every nation. That by which he offended religious Protestants was the application of their own ordinary principles to the one history in which they had been taught from childhood to see and acknowledge with exceptional reverence the working of Almighty God in the affairs of the world.

This it is which gives its peculiar character to many of the chronicles of the middle ages. It is impossible not to feel that the writers see no broad distinction between the history of the nations and times of which they are writing and that of the ancient people of God. And hence in their annals we have far more of the philosophy of history, in the true sense of the word, than was possible to any ancient author. For with all their ignorance of physical causes, which led them into many mistakes, their main principles were both true and vitally important, and were wholly unknown to Thucydides and Tacitus. But the circumstances of their times made it impossible that they should survey the extensive range of facts which lies before a modern historian. In many instances also they were led by the imperfect state of physical science to attribute to a supernatural interference of God in the world things which we are now able to refer to natural causes. That God has before now interfered with the course of nature which He has established in the world, and may whenever He pleases so interfere again, these were to them first principles. And so far they reasoned truly and justly, although their imperfect acquaintance with other branches of human knowledge sometimes led them to apply amiss their true principle. Their minds were so much accustomed to dwell upon the thought of God, and upon His acts in the world, that they were always prepared to see and hear Him everywhere, and in every event. When they heard of any event supposed to be supernatural, they might be awestruck and impressed, but could not be said to be surprised; and hence, no doubt, they sometimes accepted as supernatural, events which, if examined by a shrewd man who starts with the first principle that nothing supernatural can really have taken place, could have been otherwise explained. Besides, their comparative unacquaintance with physical science led them into errors in accounting for and even in observing those which they themselves did not imagine to be supernatural. But their first principles were true. And the modern who assumes, whether explicitly or implicitly, that the course of the world is modified and governed only by the passions and deeds of man is in his first principles fundamentally wrong. They fell into accidental error; he cannot be more than accidentally right.

Mr. Allies says:—

In the middle ages, and notably in the thirteenth century, there were minds which have left us imperishable memorials of themselves, and which would have taken the largest and most philosophical view of history had the materials existed ready to their hand. Conceive, for instance, a history from the luminous mind of S. Thomas with the stores of modern knowledge at his command. But the invention of printing, one of the turning-points of the human race, was first to take place, and then on that soil of the middle ages, so long prepared and fertilised by so patient a toil, a mighty harvest was to spring up. Among the first fruits of labours so often depreciated by those who have profited by them, and in the land of children who despise their sires, we find the proper alliance of philosophy with history. Then at length the province of the historian is seen to consist, not merely in the just, accurate, and lively narrative of facts, but in the exhibition of cause and effect. 'What do we now expect in history?' says M. de Barante, and he replies, 'Solid instruction and complete knowledge of things; moral lessons, political counsels; comparison with the present, and the general knowledge of facts.' Even in the age of Tacitus, the most philosophic of ancient historians, no individual ability could secure all such powers (p. 12).

Thus philosophical history is one of the results of Christianity. Professor Max Müller makes a similar remark with regard to his own favourite study of ethnology. Before the day of Pentecost, he says, no man, not even the greatest minds, ever thought of tracing the genealogy of nations by their languages, because they did not know the unity of the human race. The unity of mankind is naturally connected in the order of ideas with the unity of God. Those who worshipped many gods, and believed that each race and nation had its own tutelary divinity, not unnaturally regarded each nation as a separate race. So far was this feeling carried by the most civilised races of the old world, that they thought it a profanation that the worship of the gods of one race should be offered by a priest not sprung from that race. The most moderate and popular of the Roman patricians rejected the demand of the *plebs* to be admitted to the highest offices of the state, not as politically dangerous, but as profane. The Roman consul, in virtue of his office, was the priest of the Capitoline Jove, to whom, on certain solemn occasions, he had to offer sacrifice. It would be a pollution that a plebeian, not sprung from any of the tribes of Romulus, should presume to offer that sacrifice. In fact, the consulship would hardly have been thrown open to the *plebs* until the long-continued habit of intermarriage had welded the two portions of the Roman people so completely into one that the plebeian began, at last, to be regarded as of the same blood with the Furii, the Cornelii, and the Julii. The first measure by which the tribunes commenced their attack upon the exclusive privilege of the great houses was wisely chosen; it was the Canuleian law, by which marriages between the two orders were made legal and valid. Before that, patricians and plebeians were two nations living in one city, and, according to the universal opinion of the ancient world, this implied that they had different gods, different priests, a different ritual, and different temples. But the day of Pentecost blended all nations into a new unity—the unity of the body of Christ; and its first effect was, that the preachers of the new law proclaimed everywhere, that 'God had made of one blood all nations of men, to dwell upon the face of the whole earth.' The professor points out what curiously completes the analogy between the two cases, that while Christianity, by collecting into one church all the nations of the world, and by teaching their original unity, naturally suggested the idea that all their different languages had some common origin, any satisfactory investigation of the subject was long delayed by the unfounded notion that the Hebrew must needs be the root from which they all sprang. Thus, in both cases, the germ of studies, whose development was delayed for ages by the imperfection of human knowledge, appears to have been contained in the revelation of the gospel of Christ.

It is important to bring these considerations into prominence, because the knowledge which would never have existed without Christianity is, in many cases, retained by men who forget or deny the faith to which they are indebted for it. Mr. Allies draws comparison between Tacitus and Gibbon (page 14).

The world of thought in which we live is, after all, formed by Christianity. Modern Europe is a relic of Christendom, the virtue of which is not gone out of it. Gregory VII. and Innocent III. have ruled over generations which have ignored them; have given breadth to minds which condemned their benefactors as guilty of narrow priestcraft, and derided the work of those benefactors as an exploded theory. Let us take an example in what is, morally, perhaps the worst and most shocking period of the last three centuries—the thirty years preceding the great French revolution. We shall see that at this time even minds which had rejected, with all the firmness of a reprobate will, the regenerating influence of Christianity, could not emancipate themselves from the virtue of the atmosphere which they had breathed. They are immeasurably greater than they would have been in pagan times, by the force of that faith which they misrepresented and repudiated. To prove the truth of my words, compare for a moment the great artist who drew Tiberius and Domitian and the Roman Empire in the first century, with him who wrote of its decline and fall in the second and succeeding centuries. How far wider a grasp of thought, how far more manifold an experience, combined with philosophic purposes, in Gibbon than in Tacitus! He has a standard within him by which he can measure the nations as they come in long procession before him. In that vast and wondrous drama of the Antonines and Constantine, Athanasius and Leo, Justinian and Charlemagne, Mahomet, Zenghis Khan, and Timour, Jerusalem and Mecca, Rome and Constantinople, what stores of thought are laid up—what a train of philosophic induction exhibited! How much larger is this world become than that which trembled at Cæsar! The very apostate profits by the light which has shone on Thabor, and the blood which has flowed on Calvary. He is a greater historian than his heathen predecessor, because he lives in a society to which the God whom he has abandoned has disclosed the depth of its being, the laws of its course, the importance of its present, the price of its futurity.

A very little thought will show that, constituted as man's nature is, this could not have been otherwise. Man differs from the inferior animals in that he is richly endowed with faculties which, until they have been developed by education, he can never use, and appreciates and embraces truths, when they have been set before him, which he could never have discovered unassisted. This is the most obvious distinction between reason and instinct. The caterpillar, hatched from an egg dropped by a parent whom it never saw, knows at once what food and what habits are necessary for its new life. Weeks pass away, and its first skin begins to die; but (as if it had been fully instructed in what has to be done) it draws its body out of it as from a glove, and comes forth in a new one. A few weeks later it forsakes the food which has hitherto been necessary for its life, and buries itself in the earth, which up to that very day would have been certain death. There a mysterious change passes upon it, and it lies as if dead till the time for another change approaches. It then gradually works its way to the surface, and comes out a butterfly or a moth. It is now indifferent to the plants which in its former state were necessary to its existence; but yet it chooses those plants on which to deposit its eggs. We are so apt to delude ourselves with the notion that we understand everything to which we give a name, that ninety-nine people out of a hundred seem to think they account for this marvellous power of the inferior animals to act exactly right under circumstances so strangely changed, by calling it 'instinct.' But, in truth, why or how the creature does what it does, we no more know when we have called it 'instinct' than we did before. All we can suppose is that as the Creator has left none of His creatures destitute of the kind and degree of knowledge necessary to enable it to discharge its appointed office in creation, the appetites and desires of the insect are modified from time to time in the different stages of its existence, so that they impel it exactly to the course necessary for it to take, with much greater certainty than if it understood what the result was to be. How different is the case of man! Not only is he a free agent, and therefore to be guided by reason, not by mere propensity, but neither reason nor speech, nor indeed life itself, could be preserved or made of any use except by means of training and education received from others. A man left to shift for himself like the animal whose changes we have been tracing, would die at each state of his existence for want of some one to teach him what must be done for his preservation. The same training is equally necessary for his physical, intellectual, and moral and spiritual life. But he is so constituted that the different things needful for him to know for each of these purposes approve themselves to him as soon as they are presented to his mind from without; and the things which thus approve themselves, although he could never have discovered them, we truly call natural to man, because no external teaching would have made him capable of learning them unless the faculty had been as much a part of his original constitution as the unreasoning desires which we call instinct are part of the constitution of brutes. And therefore, when once developed by education, they remain a part of the man, even when he casts away from him those teachers by whom they were developed. Nero would never have learned the use of speech if he had not caught it from his mother; yet when he used it to order her murder he did not lose what she had taught him, because it was a part of his nature.' And so of higher powers, the result of a superior training. Principles which men would never have known without Christian training, are retained when Christianity itself is rejected, because they are part of the spiritual endowment given to man by his Creator, although without training he would never have been able to develope them. His rejection of Christianity results from an evil will. The parts of Christian teaching against which that will does not rebel, he calls and believes to be the lessons of his natural reason, although the experience of the greatest and wisest heathen shows that his unassisted natural faculties never would have discovered them.

Nor is this true only of individuals. Nations trained for many generations in Christian faith have before now fallen away from Christianity. But it does not seem that they are able to reduce themselves to the level of heathen nations in their moral standard, their perception and appreciation of good and evil, justice and wrong, or of the nature and destinies of the human race. In some respects they are morally much worse than heathen. But it does not appear that in these points they can sink so low, because their nature, fallen though it be, approves and accepts some of the truths taught it by Christianity. Hence, in order to judge what man can or cannot do without the revelation of God in Jesus Christ, we must examine him in nations to which the faith has never been given, rather than in those which have rejected it. Unhappily, there are at this moment parts of Europe in which the belief in the supernatural seems wanting. An intelligent correspondent of the 'Times' a year ago described such a state of things as existing in parts of Northern Germany and Scandinavia. The population believes nothing, and practises no religion. Public worship is deserted, not because the people have devised any new heresy of their own as to the manner in which man should approach God, but because they have ceased to trouble themselves about the matter at all. Lutheranism is dead and gone; but nothing has been substituted for it. The intelligent Protestant writer was surprised to find a population thus wholly without religion orderly and well-behaved, hard-working, and by no means forgetful of social duties. The phenomenon is, no doubt, remarkable; but it is by no means without example. Many parishes (I fear considerable districts) in France are substantially in the same state. The peasantry are sober, industrious, and orderly, to a degree unknown in England. They reap the temporal fruits of these good qualities in a general prosperity equally unknown here. They are saving to a degree almost incredible, so that it is a matter of ordinary experience that a peasant who began life with nothing except his bodily strength, leaves behind him several hundreds, not unfrequently some thousands of pounds sterling. But in this same district whole villages are so absolutely without religion, that, although there is not one person for many miles who calls himself a Protestant, the churches are almost absolutely deserted, and the *curés* (generally good and zealous men) are reduced almost to inactivity by absolute despair. Some give themselves up to prayer, seeing nothing else that they can do; some will say that they are not wholly without encouragement, because, after fifteen or twenty years of labour, they have succeeded in bringing four or five persons to seek the benefit of the sacraments out of a population of as many hundreds, among whom when they came there was not one such person to be found.¹

Appalling as is this state of things, the natural virtues (such as they are) of populations which have thus lost faith are themselves the remains of Christianity. History gives us no trace of any people in such a state except those who have once been Christians. For instance, in all others, however civilised, slavery has been established both by law and practice; no one of them has been without divorce; infanticide has been allowed and practised. Nowhere has the unity of man's nature been acknowledged, and, what follows from that, the duties owing to him as man, not merely as fellow countryman. And hence nowhere has there existed what we call the law of nations, a rule which limits the conduct of men, not only towards those of other nations, but, what is much more, towards those with whom they are in a state of war, or whom they have conquered. In the most civilised times of ancient Greece and Rome, no rights were recognised in such foreigners. All these things are the legitimate progeny of Christianity, and

---

¹ It should be observed that the morality said to exist in those parts of France which have so nearly lost the faith is not Catholic morality; in fact, the population in those districts is decreasing, and that (it is universally admitted) from immorality. It should also be remembered that there is a most marked contrast between these districts and those Lutheran districts of which the 'Times' spoke; in the latter, Lutheranism has died out of itself. In the worst districts of France, the Catholic religion has not died out, but has been displaced by a systematic infidel education inflicted on the people by a godless government. Lastly, even where things are the worst, there are a few in each generation who, in the midst of a godless population, turn out saints, really worthy of that name. It is seldom that a mission is preached in any village without some such being rescued from the corrupt mass around them. Nothing, in fact, can more strongly mark the contrast between the Catholic religion and Lutheranism. The subject is far too large to be discussed here, but I have suggested these considerations to avoid misconceptions of my meaning.

of Christianity alone, although they are now accepted as natural principles by nations by whom, but for the Gospel of Christ, they would never have been heard of.

I have enlarged upon this point because, not only in what he says of Gibbon, but in many parts of his subsequent chapters, Mr. Allies attributes to the influence of Christianity things which a superficial observer may attribute rather to some general progress in the world towards a higher civilisation. We shall see instances of this as we proceed. I am satisfied that the objection is utterly unfounded. I see no reason to believe that without Christianity any higher or better civilisation than that of Rome under Augustus and Athens under Pericles would ever have been attained. That those who lived under that state, so far from expecting any 'progress,' believed that the world was getting worse and worse, and that there remained no hope of improvement, nor any principles from which it could possibly arise, is most certain. Nor do I believe that those who thus judged of the natural tendency of the world were mistaken, although, by a stupendous interference of the Creator with the course of nature, an improvement actually took place.

The philosophy of history then sifts and arranges the facts which it records, and judges of them by fixed and eternal principles of right and wrong, drawing from the past lessons of wisdom and virtue for the future. It will approach nearer and nearer to perfection as the range of facts investigated becomes wider, and as the principles by which they are judged are more absolutely true, and applied more correctly, more practically, and more universally. Hence it would never have existed without Christianity, and although in Christian nations it is found in men partially or wholly unworthy of the Christian name, but who retain many ideas and principles derived from Christianity alone, yet even in them it is exercised imperfectly in proportion as they are less and less Christian.

Mr. Allies thus compares Tacitus and S. Augustine :—

The atmosphere of Tacitus and the lurid glare of his Rome compared with S. Augustine's world, are like the shades in which Achilles deplored the loss of life contrasted with a landscape bathed in the morning light of a southern sun. Yet how much more of material misery was there in the time of S. Augustine than in the time of Tacitus! In spite of the excesses in which the emperors might indulge within the walls of their palace or of Rome, the fair fabric of civilisation filled the whole Roman world, the great Empire was in peace, and its multitude of nations were brethren. Countries which now form great kingdoms of themselves, were then tranquil members of one body politic. Men could travel the coasts of Italy, Gaul, Spain, Africa, Syria, Asia Minor, and Greece, round to Italy again, and find a rich smiling land covered by prosperous cities, enjoying the same laws and institutions, and possessed in peace by its children. In S. Augustine's time all had been changed ; on many of these coasts a ruthless, uncivilised, unbelieving, or misbelieving enemy had descended. Through the whole Empire there was a feeling of insecurity, a cry of helplessness, and a trembling at what was to come. Yet in the pages of the two writers, the contrast is in the inverse ratio. In the Pagan, everything seems borne on by an iron fate, which tramples upon the free will of man, and overwhelms the virtuous before the wicked. In the Christian, order shines in the midst of destruction, and mercy dispenses the severest humiliations. It was the symbol of the coming age. And so that great picture of the Doctor, Saint, and Philosopher, laid hold of the minds of men during those centuries of violence which followed, and in which peace and justice, so far from embracing each other, seemed to have deserted the earth. And in modern times a great genius has seized upon it, and developed it in the discourse on Universal History. Bossuet is worthy to receive the torch from S. Augustine. Scarcely could a more majestic voice or a more philosophic spirit set forth the double succession of empire and of religion, or exhibit the tissue wrought by Divine Providence, human free will, and the permitted power of evil.

After this estimate of S. Augustine, he speaks of—

A living author—at once statesman, orator, philosopher, and historian of the highest rank, who has given us, on a less extensive scale, a philosophy of history in its most finished and amiable form. The very attempt on the part of M. Guizot to draw out a picture of civilisation during fourteen hundred years, and to depict, amongst that immense and ever-changing period, the course of society in so many countries, indicates no ordinary power; and the partial fulfilment of the design may be said to have elevated the philosophy of history into a science. In this work may be found the most important rules of the science accurately stated ; but the work itself is the best example of philosophic method and artistic execution, united to illustrate a complex subject. A careful study of original authorities, a patient induction of facts, a cautious generalisation, the philosophic eye to detect analogies, the painter's power to group results, and, above all, a unity of conception which no multiplicity of details can embarrass—these are some of the main qualifications for a philosophy of history which I should deduce from these works. Yet, while the action of Providence and that of human free will are carefully and beautifully brought out, while both may be said to be points of predilection with the author, he has not alluded, so far as I am aware, to the great evil spirit and his personal operation. Strong as he is, he has been apparently too weak to bear the scoff of modern nfidelity—'he believes in the Devil'—unless, indeed, the cause of this ies deeper, and belongs to his philosophy ; for if there be one subject out of which eclecticism can pick nothing to its taste, it would be the permitted operation of the great fallen spirit. Nor will the warmest admiration of his genius be mistaken for a concurrence in all his judgments. I presume not to say how far such an author is sometimes, in spite of himself, unjust, from the point of view at which he draws his picture. Whether, and how far, he be an eclectic philosopher, let others decide. It would be grievous to feel it true of such a mind ; for it is the original sin of that philosophy to make the universe rotate round itself. Great is its complacency in its own conclusions, but there runs through them one mistake—to fancy itself in the place of God (p. 31).

Those who have ever made the attempt to analyse in a few lines the genius of a great writer will best be able to estimate the combination of keen intellect, patient thought, and scrupulous candour in this criticism. I must not deny myself one more quotation :—

S. Augustine, Bossuet, Guizot, Balmez, Schlegel: I have taken these names not to exhaust but to illustrate the subject. Here we have the ancient and the modern society, Africa and France, Spain and Germany, and the Christian mind in each, thrown upon the facts of history. They point out, I think, sufficiently a common result. But amid the founders of a new science who shall represent our own country? Can I hesitate, or can I venture, in this place and company [*i.e.* before the Catholic University of Dublin, in the chair of which this lecture was delivered], to mention the hand which has directed the scattered rays of light from so many sources on the wild children of Central Asia, and produced the Turk before us in his untameable ferocity—the outcast of the human race, before whom earth herself ceases to be a mother—by whom man's blood has ever been shed like water, woman's honour counted as the vilest of things, nature's most sacred laws publicly and avowedly outraged—has produced him before us for the abhorrence of mankind, the infamy of nations? To sketch the intrinsic character of barbarism and civilisation, and out of common historical details, travel, and observation to show the ineffaceable stamp of race and tribe, reproducing itself through the long series of ages, surely expresses the idea which we mean by the philosophy of history (p. 33).

I have given a disproportionate space to this inaugural lecture, both for its intrinsic importance and because it gives a shadow of the whole plan of Mr. Allies's work, both that part which lies before us and that which remains to be published; for the volume before us is 'only a portion, perhaps about a fourth, of the author's design.' In the six lectures which it contains, he gives us an estimate, first, of the physical and political condition of the Roman empire in its palmy days; then of the force by which it pleased God to constitute the new creation in the midst of it. In the last four lectures he compares the vital principles of these two vast social organisations—the heathen and the Christian—first in a representative man of each class, then in the effects produced upon society at large by the influence of each; then in the primary relation of man to woman in marriage; and, lastly, in the virginal state; although under this last head there can hardly be said to be a comparison, as heathen society has simply nothing to set against that wonderful creation of Christianity,—holy virginity.

I know not where I have met any painting of the Roman empire so striking as that contained in the first lecture. Of the multitude of Englishmen who read more or less of the classical Latin authors, a very small proportion have ever paid any attention to the Roman empire, except as it is displayed by Tacitus and Juvenal. This is the natural result of the grace and eloquence of Livy and Cicero, much rather than of any strong preference for republican institutions. Indeed it is impossible not to be struck with the vast influence which Roman republicanism exercises in France compared with England. Nor is it difficult to account for this. France, except to a limited degree under the monarchy of July, has never enjoyed constitutional liberty. The Frenchman, therefore, who dreams of liberty at all, places his dreamland in a Roman republic. Boys who in England would rant about John Hampden are found in France ranting about Junius Brutus. For what the Englishman means when he talks about liberty is 'English liberty,' the Frenchman means the Roman republic. So much has this been the case, that even in America the war of independence began, not in any aspiration after a republic, but for the rights of English subjects. The sword had been drawn for a year before the colonies claimed independence, and very shortly before, Washington had declared that 'there was no thought of separation, only of English liberty.' What proves that these were not mere words was, that even after independence had been achieved, the leaders, who met in congress, agreed almost to a man in expressing their preference for 'an English constitution,' if circumstances had placed it within their reach. All the world knows that France became a republic chiefly because Rome in her palmy days had been so called; nay, to this hour all the terms adopted by the revolutionary party have been borrowed from classical times. Such was the term 'Citizen,' so appropriate to a people whose boast was that they were free of a city which had conquered the world, so absurd as denoting the members of a great nation in which not even centuries of extreme centralisation have prevented political rights from being exercised by each man in his own province. Such, again, was that inundation of pagan names which the revolutionary times substituted for those of the saints, and which are still characteristic of France—Camille, Emile, Antonine, and even Brute and Timoleon. This we take to be one great reason why many sensible persons in France are so greatly afraid of classical studies in schools and colleges. They say that they turn the heads of boys, especially French boys. It is highly characteristic of the man, that the officers of the House of Commons, who made forcible entry into the house of Sir Francis Burdett when he was committed by order of the House, found him reading with his little son, not Plutarch's life of Brutus or Cato, as would assuredly have been the case with a Frenchman, but 'Magna Charta.' He was not less theatrical, but he was a thoroughly English actor.

And yet I strongly suspect that out of a hundred boys who leave a classical school more than ninety believe that Roman history ends with Augustus. The university no doubt gives a somewhat more extended view. But even there Tacitus is usually about the limit. I wonder how far this feeling was carried before Gibbon published the 'Decline and Fall.'

Hence I especially value the wonderful picture of the Empire painted by Mr. Allies.

It was in fact a federation of civilised states under an absolute monarch: the municipal liberties were left so entire, that Niebuhr mentions Italian cities in the immediate neighbourhood of Rome itself which retained all through the times of the Empire and the middle ages, down to the wars of the French revolution, the same municipal institutions under which Rome had found them. They were swept away by that faithful lover of despotism, Napoleon I., to make way for the uniform system of a préfet and sous-préfet in each district. It is more important to bear this in mind because, as the revolutionists aped the manners and names of the Roman Republic without understanding them, the imperialists of France are apt to assume that they faithfully represent the Roman Empire. Now the one striking characteristic of the French Empire is that it raises yearly 100,000 military conscripts, besides the naval conscription, the police and the very firemen, all of whom are carefully drilled as soldiers. How was it under Augustus?

It is hard to conceive adequately what a spectator called 'the immense majesty of the Roman peace' (Pliny, *Nat. Hist.* xxvii. 1). Where now in Europe, impatient and uneasy, a group of half-friendly nations jealously watches each other's progress and power, and the acquisition of a province threatens a general war, Rome maintained, from generation to generation, in tranquil sway, an empire of which Gaul, Spain, Britain, and North Africa, Switzerland, and the greater part of Austria, Turkey in Europe, Asia Minor, Syria, and Egypt, formed but single limbs, members of her mighty body. Her roads, which spread like a network over this immense territory, from their common centre, the golden milestone of the Forum, under the palace of her emperors, did but express the unity of that spirit with which she ruled the earth her subject, levelling the mountains and filling up the valleys for the march of her armies, the caravans of her merchandise, and the even sweep of her legislation. A moderate fleet of 6,000 sailors at Misenum, and another at Ravenna, a flotilla at Forum Julii, and another in the Black Sea, of half that force, preserved the whole Mediterranean from piracy; and every nation bordering on its shores could freely interchange the productions of their industry. Two smaller armaments of twenty-four vessels each on the Rhine and the Danube secured the Empire from northern incursion. In the time of Tiberius, a force of twenty-five legions and fourteen cohorts, making 171,500 men, with about an equal number of auxiliary troops, that is, in all, an army of 340,000, sufficed not so much to preserve internal order, which rested upon other and surer ground, but to guard the frontiers of a vast population, amounting, as is calculated, to

120,000,000, and inhabiting the very fairest regions of the earth, of which the great Mediterranean Sea was a sort of central and domestic lake. But this army itself, thus moderate in number, was not, as a rule, stationed in cities, but in fixed quarters on the frontiers, as a guard against external foes. Thus, for instance, the whole interior of Gaul possessed a garrison of but 1,200 men—that Gaul which, in the year 1860, in a time of peace, thought necessary for internal tranquillity and external rank and security to have 626,000 men in arms.[1] Again, Asia Minor had no military force; that most beautiful region of the earth teemed with princely cities, enjoying the civilisation of a thousand years, and all the treasures of art and industry, in undisturbed repose. And within its unquestioned boundaries, the spirit, moreover, of Roman rule was far other than that of a military despotism, or of a bureaucracy and a police pressing with ever watchful suspicion on every spring of civil life. The principle of its government was not that no population could be faithful which was not kept in leading-strings, but rather to leave cities and corporations to manage their own affairs themselves. Thus its march was firm and strong, but for this very reason devoid alike of fickleness and haste.

It might have been added, that, as a general rule, the army which guarded each portion was composed of the natives of the country in which they were stationed. Roman citizens they were no doubt, but citizens of provincial extraction, and posted to guard on behalf of Rome the very country which their fathers, sometimes but a very few generations back, had defended against her.[2] This is a policy the generosity of which France dares not at this day imitate, even in her oldest provinces. To say nothing of the British army in Ireland, the Breton conscripts are still sent to serve at Lyons and Paris.

The extracts I have given will doubtless lead every reader to study for himself Mr. Allies's descriptions of Rome, and the

---

[1] Surely the author should have added the Belgian army (fixed by the laws of 1853 at 100,000), and that part of the Prussian, &c., which is raised west of the Rhine, in comparing the military force of ancient Gaul with that of the same district in our day.

[2] Champagny, Rome and Judea.

life of the Thermæ, and of the colonies, everywhere reproducing the life of Rome. Every page breathes with the matured thought of a mind of remarkable natural acuteness, and stored with refined scholarship. There is nothing of beauty or majesty in that magnificent old world which he does not seem to have witnessed and mused over.

It is hardly possible to realise all this greatness without being tempted to repine in the remembrance whither it was all hastening—that the peace of the Roman world was but 'the torrent's smoothness ere it dash below;' its magnificence only the feast of Baltassar in that last night of the splendour of Babylon, when the Medes and Persians were already under her walls, and the river had been turned away from its course through her quays, and a way left open for the rush of the destroyer into her streets and palaces. Already the mysterious impulse had been given which, during so many centuries, drove down horde after horde of barbarians from the wild North-East, to overflow the favoured lands that surrounded the Mediterranean. In the early days of Roman history the Gauls had rushed on, sweeping away those earlier races whose remains we are now exploring in the shallows of the Swiss lakes, and whose descendants are probably to be found in the Basques, and in some of those degraded castes which, in spite of the welding power of the Church, left proscribed remnants in France and elsewhere until the great revolution. That mighty wave burst upon the rock of the Capitol, threatened for a moment utterly to overwhelm it, and then fell broken at its feet. But it is not by repelling one wave, however formidable, that a rising tide is turned back. In the day of Rome's utmost power her very foundations were shaken by the torrent of the Cimbri and Teutones. They, too, were broken against the steel-clad legions of Marius, and fell off like spray on the earth. But the tide was still advancing. What need to trace its successive inroads? Every reader of Gibbon remembers how the time came at last, when the very site where Rome had stood had been so often swept by it, that of all its greatness, there remained nothing more than the sea leaves of some castle of shingles and sand, after a few waves have passed over it.

> Quench'd is the golden statue's ray;
> The breath of Heaven hath swept away
>   What toiling earth hath piled;
> Scattering wise heart and crafty hand,
> As breezes strew on ocean's strand
>   The fabrics of a child!

There even came a time when for many weeks the very ruins of ancient Rome were absolutely deserted, and trodden neither by man nor beast. No wonder that the world stood by afar off, weeping and mourning over the utter destruction of all that the earth had ever known of greatness and glory. So the sentence had been passed, in the day of her greatest glory, by the prophetic voice of the angel, who cried with a strong voice—

'Fallen—fallen, is Babylon the great, and is become the habitation of devils and the hold of every unclean spirit, and of every unclean and hateful bird. And the kings of the earth shall weep and bewail themselves over her, when they shall see the smoke of the burning; standing afar off for fear of her torments, saying, Alas! alas! that great city Babylon, that mighty city; for in one hour is thy judgment come. And the merchants of the earth shall weep and mourn over her, and shall stand afar off from her for fear of her torments, weeping and mourning, and saying, Alas! alas! that great city which was clothed in fine linen, and purple, and scarlet, and was gilt with gold and precious stones, and pearls. For in one hour are so great riches come to nought.'—(Apocalypse, chap. xviii.)

It was not the ruin of one city, however glorious, but the sweeping away of all the accumulated glories of the civilisation of the whole civilised world, during more than a thousand years. All had been embodied in Imperial Rome. In the words of my author—

> The empire of Augustus inherited the whole civilisation of the ancient world. Whatever political or social knowledge, whatever moral or intellectual truth, whatever useful or elegant arts, 'the enterprising race of Japhet' had acquired, preserved, and accumulated in the long course of centuries since the beginning of history, had descended without a break to Rome, with the dominion of all the countries washed by the Mediterranean. For her the wisdom of Egypt and of all the East had been stored up. For her Pythagoras and Thales, Socrates, Plato, and Aristotle, and all the schools besides of Grecian philosophy suggested by these names, had thought. For her Zoroaster, as well as Solon and Lycurgus, legislated. For her Alexander conquered, the races which he subdued forming but a portion of her empire. Every city, in the ears of whose youth the poems of Homer were familiar as household words, owned her sway. The magistrates, from the Northern Sea to the confines of Arabia, issued their decrees in the language of empire—the Latin tongue; while, as men of letters, they spoke and wrote in Greek. For her Carthage had risen, founded colonies, discovered distant coasts, set up a world-wide trade, and then fallen, leaving her the empire of Africa and the West, with the lessons of a long experience. Not only so, but likewise Spain, Gaul, and all the frontier provinces, from the Alps to the mouth of the Danube, spent in her service their strength and skill; supplied her armies with their bravest youths; gave to her senate and her knights their choicest minds. The vigour of new and the culture of long-polished races were alike employed in the vast fabric of her power. Every science and art, all human experience and discovery, had poured their treasure in one stream into the bosom of that society, which, after forty-four years of undisputed rule, Augustus had consolidated into a new system of government, and bequeathed to the charge of Tiberius (p. 41).

No wonder the ancient world had assured itself that, as nothing greater, nothing wiser, nothing more glorious than Rome could ever arise upon earth, so its greatness, wisdom, and glory could never be superseded. It was 'the eternal city.' It was 'for ever to give laws to the world.' The contemporary poets could imagine no stronger expression of an eternity than that of a duration while Rome itself should last. Yet was it at that very time that the eyes of a fisherman of the Lake of Tiberias were opened to see the angel ' coming down from heaven with power and great glory,' from whose mighty cry over the fall of Babylon we have already quoted some words. No wonder, when the time came that his prophecy was fulfilled, the world stood by weeping and mourning, not over the fall of a single city (such as Scipio Africanus had forecast as he watched the smoke of old Carthage rising up to heaven), but over the ruin of the civilisation of the whole world. No wonder that, even in our own age, those whose hearts have so far sunk back to the level of heathenism as to value only material prosperity and worldly greatness, still re-echo the cry—

> Alas ! the eternal city, and alas !
> The trebly hundred triumphs, and the day
> When Brutus made the dagger's edge surpass
> The conqueror's sword in bearing fame away.
> Alas! for earth, for never shall we see
> That brightness in her eye she wore when Rome was free.

But the voice of divine wisdom was far different :—' Rejoice over her, thou heaven, and ye holy apostles and prophets, for God hath judged your judgment upon her. And a mighty angel took up a stone, as it were a great millstone, and cast it into the sea, saying, " With such violence as this shall Babylon, that great city, be thrown down, and shall be found no more at all : and the voice of harpers, and of musicians, and of them that play on the pipe and on the trumpet, shall no more be heard at all in thee ; and no craftsman, of any art whatsoever, shall be found any more at all in thee ; and the sound of the mill shall be heard no more at all in thee ; and the light of the lamp shall shine no more in thee ; and the voice of the bridegroom and the bride shall be heard no more at all in thee ; for thy merchants were the great men of the earth, for all nations have been deceived by thine enchantments." And in her was found the blood of prophets, and of saints, and of all that were slain upon the earth.'

Thus total, according to the prophecy, was to be the destruction of the wealth, civilisation, greatness, and glory of the ancient heathen world, gathered together in Rome, that in the utter sweeping away of that one city all might perish together. How fully the words were accomplished we know by the lamentation of the whole world over Babylon, the echoes of which still ring in our ears. But to us Christians it rather belongs to weigh the words which follow without any break in the sacred text (although the division of the chapters leads many readers to overlook the close connection). 'After these things I heard, as it were, the voice of much people in heaven, saying, "Alleluia. Salvation, and glory, and power is to our God. For just and true are His judgments, who hath judged the great harlot which corrupted the earth with her fornications, and He hath avenged the blood of His servants at her hands." And again they said, "Alleluia. And her smoke ascendeth for ever and ever."' Here is the answer to that cry of the angel, 'Rejoice over her, thou heaven, and ye holy apostles and prophets.'

Were any comment needed upon such prophecies—any explanation of the sentence passed upon a civilisation so great, so ancient, so widely extended, and so refined—anything to reconcile us to the utter destruction of so much that was fair and mighty, we may find it in the latter half of the lecture before us. Not that our author is insensible to the marvellous beauty of that glow with which classical literature causes the figures of those days to shine before us. That would be impossible for a man of his studies. He says—

> Is not the very language of Cicero and Virgil an expression of this ordly yet peaceful rule; this even, undisturbed majesty, which holds

the world together like the regularity of the seasons, like the alternations of light and darkness, like the all-pervading warmth of the sun? If every language reflects the character of the race which speaks it, surely we discern in the very strain of Virgil the closing of the gates of war, the settling of the nations down to the arts of peace, the reign of law and order, the amity and concord of races, the weak protected, the strong ruled; in a word,

> 'Romanos rerum dominos, gentemque togatam.'

Neither, need it hardly be said, has he set the hideous pollutions of that civilisation fully before us: that is rendered impossible by its very hideousness. Let those who recoil from the horrors of what he has said—but a faint outline of the miserable truth, though traced with singular artistic force and beauty—bear in mind the while the words of the inspired prophecy, 'All nations have drunk of the wine of her fornication, and the kings of the earth have committed fornication with her'—'Her sins have reached unto heaven, and the Lord shall reward her iniquities'—'In her was found the blood of prophets, and saints, and of all that were slain upon the earth.' The crimes as well as the civilisation of a thousand years were accumulated at Rome, and both were swept away together by that overwhelming flood of fierce barbarians. Little were it worthy of Christians to mourn over a civilisation into whose very heartstrings such unutterable pollution was intertwined; especially as it was removed, not like Babylon of old, to leave behind it nothing but desolation, but to make room for that kingdom of God which was to be enthroned upon its ruins; for such was the purpose of God, that the very centre of Christendom, the very seat of the throne of Christ upon earth, on which He would visibly sit in the person of his Vicar, was there to be established, whence the throne of the Cæsars and the golden house of Nero had been swept away in headlong ruin. 'I saw a new heaven and a new earth, for the first heaven and the first earth was gone. And I heard a great voice from the throne saying, " Behold the tabernacle of God with men, and He will dwell with them. And they shall be His people, and God Himself shall be their God. And God shall wipe away all tears from their eyes."' 'And He that sat on the throne said, "Behold, I make all things new."' The full accomplishment of these words we expect, in faith and hope, when 'death shall be no more, nor mourning, nor crying, nor sorrow shall be any more ; for the former things are passed away ;' yet, surely, whatever more glorious accomplishment is yet to come, it were blindness not to see how far they are already fulfilled in the substitution of Christendom for the civilised pagan world—the setting up the throne of the Vicar of Christ upon the ruins of the palace of the Cæsars.

First among the causes of that hideous accumulated mixture of blood and filth in which heathen civilisation was drowned, Mr. Allies most justly places the institution of slavery as it was at Rome, because by this the springs of human life were tainted. It is certain that during all the long years of the duration of the Roman empire, there was among its heathen population no one human being who lived beyond the earliest childhood, who was not polluted, and whose very soul was not scarred and branded by the marks of that hideous moral pestilence. I say 'its heathen population,' because, great as must have been the evil it wrought upon ordinary Christians, I doubt not that there were those who gathered honey out of corruption, and whose justice, charity, and purity came out from that furnace of temptation with a brightness which nothing but the most fiery trial could have given to them. From slavery the whole of Roman society received its form. The author most truly says, 'The spirit of slavery is never limited to the slave; it saturates the atmosphere which the freeman breathes together with the slave, passes into his nature, and corrupts it.' This miserable truth can never be too often impressed upon men, because unhappily there are still advocates of slavery who think that they apologise for it if they can prove, as they think, that the slave is happy. As well might they argue that the introduction of the plague into London would be no calamity, if the man who brought it in upon him entered the city dancing and shouting. In ancient Italy slaves replaced the hardy rustics, that 'prisca gens mortalium,' who, though doubtless far less virtuous than they appeared in the fevered dreams of men sick of the vices of Rome in the last days of the republic, were still among the best specimens of heathen life. Wherever slavery extends, labour becomes dishonourable, as the badge of servitude, a few masters languish in bloated luxury, but the nation itself grows constantly poorer, as an ever-increasing proportion of its population has to be maintained in indolence. At Rome slaves were the only domestic servants, and after a time the only manufacturers. And yet even this is nothing compared to the evils of a state of society in which the great majority of women as well as of men are the absolute property of their masters. Horrible as was this state of things, it offered so many gratifications to the corrupt natures of those whose hands held the power of the world, and without whose consent it could not be abolished, that it would have seemed to any one who had ever witnessed the life of a wealthy Roman noble, no less than madness to imagine that any man would ever willingly surrender them.

As a matter of fact, so far was this state of society from holding out any hope of its own amendment, whether sudden or gradual, that, as my author remarks—

Of all the minds which have left a record of themselves, from Cicero to Tacitus, there is not one who does not look upon the world's course as a rapid descent. They feel an immense moral corruption breaking in on all sides, which wealth, convenience of life, and prosperity only enhance. They have no hope for humanity, for they have no faith in it, nor in any power encompassing and directing it.

Faithless and hopeless they were; but whatever this world could give they had in abundance :—

In the time of heathenism the world of sense which surrounded man flattered and caressed all his natural powers, and solicited an answer from them; and in return he flung himself greedily upon that world, and tried to exhaust its treasures. Glory, wealth, and pleasure intoxicated his heart with their dreams; he crowned himself with the earth's flowers, and drank in the air's perfume; and in one object or another, in one after another, he sought enjoyment and satisfaction. The world had nothing more to give him; nor will the latest growth of civilisation surpass the profusion with which the earth poured forth its gifts to those who consented to seek on the earth alone their home and their reward; though, indeed, they were the few, to whom the many were sacrificed. The Roman noble, with the pleasures of a vanquished world at his feet, with men and women from the fairest climes of the earth to do his bidding—men who, though slaves, had learnt all the arts and letters of Greece, and were ready to use them for the benefit of their lords; and women, the most beautiful and accomplished of their sex, who were yet the property of these same lords—the Roman noble, as to material and even intellectual enjoyment, stood on a vantage-ground which never again man can hope to occupy, however—

'Through the ages an increasing purpose runs,
And the thoughts of men are widen'd with the process of the suns.'

Cæsar and Pompey, Lucullus and Hortensius, and the fellows of their order, were orators, statesmen, jurists and legislators, generals, men of literature, and luxurious nobles at the same time; and they were this because they could use the minds as well as the bodies of others at their pleasure. Not in this direction was an advance possible (p. 159).

The author draws with great skill and vigour a picture of the moral society of the heathen world, and of the beliefs upon which the practice of the heathen rested. Into these I have no room to follow him. At the end of this lecture he shows what sights they were which met the eyes of a stranger coming from the East in the days of Nero—an execution in which four hundred men, women, and children were marched through the streets of Rome to the cross, because their master had been killed by one of his slaves. In all such cases the Roman law required that every slave in the house, however innocent, however young or however old—man, woman, or child—should be put to death. Thence the stranger passed to a scene of debauchery such as the world had never imagined, in the gardens close to the Pantheon. This stranger—

Why has he come to Rome, and what is he doing there? Poor, unknown, a foreigner in dress, language, and demeanour, he is come from a distant province, small in extent, but the most despised and the most disliked of Rome's hundred provinces, to found in Rome itself a society, and one, too, far more extensive than this great Roman Empire, since it is to embrace all nations; far more lasting, since it is to endure for ever. He is come to found a society, by means of which all that he sees around him, from the Emperor to the slave, shall be changed (p. 101).

What madness can have inspired such a hope, or what miracle, real or simulated, could fulfil it? And that, not in the golden age of pastoral simplicity, in which men looked for wonders with an uncritical eye, but 'amid the dregs of Romulus,' when all the world seemed to have fallen together into the 'sere and yellow leaf.'

He has two things within him, for want of which society was perishing and man unhappy: a certain knowledge of God as the Creator, Ruler, Judge, and Rewarder of men; and of man's soul made after the image and likeness of this God. This God he has seen, touched, and handled upon earth; has been an eye-witness of His majesty, has received His message, and bears His commission. But whence had this despised foreigner received the double knowledge of God and of the soul, so miserably lost (as we have seen) to this brilliant Roman civilisation?

In the latter years of Augustus, when the foundations of the imperial rule had been laid, and the structure mainly raised by his practical wisdom, there had dwelt a poor family in a small town of evil repute, not far from the lake of the remote province where this fisherman plied his trade. It consisted of an elderly man, a youthful wife, and one young child. The man gained his livelihood as a carpenter, and the child worked with him. Complete obscurity rested upon this household till the child grew to the age of thirty years (p. 104).

Then follows, in few words, the history of His life, death, and resurrection. These things the fisherman had seen, and in this was the power which was to substitute a new life for the corrupt civilisation of a world.

The details of the comparison which follows we may leave to be considered when the work is continued. They are drawn out with great spirit, thoughtfulness, and artistic beauty. For the comparison of the two systems in an individual Mr. Allies selects on the one side Cicero, on the other S. Augustine. An able reviewer has maintained that 'Marcus Aurelius was the person to compare with S. Augustine.' Mr. Allies has given his reasons for not selecting either Marcus Aurelius or Epictetus in the defective religious system of both. There were, however, other grounds which seem to me even stronger. To test what heathenism can do, it was necessary that the example selected should, as a chemist would say, present not a 'trace' of any other influence. Now this was impossible in the days of Epictetus or Aurelius. Christianity had then been taught and professed publicly and without restraint for many years, with only occasional bursts of persecution since Nero first declared war upon it. Its theology, indeed, was fully known only to the faithful, but its moral code was publicly professed. The Christian teachers came before the people as philosophers. It is absolutely certain that all the great Stoics, and especially the emperor, must often and often have heard of the great moral and religious principles laid down by the Christian teachers, however imperfect was his knowledge of their religious practices. But I have already had occasion to remark that men are driven, whether they will or no, to approve and admit these great principles when they are only publicly stated and maintained, although certain not to have discovered them by their unassisted reason. I cannot, therefore, but regard the religious and moral maxims of the later Stoics as an imperfect reflection of the full light of Christianity, like the moonlight illuminating without warming, but still taking such hold of the minds which have once embraced them, that they could never be forgotten. The life and practice of the imperial philosopher, I have every reason to believe, was, for a man without the faith and the sacraments, wonderfully high. Far be it from me to depreciate it, for whatever there was in it that was really good I know resulted from that grace which is given even beyond the bounds of the Church. But our knowledge of details is most meagre, while Cicero we know probably more familiarly than any great man in whose intimacy we have not lived. The thoughts and speculations which approved themselves to the deliberate judgment of Marcus Aurelius, these we know, and in many respects they are wonderful. Of his life we know little more than he chose publicly to exhibit to his subjects. The failings of Cicero were petty and degrading; but if he had been firmly seated on the throne of the Cæsars, and if we had possessed no more exact details of his life than we do of the life of Marcus Aurelius, I much doubt whether we should have been aware of them. Merivale says—'The high standard by which we claim to judge him is in itself the fullest acknowledgment of his transcendent merits; for, undoubtedly, had he not placed himself on a higher level than the statesmen and sages of his day, we should pass over many of his weaknesses in silence, and allow his pretensions to our regard to pass almost unchallenged. But we demand a nearer approach to the perfection of human wisdom and virtue in one who sought to approve himself as the greatest of their teachers.' He was condemned indeed by his heathen countrymen, but their censure was rather of his greatness than his goodness, and they would probably have been even more severe had he attained what he did not even aim at—Christian humility.

Considering these things, and especially that Cicero belonged almost to the last generation, which was wholly uninfluenced by the reflected light of Christianity, and in which, therefore, we can to a considerable degree measure the real effects of heathen philosophy, I venture to think that Mr. Allies has judged well in comparing him as the model heathen with S. Augustine as the model Christian. The comparison is drawn with a masterly hand.

On the whole, however, I incline to think that the two last lectures are of the greatest practical value, especially at the present crisis. The salt by which Christianity acts upon the world seems to be martyrdom and holy virginity. Both of them have been always in operation since the days of John the Baptist. But there are periods of comparative stillness in which martyrdom is hardly seen, or at least only at the outposts of the Christian host. At such times, it is by holy virginity that the Church acts most directly and most powerfully upon the world. This was the case in the Roman Empire as soon as persecution relaxed.

The author says—

A great Christian writer [S. Chrysostome] who stood between the old pagan world and the new society which was taking its place, and who was equally familiar with both, made, near the end of the fourth century, the following observation : 'The Greeks had some few men, though it was but few, among them, who, by the force of philosophy, came to despise riches ; and some, too, who could control the irascible part of man ; but the flower of virginity was nowhere to be found among them. Here they always gave precedence to us, confessing that to succeed in such a thing was to be superior to nature and more than man. Hence their profound admiration for the whole Christian people. The Christian host derived its chief lustre from this portion of its ranks.' And, again, he notes the existence, in his time, of three different sentiments respecting this institution. 'The Jews,' he says, 'turn with abhorrence from the beauty of virginity ; which, indeed, is no wonder, since they treated with dishonour the very Son of the

Virgin Himself. The Greeks, however, admire it, and look up to it with astonishment, but the Church of God alone cultivates it.' After fifteen hundred years we find the said sentiments in three great classes of the world. The pagan nations, among whom Catholic missionaries go forth, reproduce the admiration of Greek and Latin pagans; they reverence that which they have not strength to follow, and are often drawn by its exhibition into the fold. But there are nations who likewise reproduce the Jewish abhorrence of the virginal life. And as the Jews worshipped the unity of the godhead, like the Christians, and so seemed to be far nearer to them than pagan idolaters, and yet turned with loathing from this product of Christian life, so those nations might seem from the large portions of Christian doctrine which they still hold, to be nearer to Christianity than the Hindoo and the Chinese; and yet their contempt and dislike for the virginal life and its wonderful institutions seems to tell another tale. But now, as fifteen hundred years ago, whether those outside admire or abhor, the Church alone cultivates the virginal life. Now, as then, it is her glory and her strength, the mark of her Lord, and the standard of His power, the most *special* sign of His presence and operation. 'If,' says the same writer, 'you take away its seemliness and its continuity of devotion, you cut the very sinews of the virginal estate; so when it is possessed together with the best conduct of life, you have in it the root and support of all good things: just as a most fruitful soil nurtures a root, so a good conduct bears the fruits of virginity. Or, to speak with greater truth, the crucified life is at once both its root and its fruit (p. 382).

I must conclude by expressing my deliberate conviction that no study can be more important at the present day than that of the change from heathen civilisation to Christendom, the means by which it was brought about, and the effects which it produced. For in our day, most eminently, the Protestant falling away is producing its fruits in restoring throughout all Europe more and more of the special characteristics of heathen society. I have not room at present to offer any proofs of this, but I would beg every reader to observe for himself, and I am confident that his experience will confirm what I say. Nor is it only Catholics that are aware of this tendency. A thoughtful writer in the 'Saturday Review' six months back devoted a whole article to trace the points of resemblance between an educated English Protestant of our day and a heathen of cultivated mind. Those who feel disposed at once to regard the idea as an insult are probably judging of heathen civilisation by Nero and Domitian. Mr. Allies's book will at least dispel this delusion. In fact, it is only too obvious that there is, even in our own day, no want of plausibility in what is, at the bottom, only revived heathenism; and, in consequence of this remarkable resemblance, nothing could be more strictly practical at the present moment than any studies which show us the old heathen civilisation as it really was, in its attractive as well as its repulsive qualities.

II.

CHAMPAGNY'S ROMAN EMPIRE.[1]

I OWE my readers an apology for not having earlier invited their attention to the historical works of the Count de Champagny. They have for some years obtained a degree of popularity in France which would render any recommendation there quite needless. In England I have been surprised to find them unknown, not merely to persons of general intelligence, but to some whose attention has been specially directed to the Roman Empire. This is the more to be regretted because we have no work in our own language which exactly supplies their place; neither is it at all likely that such a work will be written. We have, indeed, from Mr. Merivale an able, learned, and interesting history of the 'Romans under the Empire.' But no man whose eyes have not been opened by the gift of faith can fully understand the history of those centuries, of which the one great and distinguishing event was the fulfilment of that prophecy of our Divine Lord, 'The kingdom of Heaven is like to leaven, which a woman took and hid in three measures of meal, until the whole was leavened.' Mr. Merivale's tone, of course, is as different as possible from that of Gibbon. Dr. Newman quotes (in 'The

---

[1] 'Les Césars.' Par le Comte Franz de Champagny. Paris: Ambroise Bray.
'Rome et la Judée au Temps de la Chute de Néron' (ans 66-72 après Jésus-Christ). Par le Comte F. de Champagny.
'Les Antonins' (ans de Jésus-Christ 69-180). Par le Comte de Champagny.

Church of the Fathers,' if I remember right) a sentence from a distinguished Anglican, regretting that the best English writer upon ecclesiastical history should be an infidel. The fact is, that Gibbon's history is in great measure ecclesiastical because his hatred of Christianity made him instinctively feel its presence, even where it was not prominently put forward, as some people are conscious when a cat is hidden in the room. Mr. Merivale's attitude towards Christianity is as different as possible, and if he wrote an ecclesiastical history it would be a contrast to that of Gibbon. But his is not an ecclesiastical history. It is only when the Church is forced upon his attention that it is noticed at all. He represents a class of minds which I suppose hardly exists except in Protestant countries—in our day I might probably have said, except in England. He believes in the truth of Christianity; he would, no doubt, be shocked to hear it doubted, much more denied; but he falls into the popular English notion, that, true as Christianity is, and important as it is in its own sphere, it is intended only for certain particular times and places. In fact, Christianity is a Sunday matter. And especially, when we read heathen histories of heathen times, and desire as much as possible to see things as they were seen by the contemporaries of Augustus or of Nero, a word about Christianity and the Christian Church would be as much out of place as if we were to fancy to ourselves Alexander the Great invading America and fighting with Montezuma (as poor Oliver Goldsmith was nearly betrayed into recording in his 'History of Greece'). Even under the Antonines Christianity is, in Mr. Merivale's view, very little more prominent. Hence, with one or two short, but, I doubt not, quite sincere recognitions of its truth, it is, as a general rule, simply ignored and forgotten in the greater part of his history.

Of course his explanation of this, to himself as well as to others, would be that he undertook to tell the story of the Roman

Empire as it has been told to us by Tacitus, Suetonius, &c., and that if there was nothing in Christianity which arrested their attention, there could be nothing which he was at liberty to mention. This, however, is simply to mistake the duty of an historian. He has to tell what is true, and nothing else. But if events of the highest importance, destined to produce most momentous results upon the happiness and welfare of many nations, were really in progress in the country and age of which he is writing, and if he has any means of tracing their development, nothing could be more absurd than that he should pass them over without notice, merely because they worked so gradually and secretly as not to arrest, at the time, the attention even of keen observers. Christianity then claims the special attention of the historian of the Roman Empire, not merely because it is the truth, and alone discloses our relations with the unseen world, but even upon much lower grounds, because its progress (even had it been a merely human event) would have been by far the most momentous event of those times, and therefore the most proper subject of the historian, even if he were personally without religion. And this would be even more his duty if so important an event had been overlooked by contemporary heathen writers; for history is never more strictly in her proper task than when she is tracing to their earliest beginnings, events which have afterwards developed themselves into an importance as unforeseen as it is momentous.

Let me give an example of what I mean. The introduction of standing armies was unquestionably the most important political change in the history of modern Europe. When introduced in one nation, all were obliged to follow the example. This at once made it impossible to continue the system of government which prevailed everywhere during the middle ages. On the Continent it led to despotic government, in England to the supremacy of Parliament. It has introduced the system of 'great powers,' instead of that before existing, of a multitude of small states with the Holy Father for the arbiter of all. It threatens results still more important—the absolute domination of two or three states, perhaps of one. Now Hallam seems to prove that this system was silently introduced by Charles VII. of France, when he was restoring some degree of order after the murderous devastation caused by the English wars. It can hardly be doubted that a contemporary Frenchman must have thought it far less important than the marriage of a daughter of France with a prince of the blood, or the wresting of some petty fortress from the English. But, great as this change was, incalculably greater was the change which was working unobserved and unremembered, in the Roman Empire, during the centuries of which the Count of Champagny and Mr. Merivale have written. This must be admitted even by unbelievers, for even they cannot shut their eyes to the fact that the spread of Christianity, however little they may love it, was at least the most important event in history. . What M. Champagny then has done is to trace the progress and effects of this great event in its earlier stages ; while the fashion with historians has been to shut their eyes and turn away their thoughts from it altogether, until at last, in the time of Constantine and his successors, it forced itself upon them. Which of the two is most worthy of a philosopher I need hardly say, even if Christianity had been merely a human philosophy, and not, as it is, the one remedy revealed by God for the evils of this world, as well as the only hope and light for that which is still unseen.

I sincerely believe that this merit of the author (and a great merit it is) is, in fact, the main fault which has been found in him by Protestant readers and critics. The 'Saturday Review,' for instance, in reviewing the second of the three works before me (which relates the fall of Jerusalem), admits that M. de Champagny's 'narrative is spirited, his learning considerable, and his description of the Roman Empire and its several provinces generally faithful and picturesque.' This is high praise to be given from that quarter to a work zealously Catholic. His 'main blemishes,' adds the reviewer, are 'credulity and ultra-judicial zeal,' *i.e.* credulity as to the narrative of the martyrs—ultra-judicial zeal in tracing the judgments of God, not a mere political catastrophe, in the great tragedy of Jewish history. The Count, he complains, 'is not content with descrying in events the swift or tardy justice of heaven. He traces it equally in their accessories and minor phenomena, and seats himself, like Minos and Rhadamanthus in Plato's Republic, before the folding doors of Orchus, sending nations, principalities, and powers to the right or left, according to his own notions of the fitness of things. But it would be hard to persuade us that, in the first century of the Christian era, even Jerusalem was more wicked than Rome. To be consistent, the Count should doom both, or show reason why the former was annihilated and the latter permitted to oppress the earth for full two centuries longer. Then, in our opinion, he ascribes too much influence to the early workings of the leaven of Christianity. He magnifies Nero's persecution, in which it is doubtful whether the victims were singled out as Christians, and not rather taken up at random as turbulent Jews, &c.'

I have given this passage in full, from a desire to do justice to M. de Champagny quite as much as to his reviewer; for I presume that when the 'Saturday Review,' highly commending the literary and historical merits of a book, finds nothing more than these as its blemishes, most English Catholics, and a very large proportion of English Protestants, will come to the conclusion that it is well worth their careful study: for, in truth, the complaint comes to this, that, while viewing the Roman Empire with the eyes of an historian and a philosopher, the author views it preeminently with the instincts of a Christian and a Catholic. Upon this charge, I must own myself unable to give M. de Champagny a verdict of 'not guilty.' Still the passage itself is remarkable, as an indication of the state of opinion and feeling spreading in England. The Count judges the nations 'according to his own notions of the fitness of things.' The writer, in more than one part of the same article, makes a rather prominent profession of writing as a Christian. Yet so much is he accustomed to regard all religious doctrines as the notions of this or that individual, that it did not even cross his mind that the Count believes and professes to judge, not by his own notions, but a divinely revealed rule. And then he cannot understand the peculiar guilt of Jerusalem. Is it possible that he has never read or heard the history of the Passion; the cry of the mad populace, 'His blood be upon us and upon our children;' or the prophecies of our Divine Lord, and His weeping over the city, while He foretold its desolation, expressly as the punishment of its rejection of Himself? I know not when I have met a more striking example of the pagan method of regarding and weighing the facts even of sacred history. Not that the writer means to be irreligious. Far from it. He even indulges in religious remarks himself. He says: 'The catastrophe of the Hebrew nation must always be profoundly interesting to Christian readers, who in its fall behold the accomplishment of a train of prophecies, and in its errors an impressive lesson on pride, stubbornness, and bigotry.' Only he has so much accustomed himself to consider belief and disbelief as a legitimate exercise of private judgment, and a thing which it would be bigotry to praise or condemn, that he cannot bring himself to believe that the rejection of God made flesh, the clamorous cries for His crucifixion, and the denial of His authority, can really have brought down upon any people so terrible a judgment. After all, these Chief Priests and Pharisees, at whose awful wickedness in rejecting the Christ of God Christians in all ages have shuddered with horror—what were they (according to modern uncatholic notions) but 'reverend gentlemen of the Jewish persuasion,' and what else was their obstinacy except adherence to the 'religion by law established' in their country?

Of the three works before me, the first, 'The Cæsars,' begins with a rapid glance at the state of Rome and Italy, and their history during the period in which the old republic was breaking up (which the author fixes as commencing after the destruction of Carthage). In the second chapter he takes up the narrative from the birth of the great Dictator Julius, and carries it on to the death of Nero. This history occupies a little more than half the three volumes. It is followed by a 'picture of the Roman world,' which, to any thinking reader, will be by far the most interesting, as it certainly is the most original, part of the work. At the same time, some readers may consider it a blemish, in a work professedly a history, that it contains, perhaps, even more of reflections upon history, pictures of the times, &c., than of narrative. I do not accede to this censure. It means, after all, little more than this—that M. de Champagny sets before us, not merely the emperors, their families, and their courts, but especially the nations, tribes, and individuals over whom they ruled. He had in fact much more right than Mr. Merivale to have taken the title 'The Romans under the Empire,' rather than 'The Cæsars.' This is a great merit, the want of which our own age has especially blamed in the historians of past times. We complain that while they tell us in detail strange and grotesque stories of tyrants, some of which would almost seem to be more in their natural place in the 'Thousand and One Nights' than in the annals of a great and grave people, they give us no means of judging what sort of lives were led by the mass of their subjects, how they spent their time, in what things they found their pleasure, to what businesses they devoted their energies, how they lived and how they died. These are the questions which M. de Champagny answers in the 'picture,' which occupies nearly half his work on the Cæsars, and which is, in my judgment, by far the most interesting part of it, and I hardly know where I should point for one more interesting. At the same time, it is one of which it is not easy to give specimens, although I shall have to recur to many parts of it as I go on.

After 'The Cæsars' came 'Rome and Judæa.' This is a history of only six years. Its main interest, of course, is in the destruction of Jerusalem and the Jewish worship and polity. Combined with this, however, is the contemporary history of Rome, which contains the strange military revolutions which followed the death of Nero.

It was a remarkable coincidence that while the Roman armies were already gathering in fatal circle round Jerusalem, destined, against the will of their commanders, to fulfil to the letter the prediction of our Divine Lord, and to consume with fire the 'holy and beautiful house' which was the glory of the Jewish nation, the only temple in the world without an idol, at that very moment the Capitol itself and the temple of Jupiter, which the Romans identified with the eternal majesty of Rome itself, should also have been consumed, in the short struggle between the supporters of Vitellius and Vespasian. It is impossible not to feel as if the Almighty Ruler of the world were teaching the nations that the old dispensations were to be swept away, and all things were now to become new.

Then follows what strikes me as one of the most interesting parts of this history—the estimate of position of the Jewish people in the Roman Empire before the last fatal war. Even under the Republic, and still more under the Empire, they were the spoiled children of the Roman State. By Julius Cæsar they were exempted from tribute in every seventh year, in which, by the law of Moses, the land was not to be cultivated. This is specially interesting, because, so far as I am aware, there is no positive testimony in the Old Testament to the actual observance of this law. Gibbon sneers at it as impossible. We must suppose either that at the time of the great Dictator it was observed more or less generally, or that he had so much reverence for the law of Moses as to make so very striking a recognition of it, even on a point as to which it was in practice obsolete. In either case, the fact is most remarkable. It was, however, but one among many. The author devotes a whole chapter ('Rome and Judæa,' vol. i. chap. iv.) to the condition of the Jewish people before the reign of Nero. The effect of the evidence which he collects from many very different quarters will, I think, surprise even those who were before acquainted with most of the detached facts. The numbers of the Jewish people had long increased far beyond the capacities of their own land, even in its then fruitful state, of which in its present barren condition we can form a very imperfect idea. Everywhere they were found, and everywhere they were wealthy and powerful. In Jerusalem itself the greatest respect was paid by their Roman masters to the national religion, the bond and pledge of their distinct nationality.

In all parts of the world the Roman legions bore before them images of the emperors, to which idolatrous honours were paid. The orderly and conservative spirit of Rome forbade that the universal custom should anywhere be dispensed with. But into Jerusalem, and Jerusalem alone, the legions were never permitted to enter without veiling them from the inhabitants of the holy city. Some pagans stealthily placed the image of Cæsar in a synagogue, and it was removed by Cæsar's representative. Inscriptions in Greek and Latin were placed at the entrance of the court of the Temple reserved to the Israelites, denouncing the penalty of death to any heathen who should trespass farther. The language of the two great conquering races, the language of empire, and the language of heathen philosophy, thus bowed down before the exclusive majesty of the Hebrew law. The Jews were even exempted from military service, that their scruples might not be offended by serving under the symbols of idolatry. The Roman State afforded its special protection to the transmission of gold from all parts of the Empire to the Temple of Jerusalem. Even before the fall of the republic, a Roman magistrate in Asia had been impeached for having interfered with it. The irritable and proud conscience of the Jews obtained respect even for its scruples. Pilate once ventured to hang upon the walls of a palace some golden bucklers consecrated to Tiberius, and marked simply with his name. The Jews complained to the Emperor himself of this flattery of the Emperor, and Pilate was reprimanded.

The toleration was carried even to worship. Pompeius in the giddiness of victory had ventured to enter the sanctuary. But the sight of that shrine without an idol had checked him in wonder and reverence. He had respected the Temple, the city, the treasure, and had directed the priests to expiate the next day the profanation which he himself had thrown upon the sanctuary. And be it observed that Cicero, while pleading for Flaccus, although he attacks the Jews, because he was acting as the advocate of one of their enemies — Cicero himself praises this moderation on the part of Pompeius. Others had been impressed with the same feeling of veneration. Hardly would a Roman in any official character so much as enter the court of the Temple, to which the Gentiles were admitted, without offering his adoration to the God of Israel. Agrippa, the minister of Augustus, while staying at Jerusalem, never let a day pass without visiting the Temple and making costly offerings. Livia, the consort of Augustus, gave cups and vases of gold. Augustus himself, though he commanded the members of his family to abstain from personal worship, not only made similar offerings, but directed that a bull and two lambs should be offered daily at his cost and in his name to that unknown God of Jerusalem, with whose greatness he had been struck. This daily sacrifice, continued by his successors and celebrated by the Jews with pious zeal, was long the pledge of Roman toleration and of Jewish submission, the seal of friendship between Rome and Jerusalem.—(*Rome and Judæa*, vol. i. ch. iv.)

The very jokes of Horace and Cicero upon the Jews showed the reality and extent of their influence on Rome itself. In our own day, for instance, no man (even in Poland or Jamaica) would, even in satire, represent himself as refusing to enter upon a matter of business because it was the Jewish Sabbath. 'The Jews,' says our author, ' caused the lamentations of the Hebrew Scriptures to resound around the funeral pile of Cæsar.' Everywhere they enjoyed the rights of citizenship. S. Paul's possession of the citizenship of Tarsus and of Rome itself was no rare privilege. In most at least of the Greek cities, they enjoyed it before the Roman conquest; the author refers to authorities proving that this was the case at Alexandria, Antioch, Cæsarea, and other cities; he adds, 'Pompeius, Cæsar, Antonius, Augustus, Agrippa, in gratitude for their enthusiasm, or their services, maintained their liberties, confirmed their exemption from military service, protected the transmission of gold to the Temple, and caused their privileges, which the Greek cities were always tempted to forget, to be inscribed in bronze.' Claudius published a decree, giving them, in all the cities of the Empire, the same privileges which they enjoyed at Alexandria. Above all, they possessed the same right of citizenship in Rome itself, and the number of Jewish citizens was so considerable that, by a special enactment, whenever the public distribution of corn (which formed so important a part of the privileges of the poorer citizens) took place upon the Sabbath, they were authorised to receive their share the day following. The fact is, that accustomed during many centuries to form a part of one or other great Empire, and placing their nationality in their religion rather than in their government, the Jews were perfectly prepared to yield a hearty support to the Roman conquerors, and wherever they were settled they came to be regarded, alike by the people and by the Romans themselves, as a sort of garrison for Rome.

To complete the resemblance between the people of Israel now and then, the Jews, in the first century as well as the nineteenth, were the men to turn their liberty to the greatest advantage. In our own day we see what that race has become, which has hardly been naturalised in the states of Christendom for sixty years, and the position they have made for themselves, not only in finance, but in politics, in science, in literature. The Jewish race is certainly one of those most richly gifted by God; for He has given it patience combined with boldness, ingenuity with energy, eloquence with finesse, sentiment with the pursuit of gain. It was then what it is now, only more entire and more near to the sources of inspiration. Then, as now, it knew how to use the liberties it had succeeded in obtaining.

In numbers the Jews were increasing, while the Greeks and Romans (by immorality and the exposure of infants) were rapidly declining in numbers. M. Champagny quotes the express testimony of Tacitus, 'They desire to increase their numbers. To kill any of their families is to them an abomination. They believe also that the souls of those killed in battle, or by the executioner, are eternal. Hence they desire to become fathers.' The Jews in the Roman Empire the author calculates at eight or nine millions. What is more remarkable was the spread of their religion by proselytism. There was all over the earth a real famine of the knowledge of any true God. This knowledge the Jews had, and although there is no reason to suppose that the desire to propagate it was widely spread among them, they could not prevent the light from being more or less seen: 'a city set upon a mountain cannot be hid.' The 'Acts of the Apostles' give us many indications of proselytes to the Law. The kings and nobles of Adiabene (a heathen dynasty which reigned to the east of the Tigris under the protection of Parthia) were converted to the Jewish religion, it is said, by the teaching of a Hebrew merchant, retained it for several generations, and sent aid to the defence of the sacred city and the Temple against Titus.

At Damascus almost all the Tyrian women followed the law of Israel. Rome herself felt the attraction. Many men, many more women of Rome, converted in different degrees, some even so far as circumcision, observed either the fasts, the abstinences, or the Sabbaths. In Horace, Seneca, Persius, Tacitus, and Juvenal, we find Rome teeming with these proselytes, the Sabbaths and fasts publicly observed, the feasts of the Jews known by everybody, lanterns lighted in the windows on the days of Jewish solemnities. Plutarch bears equally strong testimony to the notorious observance of the Jewish religion in the Greek cities. The description, 'a proselyte,' occurs in connection with the names of Roman women in the catacombs of the Jews at Rome. Dion, speaking of the Sabbath and the custom of dividing time by periods of seven days, adds :—'The ancient Greeks, so far as I am aware, knew nothing of this usage. In our day it is familiar to all men, and especially to the Romans, with whom it has become one of the customs of their country.'

The author concludes that the Jews, before the destruction of their city, were much in their present situation, with the addition of a religious earnestness and zeal which they have now quite lost.

But our conception of the position of the Jewish people would be very incomplete unless we bore in mind what Jerusalem was in itself, and especially what it was to them. It was on April 9, A.D. 68, that Titus and his army came within sight of the city, and looked down on that glorious spectacle, by which, thirty years before, 'the King of Israel, who came in the name of the Lord,' had been moved to tears.

The country round Jerusalem had not then the aspect of desolation and barrenness which in our day goes to the heart of travellers, and has inspired so many beautiful and mournful words. Five consecutive centuries of habitation and cultivation had overcome the naturally rugged soil. The olive, the fig, the vine, were flourishing on every side. Water artificially distributed enriched a land naturally unproductive. Aqueducts and subterranean channels brought water to Jerusalem, which was never in want of it amid all the sufferings of the siege. In the midst of this rich landscape, across the precipitous ravine of Cedron, the eye rested on Jerusalem; and the city, which was called by Pliny the most illustrious of the whole East, appeared encircled by a range of towers, which, being raised to a proportional height wherever the ground was lowest, appeared to be all on the same level, and encircled the city like a diadem.

But above this imposing crown of towers rose several pinnacles still more elevated. Sion, the city of David, which predominated over the whole city, dominated over in its turn by the three towers of Hippicos, Phasaël, and Mariamne, each of which, massy and glittering, seemed as if carved out of a single block of white marble. Somewhat nearer, to the left, was the tower of Antonia, the guardian over the temple. Further back, beyond the rising ground of Bezetha, which concealed the lower part of it, appeared the higher parts of the Temple, white as snow, except where its whiteness was relieved by plates of gold, and lifting to the sky the thousand pinnacles which crowned its summit. The city of David and of Solomon was not then the needy and mournful place which recalls to pilgrims the lamentations of Jeremias and the dolours of Calvary. It was a rich, strong, and powerful city. Agrippa had enlarged it almost by one half; every one of the Herods had laboured to ornament it. Pilate had built aqueducts for it. The proselyte kings of Adiabene had palaces within its walls. The Cæsars had enriched it with gifts. At once wealthy and provident, encircled with towers and filled with palaces, its citadels were places of delight, its towers soaring two hundred feet in height (the battlements of which were soon to pour out on the assailants boiling oil) contained baths, reservoirs of water, banquet-halls, and lodging for hundreds of courtiers and slaves. The frame of mountains from among which it stood out set off the brilliancy of its white marble and gold. On the left, beyond the arid valley of the Cedron, rose the Mount of Olives, the dark foliage of which threw into relief the whiteness of the porticoes of the Temple. In the background, the more distant mountains of Tekoa, abrupt, rocky, grey, as travellers see them at this day—those, at least, are unchanged.'—(*Rome and Judæa*, vol. ii. c. xv.)

Elsewhere we hear that Jerusalem was considered to surpass Rome in beauty and riches as much as it was inferior in extent. Caligula was said to have had his imagination early turned to the East by the descriptions of Jerusalem which he heard from the captive chief Agrippa, in the days when the fate of both equally was trembling in the balance, in the palace of the jealous Tiberius. The wealth of the city was so great that the value of gold and silver in Syria is said to have fallen by one-half when its spoils were dispersed by the victorious soldiers of Titus.

Well might Titus desire to preserve from destruction so noble an ornament of the Roman Empire; but Jerusalem was doomed.

Her outward beauties, rich as they were, were but the faint reflection of her true dignity, as 'the city of the Great King.' This was lost on the day when her sons cried out, ' We have no king but Cæsar !' Henceforth her outward beauty was like that which a corpse retains for a while, after the living spirit has departed from it, and now the time was come that even this should pass away.

M. de Champagny very strikingly traces the connection, as natural cause and effect, between the rejection of the true Christ and the utter destruction of the city, temple, and polity of the Jews. It is impossible to consider the amount of the prosperity of the Jews under the Empire and of the solid ends to which they turned it, without astonishment that a people so highly favoured by the rulers of the world, and turning their favour to such good account, should have broken out into a hopeless rebellion, and persisted in it with an obstinacy which almost compelled the conqueror to push his victory to their utter destruction. It was the more marvellous, because (as I shall have another occasion to notice) at that very period other provinces, even when less favoured and with much less to lose, clung to the Empire from a sense of the benefits it secured to them. It is impossible to doubt that, but for their own utter madness, the Jews might have continued to enjoy, under the shadow of the Imperial rule, the high position which they had attained, and an ever-increasing prosperity. In one passage (if I am not mistaken) the author speaks as if there existed, even then, a dislike towards them greater perhaps than that of our own days. This I cannot imagine possible. That there would be a great jealousy of a people so separate from all others, so closely united among themselves, and exciting so much envy by their exceptional prosperity, cannot be doubted. An able writer says, 'What is most hateful to a nation is another nation,' and the more the maxim is weighed the more its truth will be felt. But, to call out this hatred, the two nations must be in pretty close intercourse. This, I presume, has made France, in times past, 'the natural enemy' of England. This assuredly it is which is always endangering the good-will which for a thousand reasons ought to exist between England and her own flesh and blood in the United States. The danger in this last case would be far less if the two had not a common language. But while circumstances have impressed and are daily more deeply impressing upon the people of the States a distinct national character, their use of our language enables them to read day by day, from one end of the Union to the other, English newspapers and reviews which bring home to their feelings our distinct nationality. It is obvious at the same time how entirely wanting on this side the Atlantic is the animosity which so often shows itself on the other side. Perhaps it would not be so if American newspapers were as widely read here as English papers are in America. But I must return to the Jews. There were causes in plenty to make them more or less unpopular in the provincial cities, especially in Egypt and the East. But this unpopularity could hardly have been so great as that of the haughty Roman conquerors themselves. And except under some strange combination of circumstances (such as the madness of the unhappy youth Caligula) the Jews were certain of Roman protection for their persons, property, and privileges. Their unpopularity itself, therefore, was but a pledge for their continued fidelity to the Empire. How came it that they suffered themselves to forfeit the protection and to draw down upon themselves the full force of that arm irresistible by any earthly might?

The answer to this question the author gives in a most interesting chapter ('Rome and Judæa,' vol. i. chap. v.), in which he traces first the well-known expectation prevailing among all nations, alike of the East and West, about the time of Augustus, that a great king and deliverer, a restorer of that golden age of which the poets had sung, was immediately about to appear.

Moreover, even among heathen nations, this general expectation was so specially connected with Jerusalem, that when Nero found Rome slipping out of his grasp he had been assured by his astrologers that he was destined to found a new empire at Jerusalem ('Cæsars,' vol. ii. p. 233). Among the Jews alone this prophecy took a form distinct, definite, intelligible, for upon them alone the sun of divine prophecy had shone clearly out (like a gleam falling upon one spot of a clouded landscape), while the other nations only saw its obscure reflection. By them it was clearly understood that the times were fulfilled, the ages marked out by Daniel the Prophet had run their course, and the Prince of Peace was ready to be revealed, who was to unite all nations under his sceptre, but who was especially to be the King of Israel as well as the Son of David. The time came, universal peace was at length established, a deep silence of expectation reigned over the whole world. Bossuet sums up the history of Augustus : 'Victorieux par mer et par terre, il ferme le Temple de Janus (A.U.C. 753). Tout l'univers vit en paix sous sa puissance, et Jésus-Christ vient au monde.' 'He came unto His own, and His own received Him not.' The 'time of visitation' passed by unknown to them. According to the prophecy of Malachias, 'The Lord whom they sought came suddenly to His temple,' and they knew Him not. He had come and gone, and they were still in expectation—an expectation which like a maddening thirst grew daily more and more intolerable. For a while, indeed, they persuaded themselves that they had mistaken some detail in their calculation of the times defined by Daniel the Prophet, and that the time, instead of being gone by, was immediately to come. It is touching to read how they were compelled to abandon, one after another, each of these hopes. At last they could no longer doubt that the time was come. In every whistle of the breeze, in every light upon the sky, in every rumour upon the earth, they listened for, they looked out for, they heard, they saw, the coming Messias.

Then were fulfilled the words spoken in sorrow, and yet in condemnation, by our Divine Lord: 'I have come in the name of My Father, and they do not receive Me; if another shall come in his own name, him they will receive.' Then, according to His prophecy, arose false Christs and false prophets, saying, 'I am He,' and all the policy of the chiefs of the nation failed to prevail with the multitude not to go after them. The intense pain of long-protracted disappointment necessarily resulting from the wilful blindness which had failed to distinguish the true King of Israel when they saw Him, goaded them on to insurrection and destruction. Even when Jerusalem was already encompassed with armies, when the Christian remnant, recognising the signs given them by their Lord, had already fled to the mountains, and had found shelter under the protection of Agrippa at Pella, it was the certainty that, let the years of Daniel be interpreted as they might, the time for their fulfilment must have arrived, that impelled the Jewish people to reject all the offers of Titus and to risk upon a fortune, humanly speaking, utterly desperate, not merely their lives and families, but what was to them dearer still, their holy city, the holy and beautiful house where their fathers had worshipped, and the polity of the once chosen people. Thus in God's righteous judgment did the very expectation of the Messias become the sting which urged madly on to ruin the people and city which had refused to acknowledge Him when He came unto them.

It is impossible to resist the thoughts which crowd upon the mind in contemplating this appalling catastrophe. The whole history of the world, no doubt, is that of man neglecting or throwing away callings and opportunities given to him by God. But I can hardly err in saying that no other instance of it has been so striking, so miserable. What was the part designed in the Divine purposes for Israel, if he had been true to his vocation? Already, in spite of all his failings and unfaithfulness, he was, in the midst of the heathen world, a chosen witness to the existence, the unity, and the attributes of God. Already his witness had been heard and weighed by thousands. If the Messias had not been rejected; if even at the last moment, after the day of Pentecost, He had been acknowledged, not merely by the 'remnant,' but by the nation as a nation, the imagination strives in vain to paint to itself the blessings, both to Israel and to the world, which would have resulted. Here, surely, I may apply the words of S. Paul, 'If the loss of them was the reconciliation of the world, what would the receiving of them have been but life from the dead?' What would it have been if the synagogue in every city had been a pharos, 'shining as lights in the world, holding forth the word of life,' instead of the citadel, held by its most obstinate enemies? And the same change would have averted the destruction of the city and nation. For the fanaticism which drew down upon them the avenging sword of Rome was excited, as we have seen, by the perpetually-disappointed expectation of the coming of the Messias. Nay, the causes of their unpopularity in the Empire would have been diminished almost indefinitely by the more amiable social qualities which their hearty acceptance of the true Christ would have developed; while the fatal influence of false Christs would have been wholly prevented. I venture to think that M. de Champagny has been led to exaggerate the measure of their disfavour with other populations, owing to his knowledge of the hatred which has been felt towards them in Christian nations. It is needless to say that although in the middle ages every circumstance which had made them unpopular in the Greek and Roman cities existed in full, and even in increased form, the feeling towards them was caused, not by this, but by the recollection of their great national crime, which each succeeding generation of Jews seemed to continue and make its own, by its continued rejection of the true Christ. It is impossible to estimate the spiritual and temporal grandeur of the position which the nation would have occupied, had she but known the day of her visitation.

Miserable indeed it is to turn our eyes from that which we cannot doubt was the gracious purpose of God to the lot which she chose for herself. The events which led, step by step, to that awful catastrophe, are excellently described by M. de Champagny—how the multitudes of the nation were collected into the holy city; how all the desires even of the heathen conqueror to save it were frustrated by the obstinacy and fanaticism of the contending factions; how overwhelming was the destruction; how the remnant was condemned, as if in insult, to pay to the temple of the Capitoline Jupiter the very offering, the didrachma, which the Jews had been privileged to send from all quarters of the earth to the shrine of the true God at Jerusalem; how they were driven once and again into desperate attempts to rise; and how each effort only sank them deeper. And then comes not merely the oppression of their enemies, but (as Moses had foretold) the last degradation of their own souls. Their temple and worship finally gone, the distinction of their priestly tribe forgotten, their religion had no longer either a reason for its existence, or a means to keep it alive. It was a dead tree. The people sank as much below the religious level of the nations among which they were dwelling, as their forefathers had been above that of the heathen nations. The twilight of Judaism had been a bright light when surrounded by the dense darkness of paganism. In the clear shining of Gospel light, it lay like a dark spot amid fresh snow.

But I must not longer dwell upon the two volumes ('Rome and Judæa') which give that thrilling episode of the history of the Roman Empire, the fall of Jerusalem. These are followed by three, on the 'Antonines,' in which, besides continuing the history of the Empire and the emperors for a further period of a hundred and eleven years, the author suggests numberless most interesting trains of thought, and especially that to which I referred at the opening of this chapter, the unseen and unrecognised influence of the Church upon the whole moral and social state of the world, even while the world was still heathen. It was especially to these three volumes, though by no means to the exclusion of the others, that a distinguished French writer referred when he wrote—' Le plus beau privilége des écrivains qui pensent, c'est de faire penser ceux qui les lisent. M. de Champagny fait penser.'

Perhaps the most startling of his propositions is that more personal freedom was enjoyed by freemen under the Roman Empire than under any modern [Continental] government. Yet he proves it. He naturally thinks chiefly of France, but I believe the other Continental nations are in the same condition.

We, the proud citizens of a parliamentary monarchy, who have made revolutions when we were called subjects—*subjects* we were, and still are at every turn of our lives. We were and are unable to go from Paris to Neuilly ; or dine more than twenty together ; or have in our portmanteau three copies of the same tract ; or lend a book to a friend ; or put a patch of mortar upon our own house if it stands in a street ; or kill a partridge ; or plant a tree near a roadside ; or take coal out of our own land ; or teach three or four children to read ; or gather our neighbours for prayer; or have in our house an oratory [what constitutes an oratory?]; or bleed a sick man ; or sell him a medicine ; or (in some countries) be married ; or do any of a thousand other things which it would fill volumes to enumerate—without permission from the civil government. And this permission, we are carefully told, is always in its very nature subject to be recalled. Commonly, indeed, the government does not either authorise or forbid—it tolerates. We live by toleration. Thanks to the merciful and indulgent toleration of the civil government, we are permitted (until we receive orders to the contrary) to be born, to have a home, a family, to bring up our children, to have a God, to have a religion. Only one event there is in human life over which the government has not authority. We die without requiring its permission, but we cannot be buried without it. At certain moments we are sovereign over certain great and public matters; but in small matters of private life we are subjects, and much less than subjects. Unluckily, these small matters make up our lives, and these private matters are their most important events.— (*Antonins*, vol. ii. p. 181.)

This passage describes, in very few words, the real difference between the English and Continental ideas of government. Every successive French government, old *régime*, republic, empire, monarchy of the Restoration, monarchy of July, second republic, second empire—all have been alike in this. What we mean by 'personal liberty' has been unknown, and not even generally desired under any of them. This perpetual interference of the civil authority with every action of private life is maintained, I believe, under all Continental governments alike, chiefly because it increases the patronage of the government, by finding employment for thousands of petty functionaries. So far is this bad system carried, that, as a general rule, young men, instead of making a career for themselves, learn from their childhood to look to government patronage for their support and advancement. In England (as Mr. Göschen stated from the hustings at his late election) there is a perpetually increasing tendency, not on the part of government to interfere, but on the part of the people to call for its interference. Within reasonable limits, this cannot be avoided. In a highly complicated state of society like ours, it is no longer possible to maintain in all points the custom of our ancestors, who left everything to be done by unpaid local agents, selected by their neighbours. In London, for instance, we should be sorry to exchange the 'Peelers' for the old-fashioned constables and watchmen. But it is essential that we should observe and guard against the inevitable tendency of advancing civilisation to throw more and more power into the hands of the central government, and thus to substitute the perpetual interference of civil authorities for personal liberty and local self-government. To this gradual increase of administrative interference M. de Champagny in a great degree attributes the decay of the Roman Empire. In its earlier days, even under Caligula and Nero (however the nobles of the city might suffer under the tyranny of a madman), the mass of the provincials and the humbler classes of freemen, even in Rome, were really free. And this liberty of the Empire, the author shows, was as important in preparing the way for the successful preaching of the Gospel as were the unity and universal peace, the effects of which have so often been traced. He says : [1]—

A modern European, as soon as he leaves his home and begins to act, to think, or to live among his fellows, must assume that everything is forbidden which is not expressly authorised. Under the Roman Empire all that was not expressly forbidden was understood to be authorised. Above all, the intellectual liberty was entire. Every one talked, listened, gave and received information publicly, and as he pleased. Doctrines spread; schools raised themselves without the interference of the secular power, until it felt itself in danger, not from the general independence of thought (that misgiving had not yet been conceived), but from the special character of some teaching which arrested its attention. Even when the Imperial government resolved upon severity, its rigour might often be averted, sometimes even paralysed, by the municipal authority, which alone was on the spot and in activity in the interior of each great city. Thus the Christian teachers and apologists presented themselves as 'philosophers.' For, as a general rule, philosophers were at liberty to teach what they pleased.

This was the natural result of a state of society in which the national religion taught nothing, true or false. When a system which really exercised authority over conscience came in conflict with it, then, and not before, the civil government took the alarm, and hence Christianity alone came, after a time, to be excepted from the general liberty allowed to all philosophies.

But this liberty was a happy accident, arising from circum-

[1] There are some omissions in this extract.

stances, not grounded on principles; and hence, as the author shows, it was gradually diminished as the administration of the Roman Empire became more systematised, until, about a century after the Antonines, the prevalent system was that of 'a semi modern monarchy.'

Nothing can more strongly confirm M. Champagny's opinion that the earlier Roman Empire was 'a federation of free nations under an absolute monarch' than the feeling with which, as a matter of fact, it was regarded by the conquered provinces. Gaul was conquered, after a desperate and heroic resistance, fifty years B.C. How soon afterwards it was left practically without a controlling Roman force I do not know. Before the death of Nero (A.D. 68) such had long been its natural condition. A small army on the north-eastern boundary repelled the wild and warlike German tribes; but even this was composed of natives. In the civil war which followed, the mass of this force marched into Italy with Vitellius. A few enterprising Gauls took the opportunity to restore the national independence. Even they, however, so far from proposing to abolish the Roman institutions, only wished to establish an independent empire—in fact, to make Gaul, not Italy, the seat of the Roman Empire. Hence it seems to have been that, contrary to all precedent, the remainder of the legions was drawn into the scheme. For several months the whole province was literally without one Roman soldier. The provincials, left wholly to themselves, held a meeting of delegates from all the Gallic nations at Treves, and, after full discussion, determined (as it seems by an overwhelming majority) to continue subject to the Roman Empire.

And this was a country of free and brave warriors, conquered for the first time not a hundred and twenty years before.

Ireland has now been subject to the kings of England for about 700 years. If any conjuncture should draw out of it every British soldier except a very few of Irish origin, and if these should all be drawn into a movement for the independence of Ireland, is it likely that the representatives of the whole nation, meeting freely, and after full discussion, would resolve by a large majority that things should remain as they are?

One would almost be tempted to doubt whether, in the art of government, England herself had not something to learn from Imperial Rome.

The author is specially interested in tracing the gradual unobserved action of the Church upon the worst evil of Roman society—its slave system. As a matter of fact, all through the period of which the author treats, the position of the slave was gradually being changed for the better. In theory Aristotle had pronounced slavery an institution both natural and necessary; Dion, a century after the Incarnation of our Blessed Lord, declared it to be unlawful. In law, Augustus had confirmed to the master the power of life and death; Adrian deprived him of it, and Antoninus Pius went so far as to forbid by law even the ill-treatment of a slave. Marcus Aurelius even gave the slave in certain cases the right to demand his freedom.

Meanwhile the whole jurisprudence, contrary to the fundamental and universal law of slavery, inclined, timidly no doubt, to the acknowledgment of certain family ties between slaves. It did not absolutely forbid the separation of the wife from the husband, or of the children from their mother, for that would have been to overthrow the institution itself; but it allowed it with manifest reluctance and difficulty. Men's habits and feelings underwent a similar change. Cicero conceals, as a humiliating weakness, tears shed at the death of one of his slaves. Pliny the younger deems it an honour to have wept for his. He boasts that he considered them 'his neighbours,' and treated them as his children. As a last indication of the same feeling, monuments were commonly erected by masters, slaves, and freedmen to each other, and the posthumous testimonies of their mutual affection are numerous among the inscriptions of tombs.

In this change the author traces the effect of the teaching of the Church even upon those who did not enter her pale. The Church had treated the institution of slavery, as well as that of arbitrary power in the monarch, with all her own supernatural wisdom. She had not denounced institutions which she found in universal possession, and to demolish which would have been to undermine the fabric of existing society without substituting for it anything better. What she did was the very reverse. Leaving the old institutions of the heathen world to themselves, she set herself to teach to every one of her members first principles utterly inconsistent with them. She taught, for instance, to every one, rich or poor, bond or free, the equality of all men before God, and without altering the legal relation of master and slave, even among her own members, by any general enactment, she carried out into full action this principle of equality in all her own dealings with individuals of both classes.

In the bosom of the Church, this equality was at once realised. Christianity left to the 'city of this world' the distinctions and relations upon which it depends. But the Church, the City of God, is independent of the city of this world, and orders matters without reference to the prejudices, perhaps unavoidable, upon which the human society is founded. Inside the Church, as in the sight of God, there is neither freeman nor slave, neither Greek nor barbarian ; the Roman knight, with his gold ring and his white toga, cannot call upon the simple labourer in a tunic to make way for him. The senator who is one of the ordinary faithful, will bow down before the slave[1] who becomes a bishop. The Christian hierarchy does not proclaim war against the civil hierarchy, but is separate and distinct from it. In it the poor and the noble, the Roman matron and the female slave, kneel side by side, pray together, exchange the 'kiss of peace,' call each other 'brother' and 'sister,' and, mingled upon a common level of blessedness and greatness by reason of the eminent dignity to which all of them alike are called, receive together the body and the blood of their God.

[1] S. Callixtus, Pope, was a slave for some years after he reached manhood.

Then, just before they return to the life of the world, they are once more united by the 'Agape.' What the Agape must have been, and what must have been the importance of its bearing upon Christian equality, has not been observed as it deserves. We are no longer engaged in acts of religion—it is an action of domestic life; it is the brotherly repast of a society like those which the Greek called 'Hetæriæ,' and the Roman 'Confraternities.' Only the communities of the Greeks and Romans admitted, as a general rule, only persons of the same social condition. Here, on the contrary, in direct opposition to the usages of the ancient world, is a brotherly feast of free and slaves, men and women, workmen and senators. The master sits side by side with the slave, whom he bought in the market for sixteen pounds sterling—worse than that, side by side with the freedman whom he emancipated the day before—worse than that, side by side with a poor 'hand' who never had the honour to be connected with him either as freedman or as slave. It is the custom to exclude all women from solemn feasts; but at this not only women, but waiting-maids and sempstresses are admitted. To supply this feast, the bread eaten by the poor has been presented by the rich; but the gift would not have been received unless the rich had consented to eat it in common with the poor—if they had not added the alms of their society to the alms of their bread. We find from S. Paul that reluctance was sometimes felt upon this point; that there was sometimes a desire to take the 'Agape' apart; that some of the rich would have liked to have luxuries in a separate corner, and have left black bread in another corner to the poor. But of this S. Paul would not so much as hear. He maintained this singular institution of the 'Agape' strictly on the principle of equality, community, and fraternity. Thus might be said of the 'Agape' what was said of a feast of a widely different degree of holiness and majesty, 'We are all one body, for we are all partakers of one bread.'

Year after year, throughout their whole lives, during several generations, did these practices form the habitual custom of many thousand Romans, men and women, among whom many were rich and noble, but many more were poor or slaves. It was not in the nature of things that, by degrees, some whisper of what was thus going on close to them, among their own neighbours, friends, and kindred, should not reach the ears even of the heathen. Even after the original security of the Church had been broken by the persecutions of Nero, she often enjoyed peace for many years together. During such times, and (we may be sure) still more when any new persecution was beginning after a long intermission, the peculiar doctrines and practices of the Christians must have been the talk of ten thousand assemblies and domestic circles. They must have attracted the same sort of attention which we know as a matter of fact had, long before, been given to the customs of the Jews. They must have been criticised, defended, laughed at, and praised by thousands. No doubt, the wildest accounts would be given of them (this we know, from the writings of the apologists, actually was the case), yet they could hardly be more misunderstood or more misrepresented than the doctrines and practices of Catholics have been in our memory, and, indeed, still are, in London at this day. Under these circumstances, it is hardly conceivable that the feelings and customs of Christians about slaves should not, more or less, become known in general society. Here, then, we have a cause strong enough gradually to affect the thoughts and conduct of others; for truth needs only to be set before men, and it will commend itself to them. Not that they always act upon it. That, unhappily, is too often prevented by the corruption of their wills; but on the whole they will approve it, and, when not under special temptation, they are likely by degrees to imitate, as far as they can without inconvenience, those who do act upon it. Just such was the imperfect imitation in the Roman Empire of the Christian practice with regard to slaves. No other account which can be given in any degree explains the unquestionable fact of such a change for the better as actually took place. Here was a cause which we know to have been in operation. Its natural effect would be exactly what we know actually happened; under these circumstances, I do not see how anything except obstinate prejudice can make any man hesitate to believe that the silent influence of Christianity was the real cause of the improvement in the law and practice of slavery under the Antonines. It is what Bacon would call the test of the *vera causa*.

But there is an effect of slavery more fatal, perhaps, to a State than even its effect upon the master or upon the slave. This is its effect on the mass of those too poor to possess slaves. Wherever slaves are numerous, labour becomes a disgrace to freemen, however poor, as being the badge of a servile condition. This fatal social poison has worked alike in the ancient and the modern world—and not least at Rome. The agricultural labour which had once been the honourable employment of consuls and dictators, had now been turned over to 'fettered limbs and branded faces.' This evil, however, the Church met as directly as the other. The easy manumission of slaves was part of the Roman system. The Church did not command it, but unquestionably, in practice, encouraged it. It is plain, therefore, that besides masters and slaves, she could not fail to contain a large multitude of poor freemen. M. de Champagny paints most powerfully how she would not only attract many already poor, but how the fact of conversion would make poor many who before their conversion were well provided for. (' Antonins,' vol. ii. p. 156.) There were multitudes who had no alternative but either to labour hard for their daily bread, or else to obtain it by falling back into heathen rites or heathen morals. Something very similar is continually seen among ourselves, among converts of a class somewhat higher. At Rome, besides many slaves set free by Christian masters for the love of Christ, there were many free men and women escaped from the service of the temples, the circus or the theatre, the prætorium or the basilica, or from ways of life still more openly immoral. For the words of our blessed Lord to the proud Pharisees were fulfilled to the letter: 'The publicans and the harlots enter into the kingdom of God before you.' All these had been arrested, instructed, regenerated; but they had still to be fed. And how could this be done? Only by their being taught to imitate Him who toiled for His daily bread in the workshop of S. Joseph at Nazareth. 'The mass of the liberal professions were difficult, if not impossible, to a Christian.' This the author shows at length. Either, then, they must be handicrafts; or they must be supported by the alms of the Church; or they must fall back into heathenism; or, finally, they must starve. It was under these circumstances that S. Paul laid down the rule that 'if any man would not work, neither should he eat,' and admonished those who desired to live in idleness, 'to work quietly and eat their own bread.'

Moreover, the labour of a Christian had a value, which heathen labour, even if it could be obtained, had not.

The one (says the author) was enervated by debauchery, the other purified by fasting and strengthened by continence. The one smarted under the contempt which, in heathen society, attached to manual labour. Under a sense of disgrace, by stealth, blushing at his disparagement of himself, he performed the servile work to which his poverty condemned him. The other knew, indeed, that it was as a penalty that he was condemned to labour; but it was a penalty imposed upon him in common with the whole human race; and he felt that the man who accepted this necessity bravely, humbly, cheerfully, found in it not shame but honour. Bishops, saints, martyrs, apostles—a God Himself—had accompanied or gone before him in his toil. The one, by reason of the contempt which pressed upon him, found himself deprived of assistance, consolation, advice, credit; the other, free in the bosom of the Church from this contemptuous prejudice, and to whom the Church gave the rich, the learned, the senator, as his companions at table, his friends, his brethren, could talk with them, in the brotherly intercourse of the 'Agape,' over the necessities of his toil and the wants of his family; could take counsel from their superior education, be encouraged by their friendship, be even aided by their denarii. 'From him that would borrow of thee,' said the Gospel, 'turn not thou away.' Would it be possible to refuse a few denarii for the repair of a broken tool, or the purchase of the raw material of his manufacture to the brother who had just shared with you the cup of the Agape, and to whom, in the Holy Mysteries, you had just given the kiss of peace? Capital and industry—the two grand personages of the modern social drama—the one with his toga, his gold ring, and his white hands, the other with simple tunic and horny hands, met and embraced, and dipped their hands into the same dish, in the Agape, and contracted an alliance such as the ancient world had never known. In one word, modern industry, with its thousand productive schemes for bringing together capital and industry, was all in its germ in the Agape, and in the workshop of the Christian (p. 139).

My space forbids me to follow M. de Champagny farther, and trace the effects of Christianity upon a world which was not yet aware whence it had borrowed its new principles, as they showed themselves in private life, the relations of husband and wife, of father and children, and of rich and poor. That such an effect should have been produced was to be expected, for the moral and social principles which Christianity enunciates, high and holy as they are, are such as man's natural reason, if it would not have discovered them, neartily accepts and embraces when proposed to it. Passion, too often carries him away in practice; but his 'inward man delights in the law of God,' and so would it surely be with the higher mysteries of the faith as soon as they are declared, if man's heart were not perverted.

And this leads me to believe that even in countries which have once been Catholic, and have unhappily forgotten their old faith, there will generally be left behind it a residue of moral and social principles which men would never have discovered for themselves, although, having once learned them, they call them natural principles; as, indeed, they are in this important sense, that the natural conscience receives and bears witness to them. For instance, has the world ever seen a civilised country which was never Christian and was free from the institution of slavery? In our day it is denounced even by men who avowedly reject Christianity; but I believe that, had Christianity been unknown, the whole civilised world would now, as much as in the days of Aristotle, have agreed in considering it natural and indispensable. There are aspects in which this thought is encouraging Christendom, or at least Christian nations, may sink deep, but, except in moments of frenzy (like that of Paris in 1793), they are hardly likely to sink so low as civilised nations before our Blessed Lord came in the flesh. Individual Christians may, by rejecting greater light, be far more guilty than individual heathens; but nations can hardly again be covered by darkness so gross. This is in some degree a consolation under the miserable fact to which it is hardly possible for a thinking man to shut his eyes. Modern Europe has long been becoming, in many important particulars, more and more like the heathen Roman Empire.

To revert to one point of this daily increasing resemblance. The time which has passed since standing armies were introduced into Christian Europe has been (compared with the life of nations) very short. In England, the system was quite in its infancy under William III., on the Continent at the era of Charles V. and Francis I. The momentous political changes which it has already effected I have very briefly enumerated. What more is it destined to work? At Rome the same system can hardly be said to have existed before the era of Sulla and Pompeius. In the next generation it had swept away the ancient republic, and some generations later it established the principle that the government was to be administered, not by the Senate any more than by the populace, but by the creatures of the army. In France I can hardly wonder that the events which have marked the last few years have led thoughtful men especially to turn their eyes to the Roman Empire, and to consider how the evil of the military system of ancient Rome may be averted from modern Europe. This tendency has, no doubt, been greatly increased by the systematic repression of political opinion, which is the less excusable because it is combined with an extreme licence in the avowal and diffusion of such as are only unbelieving and anti-Christian. Men who are not allowed to say what they think of France under Napoleon will naturally try how far they can suggest it by speaking of Rome under the Cæsars. It is impossible, I think, to read the reviews and magazines published in France, and even many grave books on ancient history, without feeling that this necessity of saying in a parable what cannot be said openly has been a serious injury to history.

But even where this does not exist, it is evident, and it is unavoidable, that the history of the ancient empire must have an interest for men of our generation which it had not for their grandfathers. While the ancient European dynasties were still ruling, more or less, on the ancient principles, the history of the fall of the Roman republic and of the early Cæsars seemed so strange to many men that they could hardly fancy the events to have happened in this same world of theirs and ours. In our day no man can write or even read the history of the Roman Empire without being struck with parallels in the history of the European, and especially the French, revolutions. Thus M. de Champagny (who is, I think, quite free from the desire to make ancient history speak of modern politics whether it will or not) says the fall of Sejanus was but an anticipation of the 9th Thermidor. But the resemblance by which he is most painfully impressed, and which has struck thinking men of the most widely different views, is that for many years past the public policy of all the European nations has fallen back upon heathen principles. If there are those who doubt this, it must be because they identify heathenism with idols, temples, and the like, which have little attraction for modern Europeans. But these things had already lost their power over men before heathen society—' the City of the World,' as S. Augustine calls it—had come to its height and perfection. M. de Champagny has a very interesting chapter, which he calls 'One

Word on Modern Paganism.' He makes its essence to consist in the adoption of two principles, upon which, he truly says,

Roman antiquity founded its whole social system. [These are: first,] that the duty of man to the community of which he is a member, and especially towards the nation, is superior to all other duties; and next (which is the converse of this) that the society to which a man belongs has an absolute right over him. [Upon this he remarks that] the Christian religion lays down exactly the opposite; the great duty, the great foundation of the social order, is, not the love of an abstraction which is called our country, but the love of a real being, called our neighbour. Patriotism is not condemned but transformed by Christianity. It is one of the shades of this love. Christian patriotism is nothing more than a special love for certain men, in close relations with whom it has pleased God that we should dwell,—a law holy and venerable, but still a secondary law, a mere fragment of à superior law which includes it, and is supreme over it. The country, in fact, under the Christian law, is no longer an abstract mysterious being, something superior to man and approaching Divinity; it is simply an aggregate of men, and as such subject to all the same obligations with the human being himself, to all the rules of justice and charity towards all men, whether citizens or foreigners, friends or enemies.

Hence (he adds) the society has duties towards the foreigner, and no society, race, tribe, caste, or nation may bear an exclusive love to itself, or seek its own welfare by means of the sufferings of others. National hatred, the oppression of one race by another, the spirit (I do not say of aristocracy, but) of caste, which leads one race to claim a radical superiority to another, these are things purely pagan and rejected by Christianity; they transgress the great law of justice and charity, they break Christian unity, they spring from a forgetfulness of the double fraternity of man in Adam and in Christ.

In like manner, under the Christian law, the community has its duties towards each of its individual members as much as each member has duties to it. Under the Christian law no power is absolute, no authority is really without limits, because none dare overstep the boundary imposed upon it by the conscience enlightened by the faith; and these bounds are much narrower than people fancy. Christianity accepts equally all forms of government, whether kingly or republican, aristocratic or popular; whether limited by positive laws or only by the power of custom, by conditions made with men, or only by the duties imposed by the laws of God—the power is still equally the ordinance of God, not in its form (which is a thing of human origin and variable), but in its essence, which is necessary to communities. Christianity, indifferent to political squabbles, which are often very vain and wretched, accepts all equally, and condemns nothing but despotism, if by despotism is meant, what ought to be meant, *power unconnected with duty*, an authority which believes that it has all rights over men, even the rights refused it by the law of nature and by the revealed laws of God . . .

Thus have perished the two fundamental principles of heathen society—nationalism abroad and despotism at home . . .

Modern paganism, in direct opposition to Christian faith, has moulded its politics like those of ancient paganism. The City it has made its temple. It once more deifies the public interests. Of the fiction called one's country it has made its God.

Next he goes on to show that all resistance to the Church (for instance in the eleventh, twelfth, and fourteenth centuries) has taken this form. The Protestant Reformation made gods of kings. Even in Catholic nations monarchs adopted a principle so flattering to them. Then came the Great Revolution. Its fundamental delusion was the same into which the kings of the eighteenth century had fallen—that man's highest duty is to the community, and that the nation has no duties either towards its own members or its subjects. In a word, it was the rejection of the authority of God and of His Church. The fullest display of this principle was in 1793; but 1793 has passed away, and we still maintain the same principles. He concludes :—

It seems to me that we are living in the times of Augustus. We are coming out of a revolutionary crisis, as the Romans were then coming out of the crisis of the civil wars . . . . But Augustus, without either knowing or desiring it, was preparing Tiberius.

Moreover, the tyranny of the Cæsars had one special characteristic, in which every modern tyranny, whether it will or no, is forced to resemble it. It was brought into collision with a power with which no former tyranny had had to do—the power of conscience, the principle openly avowed in direct opposition to its unlimited claims—'We ought to obey God rather than you.'

I have analysed the more carefully this remarkable chapter,[1] (which I ought to mention ends with a strong expression of the author's hopes, in spite of all threatening appearances), because, on the one hand, I consider the general truth and importance of its argument unquestionable; and yet I feel, on the other hand, that there are in my own country some distinctions, the neglect of which might lead superficial observers to doubt or deny it. Wherever a 'strong government' is the taste and custom of the nation (as it is eminently in France), the rejection of the authority of the Church leaves the national government unlimited and irresponsible. It takes away at a stroke the only authority to which kings or rulers were before amenable. This is clear. In England, in our own day, it is, I need hardly say, by no means the national habit to assume that anything is right because it is done by the English government. It would, therefore, seem absurd to say that by taking away the control of the Church we have put the English government in the place of God. When the change of religion first took place, such was notoriously the case, and Wolsey, after his fall, while surrendering into the hands of the tyrant all he had, had but too much reason to beseech him to remember 'that there is both a heaven and a hell.' Perhaps his conscience told him that he had neglected to impress the lesson, as he ought, in the time of his court favour. Unhappily for Henry VIII., he had those around him whose interest it was to make him forget it, or at least to persuade him that kings need think nothing about hell. But worship of the monarch, like that of Cranmer, did not suit the national taste, and circumstances

---

[1] 'Les Césars,' vol. iii. p. 385.

have long since abolished it. Still, although the idol has been changed, the idolatry continues. It is evident that the will of the nation and the nation itself, much more than the national government, is the especial idol of Englishmen. And yet even this seems to me less characteristic of England than of some other nations. For instance, every Frenchman is at once set on fire when he hears the very words 'the glory of France;' but I much doubt whether speeches about the 'glory of England,' continued for a year together, would reconcile any considerable number of Englishmen to a penny additional on the income-tax. The annexation of a new province to France by any means, however dishonourable, throws almost every Frenchman of every class and every party into a thrill of ecstasy which an Englishman is incapable of feeling about any public event. No less a man than De Tocqueville (unless I am mistaken) deliberately declared that he believed the annexation of Belgium would be most unjust; but that if Napoleon III. should commit that injustice, he would acquire such a claim to the gratitude of every Frenchman, that he for one would never afterwards oppose his dynasty. I believe the feeling is universal among Frenchmen, with the exception of a handful of men whose love even to France is overpowered by their love of the liberty of the Church, to which they believe that the annexation of Belgium would be a serious blow. All honour to men who, though French, yet care more for the glory of God than even for what is called 'the glory of France.' All honour also to M. de Champagny, who has ventured so boldly to assail the spirit of pagan patriotism, which is the idol of his country.

In England, unless I deceive myself, not only is the national government more the servant of the nation than its idol (and the Englishman is willing enough to 'wallop his own nigger'); but the worship of the *patrie* itself is much less general and enthusiastic than it is in France. No one feels even the will of the nation to be his highest law. Very few would feel any scruple about breaking a law when it can be done safely. Perhaps no one would scruple to abandon his nationality altogether, and become a citizen of some foreign state, however the step might be forbidden by law and by the national feeling—if it suited his own interests.

And yet heathen principles of government are at least as strong in England as in France. Individuals, no doubt, there are, in some numbers (even out of the Church), who sincerely endeavour to regulate their own conduct by the rules and motives laid down by the Christian religion, as they understand them. But no one, I presume, would say that any attempt is made to refer to or recognise those rules in the management of public affairs ; very few, probably, would think it either desirable or possible to do so. Let me illustrate my meaning by an example. Mr. Gladstone is notoriously a most sincere believer in the Christian religion as understood by High Anglicans. He firmly believes, therefore, not only that all men share one common nature, but also that that nature has been assumed, once and for ever, by the Eternal Son of God, who, in it, has sat down on the right hand of the Father. And yet it is certain that, if in a debate (say on the late Jamaica affair), Mr. Gladstone were to open or wind up his speech by laying down that stupendous fact as the basis of all he said, he would most materially injure, perhaps destroy, the eminent political station which he has earned by his unrivalled powers and high character. His speech would be universally pronounced either a sign of temporary insanity or (worse still) of the most wretched taste and fanaticism. Now, this is the more remarkable, because no one (not even an infidel) will deny that the awful fact has the most direct and important bearing upon the subject; for the duties of a Christian to men of widely different races immediately result from it. It may be said that such a speech would be out of place, because there are Jews in the House of Commons. But, however plausible an explanation.

that is certainly not the real reason of the feeling, because it would have been quite as strong before the first Jew was admitted. The simple truth is, that in England all religious doctrines are recognised as 'open questions,' upon which each individual has a right to his own opinions, and as to which no one has any right to assume that his own convictions, however strong, are unquestionably true. What makes this plain is that there are other principles which any man may, without offence, take for granted, although they are not universally held; because they are admitted by the nearly universal consent of the English people. For instance, there may be in the House of Commons some two or three men who prefer a republican to a monarchical form of government; yet no man would be blamed who publicly grounded his vote upon any question upon his conviction that an opposite course would be inconsistent with monarchy. For (while individuals are free to hold the opposite opinion) the maintenance of the monarchy is one of the things which the mass of the nation considers necessary and fundamental. Again, we all know that to assume in the same manner the truth of the great Christian doctrines would formerly have seemed quite natural. Under Henry V., for instance, or Edward III., fine specimens of English character, such a thing would surprise no one, whether in a speech, an act of Parliament, or any other public paper.[1]

---

[1] Since this was written I have quite accidentally fallen in with an instance which illustrates my position. It is a pardon (in Rymer) to four men condemned for high treason. The preamble is as follows :—

'Reducentes in memoriam qualiter supremus Judex (cujus verba taliter testificatur Scriptura Sacra *Mihi Vindictam et ego retribuam*) nonnullas Personas nobis infideles tetigit et percussit anno ultimatim elapso.

'Qualiter etiam Sacrosancto Die Veneris, qui jam instat, Salvator Noster Jesus Christus gloriosam Passionem suam usque ad Mortem pro salute nostra pertulit et sustinuit.

'Et qualiter a Cunabilis nostris, singularem et internam Devotionem ad Beatissimam, gloriosissimam et intemeratam Virginem Mariam Dei Genitricem hucusque gessimus et habuimus et ad praesens gerimus et habemus, de cujus

It is plain, then, that the principle upon which public affairs are now regulated is this—That we may assume that Christianity is true, but that no man has a right to assume that any one particular doctrine or fact is a necessary part of Christianity, that being merely a matter of private opinion. He may profess to support the Established Church, because that is a political institution, but still he must not allege, as the ground of his support, that its doctrines are true; for who can say (the nation feels) whether they are or not—it is a matter of opinion.

And yet some fundamental principle there must be, which English statesmen are obliged to respect. If it is not any one Christian doctrine or rule, nor yet the will of the government, or even of the nation, what is it? I should be inclined to answer in one word—that it is 'Civilisation.' No public man among us must act except on 'principles becoming a civilised nation.' Civilisation is here taken in its ordinary sense. There are some, indeed, who say that it implies the highest Christian principles. Such is not the sense in which the word is commonly used. For instance, no man would say that the Romans under Augustus, or the Athenians under Pericles, were uncivilised. What the word really expresses is the whole of that collection of qualities, moral, social, intellectual, &c., which result from an habitual life in a

Assumptione magna et solemnis Festivitas in universali Sacrosanctâ Ecclesiâ Catholicâ, præsertim et præcipue et singulari devotione recommendanda in Devotissimo Regali nostro Collegio Beatæ Mariæ de Eton juxta Wyndesoram infra breve celebrabitur.'

He adds, especially, that Eugenius IV. and Nicholas, the reigning Pope, had granted the college great indulgences, and then continues:—'Considerantesque nedum præmissa, verùm etiam multimodas alias gratias Nobis per Altissimum anno ultimatim elapso exhibitas et ostentas.' Sharon Turner, I find, mentions the Feast of the Assumption, the Friday, the text of Scripture, and the 'multimodas gratias,' as 'four strange reasons.' He does not allude to the other reasons, I shrewdly suspect, because he could make neither head nor tail of them. For what had indulgences to do with a pardon? My point, however, is that no one at the time would think these 'strange reasons.'

civil community, and which qualify men for such a life. It does, therefore, imply many qualities which Christianity immediately tends to produce—justice, mercy, courtesy, habitual consideration for the wishes and feelings of others, &c. But these qualities (although they can hardly be formed in their perfection except by Christianity) may in a great degree be produced, and still more may be admirably simulated, by the habits and intercourse of civil life. But civilisation implies many other things which Christianity, at the utmost, only indirectly tends to produce—such, for instance, as financial, political, and social science; the improvement both of the fine and, much more, of the mechanical arts; and the subjection of the material world, animals, vegetables, metals, &c., to the service of man. Although, therefore, the perfection of civilisation more or less implies the presence of some very high qualities, which can only be matured by Christianity, yet (inasmuch as the effects which these qualities produce upon society may, in a great measure, be obtained by other means—namely, by the training to be derived from civil and political life), and as many other things enter into the idea of civilisation with which neither Christianity nor moral perfection has any immediate connection, we cannot deny that civilisation, in a very real sense, may exist without Christianity; nay, more, that a heathen community may, accidentally, be more civilised than some Christian communities. Indeed, it will hardly be doubted that one of the most important steps in civilisation is the separation of military from civil life and duties. The English people, for instance, are at this moment better qualified for civil life than they would be if every man among us were at all times liable to be called upon for military service, and if no man (except a priest) could by possibility attain any high position in the State or the Law without actually spending a large portion of his life in warfare. Mr. Gladstone, for instance, or Sir Roundell Palmer, could hardly discharge the duties of their offices as they do, if they were obliged, as a matter of course, to lead in person some military expedition or other every summer, and to spend most part of it in the camp. Yet this has generally been the condition of public men in Christian nations; while there have been heathen countries entirely exempt from it.

I may conclude, then, that civilisation in its true sense, and much more as it is and will always be understood by the majority of men, does not necessarily imply either Christianity or even the highest moral qualities, and that it gives a proportionable importance to intellectual cultivation, and still more to the studies and arts which minister to material prosperity, which is quite inconsistent with the first principles of Christianity.

And if so, then a nation which makes civilisation, and not revealed religion, its practical rule in the administration of public affairs—in fact, makes material prosperity the chief good, and, by so doing, really and truly, so far, falls back into heathenism. I cannot imagine that any thinking man can deny this; or, again, that he can doubt that the public affairs of our own country are thus administered. One night's attendance upon the House of Commons, or the study of one number of the 'Times,' would surely convince him.

But I must go much farther than this. It is plain that thinking men, who themselves accept, without scruple or hesitation, what I have called the principles of modern heathenism, as the only right and safe principles, are forcibly struck by the fact, that (however true they may be) they are in sharp contrast and opposition to the fundamental principles of Christianity.

In proof of this consciousness I would refer to the 'Saturday Review.' There is, perhaps, no journal which so accurately and fairly represents the political, social, and moral standard of educated Englishmen in our own day. It is written with singular ability and moderation, and (appearing weekly) it is free from the necessity of hasty writing, which is a condition of daily newspapers. Moreover, it would be quite unfair to call it an anti-religious paper.

A few months ago appeared an article on 'The Dead Virtues.' It mentioned especially purity, poverty, and (if I remember right) humility. It showed at some length that they have no place in the modern system of modern Englishmen; nay, that poverty especially is admitted to be an impediment to religious improvement, and it contrasted with these facts the well-known texts of the New Testament on the subject. The writer did not attempt to reconcile or remove the contradiction, but merely thought it worth noticing as a fact.

In a remarkable article on the late Lord Elgin a parallel was drawn between him and Agricola. It was suggested that the greater fame of Agricola has come in great degree from the accident of his having Tacitus for his biographer; and the author went on to say (as a general remark) that he had been much struck by the remarkable resemblance of the great English governors in India and elsewhere to the great heathen statesmen and administrators.

Nearly at the same time there was an article on the resemblance of the Sadducees among the Jews to educated Englishmen, and (if I remember right, it was said in so many words) to Saturday Reviewers. This bears closely upon my argument, because the Sadducees were clearly the heathenising party among the Jews. The writer pleaded that our Divine Lord, although stating that the Sadducees had 'erred,' reserved for the Pharisees all His most severe censures. This seems in fact to have been because the special objects of His preaching were those 'who sat in Moses' seat,' *i.e.* the religious leaders of the Jewish people. The Sadducees were rather a heathen than a Jewish school.

In commenting upon the funeral sermon of the Dean of Westminster upon Lord Palmerston, whom the same paper especially commended as being strictly and eminently the English statesman, and therefore especially qualified for the place he had occupied, it went on to admit the difficulty of Dean Stanley's task, on the ground that it was 'not easy in any way to make of Lord Palmerston exactly a *Christian* hero.'

Lastly, a few weeks back there was an able article on the government of the coloured races in our colonial and foreign dominions. It was occasioned by the Jamaica affair, and laid down as a principle, that if we are to retain India or to keep the peace in colonies where the negroes are numerous, we must act upon principles precisely opposite to those laid down in the Gospels.

I might greatly have strengthened my argument, had space allowed, by quoting the *ipsissima verba* of these articles, and I doubt not I could with a very little trouble have found many more, bearing perhaps even more directly upon the subject. Those I have enumerated have all appeared within the last few months, and are such as I happen to remember without having the paper at hand. They are enough to prove my position, that thoughtful men, writing in the spirit of the day, are struck with the opposition between their own principles and those of the Gospel. I can but repeat M. de Champagny's account of the matter. The principles of heathenism are merely those of nature. When the supernatural is displaced, they resume possession of themselves. The misery of the heathen world, (besides the lack of Christian graces), was that it was without fixed principles, without unquestionable facts, with regard to the moral and religious world. There, all was uncertainty and dispute, while material objects, (let philosophers reason how they would), were ever close about men and pressing to obtain full dominion. With the mass of men, certain and pressing things carry the day against those which are unseen and only conjectural.

In those which we call the 'dark ages,' faith made the unseen world to the mass of the European nations more near and pressing, as well as greater, than the world seen. Men were under strong temptations. Except ecclesiastics, every man had always a sword in his hand. Civilisation was far less general than it is now; for men always accustomed to decide everything by violence were disqualified for civil society. But even in the most unlikely men, and in those whose actions are least pleasant to contemplate, we find, all of a sudden, the strongest sense of the unseen and supernatural, not as a mere acknowledgment, but working out of their minds against their own wish. The great rebellion of the 16th century against the principle of faith has left the mass of men with nothing certain except objects of sense, and no rule except human civilisation and material advancement.

So much has this uncertainty got possession of them, that they are unable so much as to understand the posture of mind of those who retain the old faith. I was reading a few days ago a criticism upon the lecture delivered by our late Cardinal-Archbishop before the Academia of the Catholic religion, in which he considered the objections to the genuineness of the robe of the Blessed Virgin at Chartres, and to the account of the martyrdom of S. Ursula and her companions at Cologne. The critic complained that the Cardinal was wholly incapable of seeing what evidence is. This seemed odd; but it appeared that he supposed the Cardinal to have undertaken to prove, for instance, that the robe attributed to our Blessed Lady was really hers; as he would prove a murder against a prisoner. He did not see that the argument was not addressed to this point at all; that it was merely intended to prove that the common objections to the genuineness of the relic were without force. The fact was, the two minds approached the subject from opposite sides. The Cardinal began by assuming that an object was likely really to be what it was attested to be by an unbroken tradition of more than a thousand years. All he wished to show was that, when examined by unbelievers, it turned out to be exactly what it certainly would be supposing it to be genuine. The critic assumed that the tradition was false. He demanded, therefore, how do you prove the genuineness of the relic? and, of course, was disappointed when the Cardinal did not do what he had never thought of doing. This was no matter of faith; yet it illustrates my meaning, for it is clear that the mass of educated men in our day approach the supernatural objects of faith in the same spirit. They come with minds emptied of the tradition of eighteen hundred years, and demand proof of every detail. The appropriate proofs are not wanting: but, meanwhile, they are, like Agricola with Britain to conquer and pacify, too busy to examine the proofs of things, which it is the happiness of Christians to have learned as first principles at their mother's knee.

And hence the peculiar interest of the Romans under the Empire in our day. What may be coming I know not. I am struck with some great points of resemblance between two eras. But I know that the past never exactly reproduces itself;—much more, that the world is not governed by any iron law of necessity; so that, even if things were at the worst, it is left to our own labours and prayers to avert the catastrophe which once before fell upon it. The great lesson of the work before me is well stated by a French critic (M. de Meaux, in the 'Correspondant'):—"It is useless to ask of history how far man's reason can go by its unassisted powers. What history proves is that this reason never does find its way so absolutely without a higher light. The primitive revelation and the Christian revelation have been successively given to it by its Creator to complete it by surpassing it. Between these two revelations I seem to see heathen antiquity finding its way through a long and dark subterranean passage, both ends of which open into the light of day and the sunshine. At the point where the light which illuminated the entrance of the cavern loses itself in thick darkness, the stronger and fuller light, which blazes at its outlet, begins to penetrate. This is the point which Roman society had reached at the period before us. Let it press towards the light of the new rays which invite it onward. Let it take a new life, and not sink fatigued.

Above all, let it not conceive a fatal love for the thick darkness to which its eyes have become habituated; and before long it will see the sky over its head, and will breathe the free and pure air.'

How rash it would be to reason confidently from the points of resemblance to any similar result of these two great civilisations of the world, will appear, if we consider for a moment their most striking differences.

The basis of Roman society was slavery. The peculiar form of that slavery was, that the slaves were, in the main, of the same races, or at least races nearly allied to that of their masters. The civilised world at present knows nothing at all analogous to this. So far as I know, the only civilised nation which, in this respect, at all resembled modern Europe, was Judæa; in which, so far as we can trace, slavery, though not strictly unknown, was within exceedingly narrow bounds. It is striking how little trace we find of the institution in the Gospels; and M. de Champagny remarks that Josephus never so much as alludes to it in his history. Elsewhere, it was the very foundation of the social system. Modern authors have been much in the habit of comparing the neglected labouring classes to the slave-class of antiquity. This has sometimes had too much foundation. But the change which emigration to the new world has already wrought, and which it is likely to carry to a degree of which we are wholly unable to forecast the limits and the result, entirely overthrows any such calculations. Above all, the Catholic Church is in possession of the modern world to a degree which the ancient world never knew. All appearances seem to show that the present is one of the critical periods of history, when what is old is falling away of itself, rather than being swept away. Our work is to see that we are not wanting to our children; that we leave to them, unbroken, the inheritance of truth. They in their turn will be called to struggle and contend for it. In the world, as God has allowed it to be, there is no time for any generation to imagine that it has as yet entered into rest.

III.

CHAMPAGNY'S CÆSARS OF THE THIRD CENTURY.[1]

In the three volumes before me M. de Champagny completes a great work, undertaken many years ago; and to the earlier part of which I have already called the attention of my readers. It is to any man no small blessing to have been led to select as his own some undertaking the achievement of which is, in itself, important, and for which he is adapted by his position, talents, and attainments. It is a greater blessing still when, after having selected it with judgment, he has not been diverted from it either by human frailty or mutability, or by the distractions and accidents with which in every age the life of man is beset. His happiness is greater still, if the great task, wisely undertaken and perseveringly pursued, is not broken off unfinished by the shortness of human life. This accumulation of happiness, denied to so many great thinkers in every age, has been conceded to few of those, who, in our own, have devoted themselves to a subject of which a thoughtful mind can hardly become wearied, although its extent may alarm any ordinary diligence,—the history of the Eternal City, which shines with a double glory, as the centre and metropolis of all that is great, first in the natural order, and subsequently in the kingdom of God Himself upon earth.

The great work in which the History of the Rise of Rome was

---

[1] Études sur l'Empire Romain. Les Césars du Troisième Siècle. Par le Comte de Champagny, de l'Académie Française. Paris, Ambroise Bray, 1870; 3 vols.

illustrated by the genius and learning of Niebuhr, was cut short by his death before he had begun the narrative of the Second Punic War. Arnold left the history of that war nearly ended. Gibbon was spared to finish a gigantic work. His record of its commencement and its completion contrasts, as might be expected, so sadly with the language of M. de Champagny that it may be worth while to compare the two. 'It was at Rome, on the 15th of October, 1764, as I sat musing amidst the ruins of the Capitol, while the barefooted friars were singing vespers in the Temple of Jupiter, that the idea of writing the Decline and Fall of the city first entered into my mind.' 'It was on the day, or rather night, of the 27th of June, 1787, between the hours of eleven and twelve, that I wrote the last lines of the last page, in a summer-house in my garden. After laying down my pen, I took several turns in a *berceau*, or covered walk, of acacias, which commands a prospect of the country, the lake, and the mountains. The air was temperate, the sky was serene, the silver orb of the moon was reflected from the waters, and all nature was silent. I will not dissemble the first emotions of joy on the recovery of my freedom, and, perhaps, the establishment of my fame. But my pride was soon humbled, and a sober melancholy was spread over my mind, by the idea that I had taken an everlasting leave of an old and agreeable companion, and that, whatsoever might be the future fate of my history, the life of the historian must be short and precarious. . . . The rational pride of an author may be offended rather than flattered by vague indiscriminate praise, but he cannot, he should not be indifferent to the fair testimonies of private and public esteem. Even his moral sympathy may be gratified by the idea, that now, in the present hour, he is imparting some degree of amusement or knowledge to his friends in a distant land, and that one day his mind will be familiar to the grand-children of those who are yet unborn.'[1]

[1] Gibbon, 'Miscellaneous Works,' vol. i. pp. 129 and 170.

To the self-styled philosopher—'Myself'—'my posthumous fame,' is all in all; the highest thought to which he soars is that of the amusement of friends in a distant land. Now turn to M. de Champagny.

Thirty years ago he wrote—

Such an undertaking cannot be the work of a few days. As the Apostle teaches us, 'We know not what shall be on the morrow,' and we ought to say, 'If the Lord will, and if we live we will do this or that.'—(*Cæsars*, vol. i. xxii.)

He now ends—

Here I bring to a conclusion, not without emotion, these labours [*Études*] upon the Roman Empire, which have occupied more than forty years of my life, and which, by God's help, have supported and consoled me through the trials of private life, and through the revolutions of our national life, the former very bitter, the last, whatever else they may have been, full of suffering. . . . .

In following the course of history from Julius Cæsar to Constantine, I have travelled through twelve generations of men, before whose eyes was carried out the greatest revolution, intellectual, moral, and social, which the history of the world exhibits; a revolution which has no equal in the past, and which, I fear not to pronounce, will have none in the future—the revolution which made the world Christian. Whence did it come, and how was it brought about?

Whence did it come? I have several times touched this question, and it has been discussed by others, with much more of completeness and eloquence than I could pretend to. On one side are records, ancient, clear, simple, positive, which, until the last few centuries, have been understood literally by all mankind, and which, literally understood, give, in a single word, the full and complete solution of this revolution—the intervention of God in the course of this world. On the other side, there are theories, ingenious no doubt, profound we are assured, supported by a mighty armament of learning, learning accumulated from every quarter, and still more by a mighty power of imagination, by a self-confident criticism which throws scorn upon ordinary men, and rather lays down the law to them than aims at convincing them. These theories, while in other respects divergent and contradictory, agree only in accounting for this great event by causes of which it is not always easy to give any account. Between this record, so simply historical and literal, on the one side, and these theories so unintelligible and conflicting on the other, each man can judge for himself; not to say that the controversy does not exactly form part of my subject.

But as to the second question, how was this revolution brought about? That it has been the whole object of my labours to explain.

After all, was there any need of so much labour? Is there not one fact, as plain as the day, and of which nothing can get rid—one fact notorious even to those whose knowledge of history is the most elementary? At the death of Augustus there was not so much as one Christian in the world; at the death of Constantine, three hundred and twenty-three years later, more than half the world was Christian.

And was this change brought about by material force, by the authority of princes, or by the insurrection of peoples against their princes? There may no doubt be a question whether or not this or that emperor was a persecutor, and to what point the persecution was carried; whether it was made chiefly by the authorities or chiefly by the multitude; whether it was chiefly political or chiefly popular. It is possible, with Dodwell, to reduce the number of martyrs to the lowest possible estimate, or with others to count them by millions. There are questions of detail, upon which discussion is possible; and legends which may, rightly or wrongly, be considered apocryphal. But what is certain is this—that all through these three centuries, force, whenever and in whatever degree it was employed, was always employed against and never in support of Christianity. Force, whether that of the emperor or of the people, the executioner or the rioter, all along acted a part which, if not constant, was at least habitual. The mild Marcus Aurelius himself speaks of the Christians as a set of people accustomed to go to death, from which it follows that it was an habitual practice to lead them to it. The one thing certain is that persecution, more or less violent, now and then suspended, but soon renewed, was the legal condition of the Roman Empire. Christianity was all along a thing proscribed, to which some emperors, more humane than the rest, now and then allowed a short respite; but always a thing proscribed, against which the proscription was never long in resuming its course.

And what force was it that resisted the force thus exerted against

Christianity? Where is there any mention of an insurrection, a league, or a riot among the Christians? Here was no league of Smalkalde, no conspiracy of Amboise, no 'oath of the tennis-court' (*serment du jeu de paume*, *June* 20, 1789), no one of the ordinary circumstances of a revolution. Those who were proscribed concealed themselves, or fled; those who were arrested suffered death without resistance. That is all that can be said. And this is repeated thousands of times (no one, not Dodwell himself, denies that), and each succeeding age saw it repeated more frequently. Every time that force resolved to destroy, it found a greater number to be destroyed, and those whom it destroyed were more numerous. Insomuch that, at last, this war, in which the one party only inflicted death and never suffered it, while the other only suffered and never inflicted it, ended in the triumph of that party which died over that which slew. The sword fell shivered against breasts which offered themselves to it.

And this event stands by itself in the history of the world. This universal resignation, this courage so heroically so constantly passive, and still more this triumph won only by dying, has no single parallel in history. People try to persuade themselves that the sword cannot triumph over ideas. For the honour of the human race one would gladly have it so, but it is a delusion. Ideas, doctrines, and religions have been conquered by the sword. Budhism was resisted by force, and was driven out of India, the land of its birth. The religion of Zoroaster was extirpated in Persia by the sword of the Mahommedans. Druidism was swept away out of the Gauls and Britain; nor did it find any place of refuge elsewhere.

Sometimes, no doubt, ideas have overcome force, but only when they have employed force in their turn; when, being persecuted by the sword, they have, rightly or wrongly, taken up the sword to resist. Mahommedanism was victorious because it took up the sword. Protestantism has reigned in Europe because it has met fire and sword with fire and sword. Both one and the other may have had its missioners, but neither would ever have triumphed, if it had not also had its soldiers. No sect, no religion has ever encountered the sword with the absolute passiveness which was the characteristic of the primitive Christians, or if there has been any one which ever practised it, that one has been crushed. Christianity alone, so far as I can learn, has ever submitted itself in this manner; Christianity alone, most unquestionably, has ever gained such a victory by so submitting itself.

Is it not clear that it was only by a Divine power that this triumph over all human power could have been won? The question as to the origin of Christianity is solved by the other question of the means by which it accomplished its victory. It was victorious here below, only because it had its origin from above.

This conclusion is so evident, and the facts on which it rests so incontestable, that if I had only to prove it I need not have undergone so much labour, nor traced so many historical facts nor raised so many questions. But my object in writing was not merely to give a proof of Christianity but to kindle the love of it.

Consider well this point. Our age honours with the name of ideas, many interests and many passions; and with the name of questions of principle, many mere questions of fact. Most of the objects on which it is occupied are things merely transitory—human institutions not Divine laws,—facts which pass away, not truths which abide. But the great, the eternal question, turns upon higher truths. Slighted, treated as if they were forgotten, systematically thrown into the shade, and only spoken of in vague terms—all this they may be. But they come back, they force themselves on men's notice. Then men are compelled to resort to an utter, brutal, absolute denial of God, of truth, of themselves, and they will more and more be compelled to do so.

More and more decidedly will two things confront each other, leaving in obscurity all that lies between them. On one side atheism the most cynical and radical; on the other, Christianity the most strictly practical. To make a decision and take part with one or the other will be a matter of necessity, no middle position will any longer be tenable.

While then this, the great struggle of our age, is in progress, how can any man, however powerless or obscure, be content not to bring his humble aid? To speak more strictly, while the great labour of all ages for the building up of truth in the heart of man is in progress, woe to him who, having the truth in his heart, does not labour in her cause, and contribute his little grain of sand to that monument built up of human thought of which the builder is God. In proportion to the limited degree of power vouchsafed to my intellect, and to the goodwill which I have been able (however wavering) to maintain in my heart, I have striven to contribute to this labour. It has almost occupied my life, and I regret that it has not occupied it more entirely. In the midst of the discouragements of human life mental labour is a great consolation and a great support; but even mental labour itself becomes weary, distasteful, burdensome to the soul, except when it is undertaken in the cause of good, of truth, of God.—(Vol. iii. p. 485 *et seq.*)

It was to exhibit the contrast of M. de Champagny's tone with that of Gibbon that I began my notice of his work by this long quotation from its conclusion. But I do it not without misgivings, for, taken alone, it would give an unjust as well as inadequate notion of that work. It might not unreasonably lead a reader to expect merely a history or estimate of the progress of Christianity in the Empire. The fact, however, is so much the opposite, that he may read whole volumes without having the idea directly suggested to him. Confident of the Divine origin of Christianity, M. de Champagny has never been tempted to doubt that any picture of the age in which it was first given to mankind, and of those during which it was gradually working its way from obscurity to universal dominion, will best illustrate it, in proportion as the account itself is most true and lifelike. And hence, although it may, and no doubt was, from first to last, the cherished motive of his inmost heart to illustrate the struggles and the triumph of the Church, yet the means by which he has sought that object are none others than unusual fidelity and life in his picture of the history and manners of the first three centuries. His desire has evidently been that expressed by the illustrious Niebuhr: 'Would that I could write history so vividly, that I could so discriminate what is fluctuating and uncertain, and so develop what is confused and intricate, that everyone as soon as he heard the name of a Greek of the age of Thucydides or Polybius, or of a Roman of the days of Cato or Tacitus, might be able to form a clear and adequate idea of what he was.' Nothing could more strikingly illustrate the contrast between history as it is in our own day and as it was a century ago, than that men should now propose to themselves such an object. That it should be fully attained is, no doubt, impossible; but M. de Champagny has at least aimed at the highest excellence, and if he has in any degree fallen short of it, he has more nearly succeeded than any writer known to me.

It might, no doubt, be suspected that a man who wrote the history of the heathen empire, with the Church ever nearest to his heart, would be under a strong temptation to sacrifice truth to his own prejudices. To this it would be an easy and true reply, that every man who has been brought into any relations with Christianity must of necessity either love or hate it; and that hatred is even more inconsistent than love with historical impartiality. In truth, however, there is much more to be said. The great difficulty of historians, in every age, is to give a picture, in any degree expressive and true, of the people and the times of which they write, not a mere record of their disasters and wars, and of the fortunes and disputes, triumphs and conquests, of their emperors and kings. Oh how precious would have been the information which the least imaginative of the ancient writers could have given us, if only he had been able to foresee that the whole fabric of society as he saw it was about to be swept away, and that times would come when the heirs of a new civilisation, unlike that of his own day as well as distinct from it, would, above all things, prize lively pictures of the daily habits of the men of the world that has passed away; and would labour assiduously to piece together, at the best very imperfectly, out of chance fragments collected here and there, from poems, histories, orations, letters, and philosophical treatises, a sort of mosaic, which, after all, would by no means equal the picture that might have been given in a few pages by any writer under the Roman Empire, who possessed, even in the most moderate degree, that talent for observation and word-painting by which many writers of our own times have been distinguished. Unfortunately one of the main difficulties of the historian of the Roman Empire, is not merely the inferior quality but the absolute dearth of materials. The periods for which we have any contemporary writer, or even one who, though not contemporary, commands belief by his accuracy and truthfulness, are quite the exception. Every now and then there is a period upon which exceptional light is thrown by some happy accident, like that which enables us to read the whole history of the last agony of the Republic, in the letters, speeches, and philosophical works of Cicero. But these are few and far between; and there are cases in which we are able to infer that a particular period must have been marked by important changes, rather from the results which they produced than from any positive record of them. There are parts even of the reign of Augustus himself about which very little is known. Above all, even when we know most of the historical events of any period, we have at best very poor and disjointed scraps of information about the life and manners of the mass of the people. And the little we have of this sort is chiefly in the Christian writings. The Acts of the Apostles give us a much better idea than any other book how people lived in the Greek provinces of the Empire under Nero—how the population was mixed of Jews and Greeks— how many of the Greeks, especially the more religious of both sexes, had already been attracted by the pure theism of the Jews —how some had actually submitted to circumcision, and had become proselytes, while many more devoutly worshipped the One God, without feeling themselves bound (as it is plain they were not) to put on the yoke of the law of Moses. Then, again, as to the relations of the populace, and of the municipal magistrates to the Roman governors; the practical use of the privileges of the Roman citizen; the appeal from the sentence of a local judge to the Roman people, at that time represented by Cæsar—what heathen writer of the same age gives us, in so small a compass, so much real and lifelike historical information? The same is true of later periods. The letters of S. Cyprian, for instance, unveil to us much of the under working of society in Roman Africa at a period in many respects of great interest, and about which we are most scantily supplied with any professed history. He became Bishop of Carthage A.D. 248 (the fourth year of the Emperor Philip), and was martyred A.D. 258 (the fifth year of Valerian). Yet Gibbon writes the history of those times without so much as alluding either to Cyprian himself or to the persecutions, from one of which he hid himself, continuing the administration of the Church in letters which have been preserved to us, while in another he received the crown of martyrdom. In a later volume, no doubt, he relates, in his own scornful tone, the history of S. Cyprian, in his well-known chapter on 'the conduct of the Roman Government towards the Christians from the reign of Nero to that of Constantine,' but only for the purpose of proving how slight, even in the times of most violent persecution, was the danger of the Christians; and how great the moderation and forbearance of the persecutors. It can hardly be doubted that if any collection of letters had been preserved, written by and to the leader in any one school of heathen philosophy at that period, Gibbon would have seen that it gave him an opportunity of throwing upon the scanty remains of its history an unexpected gleam of real light. But Cyprian he could not bring himself to forgive for being a Christian, a bishop, a saint, and a martyr, and his name was therefore passed over in the history. And the chapters in which mention is made of Church affairs are so little connected with the rest of his work, that a well-meaning editor, some forty years back (Bowdler), thought he should in no degree lessen the historical value of Gibbon's work by leaving them out altogether. He has, therefore, presented us with a history of the Roman Empire in which no mention at all is made of the very names of any of the great Christian heroes, although they were not only the most remarkable men of those times, but also the men of whom most is known. Yet to Gibbon at least he really has done no injustice; for Gibbon was as unconscious as himself that their lives, actions, and deaths formed any part of the history of those times. It would not be easy to find a stronger instance of the injurious effects of anti-religious prejudice, even upon the literary powers of a really great writer.

M. de Champagny, on the contrary, invests his volumes with the most lively interest, by mixing the narrative of the Church— its spread, its contests, its sufferings, its martyrdoms—with the secular history of the decaying Pagan Empire. No other work with which I am acquainted does this to the same degree. We have histories of the Cæsars, and we have ecclesiastical histories; but none which blend the two subjects into one, like the volumes before me. The political and military history is as carefully drawn out as if it were the only subject of the book; and yet the relations of the Empire to the Church, the sufferings, perils, and conquests of the divine kingdom, the heresies which strove to corrupt it, and the labours of the saints by whom they were encountered, are all given in their place. The result is, that we not only see the gradual growth of the 'kingdom of heaven,' from the time when it was sown as a grain of mustard seed until its branches overshadowed the whole earth, but we see also its connection with the events of each succeeding generation, and especially how its peace and its sufferings depended upon the varying characters of the different inheritors of the power of Augustus and Tiberius.

Another circumstance, to which his hatred of the Church and of Christianity necessarily blinded the eyes of Gibbon, and which, as far as I remember, has passed unobserved, even by our latest English historian of the Cæsars (who could not, without gross injustice, be classed with him), is that to which I called attention in my notice of the earlier portion of M. de Champagny's book, but which naturally becomes more prominent as we proceed further with the history—the leavening even of heathen manners and legislation, and, still more, of the best heathen philosophers, by the ever-increasing influence of Christian faith and morals. As a tide, silently filling up some wide-spreading inland harbour, surrounds and covers, or else bears upon its bosom every object which it finds there, so was Christianity insinuating itself into every province, every city, every family of the great heathen Empire ; and penetrating, or sweeping before it every established institution. At last a time came when, although there were still many heathens, there was probably not one who had not all his life been in intercourse with companions, friends, instructors, sisters, mother, by whom the great principles of Christian religion and morality were taken for granted rather than maintained. It was impossible that such a state of society should not modify, silently but profoundly, the thoughts and maxims of every heathen who aspired to anything higher than a mere animal life. Many of them, indeed, had an intense hatred for the Christian religion. That could not but be. But even those who hated it most could not shut their eyes to the truth and beauty of its moral and social principles. So great is the power of sympathy, that any man who lives for years in familiar intercourse with those who assume, as first principles, maxims which he rejects when formally stated— nay, which in his conscience and reason he feels to be false and evil—will yet try in vain to keep himself wholly uninfluenced by them. This is the great danger experienced by those who, while they deliberately intend to serve God above all things, are obliged, or induced, to live for years with persons in many respects perhaps attractive, but who take for granted that the practical objects to be aimed at in life are worldly pleasures, or honours, or material prosperity, or (even if their pursuits are higher than these) mere intellectual cultivation. The same again is the cause of the danger to which, in our own country especially, Catholics are exposed from the tone of the periodical press. There is no fear of their finding in the 'Times' or the 'Saturday Review' arguments which, as mere reasoning, could be formidable to their faith; for they can hardly fail to see that the writers (however on other subjects well-informed as well as able) are quite ignorant what Catholics really believe, and unable to understand the grounds on which they believe it. And yet their spiritual health is gradually undermined, as if by living long in an unwholesome atmosphere. An infection like this, combined with the natural voice of conscience, gradually produced an exactly opposite effect upon thoughtful heathens, who were surrounded by Christians. No man, for instance, hated Christianity more than Julian the Apostate; yet the great object of his reign was to introduce into the notions and manners of the heathen, and especially of the heathen priests, as much as possible of Christian theology and morality.[1] And, doubtless, the feeling of the most respectable heathens, however they may have shared his hatred of the Christian religion, must have been one of regret that so many men and women, in other respects estimable and even admirable,

---

[1] 'Julian beheld with envy the wise and humane regulations of the Church, and he very frankly confesses his intention to deprive the Christians of the applause as well as advantage which they had acquired by the exclusive practice of charity and beneficence. The same spirit of imitation might dispose the emperor to adopt several ecclesiastical institutions, the use and importance of which were approved by the success of his enemies. But if these imaginary plans of reformation had been realised, the forced and imperfect copy would have been less beneficial to Paganism than honourable to Christianity.'—Gibbon, chap. xxiii. 'As to his theology,' Gibbon says, chap. xxii., 'it contained the sublime and important principles of natural religion. The pious emperor acknowledged and adored the eternal Cause of the universe, to whom he ascribed all the perfections of an infinite nature, invisible to the eyes and inaccessible to the understanding of feeble mortals. The Supreme God had created—or rather, in the Platonic language, had generated—the gradual succession of dependent spirits, of gods, of demons, of heroes, and of men, and every being which derived its existence immediately from the First Cause received the inherent gift of immortality.'

should unfortunately be Christians. Thus it came to pass, all through the first three centuries, as Christians became more and more numerous and better known, and their influence more widely spread, that, although the old heathen religion was dying out, and the military, political, and social aspect of the Roman Empire was one of progressive decline, there was still, in one respect, a constant advance. The moral and religious principles which approved themselves to the thoughtful heathen in each generation, were higher than those of the age before. To adopt, in a most real and worthy sense, one of the most unmeaning terms of our day, there was a constant 'progress.'

We have, happily, unusual means of tracing this progress; for it pleased God that just before Christianity was given to the world there was exhibited to it a living example of the highest wisdom and virtue which heathenism could attain, in a man whose exalted station attracted to him the eyes of all his contemporaries; and whose prominent literary and oratorical talents have placed his letters, philosophical treatises, and orations among the most highly-prized of the comparatively scanty remains of ancient literature which have come down to our own day. We know Cicero as we can hardly know any one of our own countrymen, except those with whom we have spent our lives in habits of intimate familiarity. We are, therefore, able to compare his knowledge and acceptance of the great principles of moral and social duty, with those of men, in all other respects his inferiors, two centuries later. M. de Champagny, when speaking of Marcus Aurelius, thus sums up the comparison :—

Beyond a doubt a new progress has taken place. From Cicero to Seneca, from Seneca to Epictetus, from Epictetus to Marcus Aurelius, the light has been gradually increasing. Assuredly it was not that the philosophical ideas of those who came later were either higher, or clearer, or more true; in them the theory of philosophy was always either poor or wanting. In this respect Cicero could have taught much to those who came later than himself. But this spontaneous drawing towards virtue, independent of the metaphysical ideas which in this respect are more frequently an incumbrance than an assistance, this taste for what is good, which already showed itself through all the impurity of Seneca, which shone out in Musonius, which was so strongly marked in Epictetus, is seen more clearly still in Marcus Aurelius. It is evident that in the course of something more than a hundred years the conscience of the human race has been awakened. Hence is all the merit of these men, all their glory. They have, to speak truly, no other philosophy than this sentiment of right developed and perfected. Marcus Aurelius, for his part, carries it to the very verge of Christianity. If not quite humility there is modesty, and something that goes beyond modesty; if not charity there is beneficence; if not Christian mercy there is mildness; if not the love of the neighbour there is at least love of mankind; if not the prayer of the Christian there is the prayer of the philosopher. The soul has put off Paganism although not yet clothed with Christianity. —(*Antonins*, vol. iii. p. 15.)

Marcus Antoninus was the latest of the heathen philosophers whom M. de Champagny was at liberty in this passage to contrast with Cicero. But the case would have been stronger still, if he could have gone later, and contrasted him with Porphyry. Porphyry no doubt has, very justly, a bad name among Christians, because, living as he did immediately before the final victory of Christianity, and having been, to say the least, brought into close contact with it, he not only remained a heathen, but published a work in thirteen books against the Christians. These things, naturally and justly, tell against the man; but in his case, as in that of Julian, they give us a more striking example of the gradually increasing influence of Christianity, as it became better known, even upon these philosophers by whom it was least loved.

The idea of God, One, Supreme, and Lord of all those inferior beings, which were still by a sort of courtesy styled gods—that idea which we have already found in so many of the heathen philosophers who were contemporary with Christianity—is more distinct than ever in Porphyry, who came later, and was more familiar with Christian thought. He pronounces a sentence laconically energetic and containing in itself a complete demonstration of the existence of God. 'The One must of necessity come before the many.'[1] The idea of the purely incorporeal Being, which was so often obscured by clouds in the phraseology of the Greek philosophers, stands out here in a clear light. He conceives of God—or, if you will, of the first God—as unchangeable, without parts; present everywhere, because He is not anywhere present corporally. The relations of man to God, the supernatural life, the communication of the soul with the Divine Being by a pure act of the mind and without recourse to *theurgia*;[2] prayer offered in a generous and pure spirit almost unknown to heathen prayers, nothing of this is unknown to Porphyry. He is indignant at the merely earthly and material character of Pagan piety and Pagan thought. 'That prayer which is accompanied by evil actions is not pure, and cannot be accepted by God. The wise man is the only priest, the only religious man, the only one who knows how to pray.' What follows seems quite Christian. 'Religion has four principal foundations: Faith, Truth, Hope, Love. Faith is necessary because there is no salvation save for him who turns himself towards God. It is necessary to give all diligence to apply oneself wholly to know the truth with regard to God. When He is known, it is necessary that He should be loved. When He is loved, it is necessary to feed the soul with noble hopes.'

Porphyry again, after many other philosophers, no doubt, but in a manner much more distinct than they, requires that the soul should break the links which bind her to the body, separating herself from the passions and from the slavery of the body. The body is a burden which is ever weighing us downwards. The body is not oneself. 'I am not this tangible being which is the object of the senses; I am a being very different from my body, without colour, without shape, not to be apprehended by human hands, but only to be apprehended by the thoughts.' But if I allow myself to be ruled by this appendage

---

[1] Πρὸ τῶν πολλῶν ἀνάγκη εἶναι τὸ Ἕν.

[2] Theurgia, St. Augustine says (De Civitate Dei, x. 9), is distinguished by the heathen philosophers from göetia:—'Conantur ista discernere, et illicitis artibus deditos, alios damnabiles, quos et malificos vulgus appellat, hos enim ad *göetiam* pertinere dicunt; alios autem laudabiles videri volunt, quibus *theurgiam* deputant.' He condemns both as magical and unlawful.

alien from my being, and which is no more myself than the chaff is the grain; if I cleave to the senses which, like an iron nail, fasten together two things so different—the flesh and the spirit—I no longer know how to live my proper life. Unless I know how to put off this vestment of the flesh and its affections, so as to run free and unimpeded the course of life, I am lost. Even after death, the soul which has loved the body is weighed down towards low places, and lives a life degraded and gross; but the soul which has subjugated the body, and separated herself from it, which it is the mark of the philosopher to do, that soul will live a celestial life. The former is charged with gross vapours, and, drawn down by their weight, its habitation will be hell—that is ignorance, childishness, and eternal darkness; the latter, free, disengaged, will mount on high with the spirit ($\pi\nu\epsilon\tilde{\upsilon}\mu\alpha$) which she has received from on high, and which no burden will weigh down, she will mount higher than the stars, she will live in a divine sphere and in an ethereal body.

Porphyry, in fact, understood that man is a fallen creature; and that the soul of man, united to his body under the conditions in which that union actually exists, no longer lives in its original dignity. We must needs live after the spirit; and we are in some measure condemned, as if by force, to live after the flesh. 'We have fallen from a higher abode, to which we must return by raising ourselves upon two wings absolutely necessary to us—resistance to things of earth, and desire for things divine. We are exiles who would fain return to our country, to that invisible and spotless abode which was once ours by right.'

And to mount thither, Porphyry well knows, suffering is necessary. 'We cannot return by running the race of pleasure. Mountains are not climbed without fatigue or without danger. The path which leads to the summit is none other than vigilance, and the remembrance of the fall which has thrown us down so low as we are.'—(Vol. iii. p. 198.)

To any man at all conversant with the works even of the best and greatest of heathen philosophers, the only difficulty in reading these words is to remember that they were not written by a Christian, and in consequence he naturally judges of them by a standard far more severe than he would think of applying to any merely heathen philosopher. For in them we are struck to find any point on which they have attained the knowledge of religious truth, while in Porphyry there is so much that is purely Christian, that our minds instinctively turn rather to the points on which he falls short of Christian teaching, and contradicts it : for instance, no one who believed that the Word has been made Flesh, would regard the body, as he did, as in itself evil. It is here that the strictest Christian asceticism is divided by a broad line from Gnosticism.

But to say nothing on this subject, let me observe that the facts of history are quite inconsistent with any explanation which would account for this gradual elevation of the religious teaching of the heathen philosophers of the first three centuries by anything else than the gradually increasing, though unacknowledged, influence of Christianity with which in each succeeding generation they were brought more and more closely into contact. It cannot be attributed to the natural progress and advancement of the human mind during a period of high civilisation. For beyond a doubt the three centuries between Augustus and Constantine were not a period of intellectual and social development, but of decline. And again, this solution is contrary to facts ; for the Christian thinkers and teachers during the same period, so far from improving upon the principles of their first teachers, made it their highest ambition not to fall below them. This, indeed, was only to be expected by those who know that Christianity was not invented and matured by men, but revealed by God. How it can be accounted for by those who deny its Divine origin one does not see. Such, however, was the fact. During three centuries there stood side by side, in the Roman Empire, acting mutually on each other, two rival systems of religion and morals ; on the one side Christian faith and grace, originating and taking root among classes overlooked and despised by the wise men of the age, and only gradually, as they became more prominent, forcing themselves upon their attention; on the other, the theology and philosophy which had already been developed to the highest excellence which its nature admitted, by the genius and labours of all the greatest minds of the civilised world, from the day when Socrates began to teach at Athens to the day when Cicero held out his head to the satellites of the Triumvirs. And the result was, that the teaching of the despised and unrefined Galileans, although, at a later period, some of the greatest and most gifted minds that ever existed on earth devoted all their energies to cultivate and promote it, never attained to anything higher than had been taught by the unlettered men who first propagated it; while that which, before this period began, had engrossed all the greatest men of the world during many centuries, which had already long passed the age of growth, and which promised nothing but decay, gradually admitted into itself many principles before unknown to it, each of which had been from the beginning a first principle of the rival system, and more and more of which were adopted by the philosophers, exactly as the society in which they lived became more and more deeply imbued with that system. Could anything more strongly prove that the improvement of the systems of the philosophers was due, not to any principle of internal growth and development, but to the external influence of Christianity?

In mere notions of religion, also, considerable advance seems to have been made from the same cause, even by men who so far from becoming Christians were among the vilest of heathens. Such at least is the opinion of M. de Champagny, and it seems to me well-founded. Heathens of old times had always been ready to admit new gods. 'The policy of the emperors and the Senate,' says Gibbon, in words often quoted, 'so far as it concerned religion, was happily seconded by the reflections of the enlightened, and by the habits of the superstitious part of their subjects. The various modes of worship which prevailed in the heathen world, were all considered by the people as equally true, by the philosopher as equally false, and by the magistrates as equally useful. And thus toleration produced not only mutual indulgence but even religious concord.' That is, of course, that the worshipper of the gods of Rome had no feeling that he did anything inconsistent, in offering sacrifice or worship according to the rites of other nations to the gods whom they worshipped. This was the fundamental principle of heathenism, and, so far as I know, it was only among the Hebrew people that the idea of one religion exclusively true ever existed in the ancient world. But late in the history of heathen Rome, one emperor conceived and attempted to carry out the idea of one supreme god, and one universal religion. He did not indeed deny the existence or forbid the worship of other gods, but he made them all subordinate to the one supreme Syrian god, to whom he had been priest before he attained the Empire, and whom he installed at Rome. The vile moral degradation of this young tyrant, and his doubtful sanity, have induced most writers to suppose that this was merely a wanton freak of the Emperor Elagabalus. M. de Champagny is inclined to think that there may have been in it something deeper.

Under all this, may there not have been a thought in some degree serious?—some degree of belief in the rites practised? Not in the boy Cæsar, of course, in whom rottenness had come before ripeness, corruption before manhood. But in his mother, perhaps, or in some of those around him, the project existed of uniting in the worship of the god of Edessa, all the worships of the Empire. His temple was the dominant temple in which were to meet, directly or indirectly, the prayers and homage of collective humanity. Whatever Rome had of venerated symbols, of sacred and mysterious talismans, was unpityingly summoned to surrender to it. The Emperor-Priest caused himself to be affiliated to all the priesthoods, in order to learn their secret emblems, and to bring their gods to the feet of his god. [The enumeration which follows is striking and picturesque, but we have not room for it.] His idea, or that of those by whom he was directed, was the fusion into one of all the Pagan religions. 'He said,' says Lampridius, 'that all gods were only the servants of his god, some of them his chamberlains, some his guards, some his ministers. It was not merely the religion of Rome that he desired to abolish, it was throughout the whole world that he would have his god Elagabalus alone and everywhere the object of worship.'

Nothing probably could appear to a heathen a stronger sign of madness than this desire to unite all mankind in one religion. But the wretched youth who conceived it had been brought up in Syria, and the religion of the Jews and Christians had unquestionably some attraction for him. We are expressly told that he resolved to unite in one, not only all the heathen religions, but 'that he would bring to his temple of Mount Palatine the religion of the Samaritans, that of the Jews, and that of the Christians, that so the priesthood of Elagabalus might hold in possession the secrets of all the religions of the world.' He even submitted to circumcision, and abstained from pork—strange notion for a youth who knew not what abstinence from anything meant. But there is positive testimony that his mother's sister, if not actually a Christian (which is one account), had received instruction in Christianity; and there seems little doubt that it was the Christian idea of one God and one Church for all nations, of which he had laid hold, and which he corrupted as he did all else that he touched.

I have devoted a disproportionate space to the development of M. de Champagny's estimate of the indirect and unacknowledged influence of Christianity on the Roman Empire, both because I think that he most clearly establishes the fact; because, so far as I have observed, he is the first writer upon those times by whom it has been brought out; and because, moreover, it gives to this portion of the history of the Roman Empire the interest which it wants in the hands of other historians. Nothing can be more dreary than the narrative of mere decay and corruption—a ruin physical and moral. From Gibbon's picture of the period between the accession of Commodus and the accession of Constantine, I cannot help turning with a disgust almost unrelieved. That the barbarians were like wolves baying round a mountain village on some winter night is really the only redeeming feature in it, for it is the only one which presents the hope of something better in the distant future. M. de Champagny, with surprising skill, has contrived to make this period interesting and attractive. This is in great measure because he keeps constantly before us the blessed truth, that this Empire, slowly dying away, not of any external dangers or assaults, but of its deep, internal corruption, held within it a life distinct from its own, which was daily increasing in strength, and preparing to take possession of the new world which was to succeed, when the wretchedness of the old world should no longer be endured by God or by man. I am reminded of the ceremonial so often mentioned in these volumes, and which formed a standing part of the funeral rites of an emperor. At the moment when the pile by which his body was to be consumed was kindled, an eagle, which had been concealed within it, was released, and soared away through the sky. Like it, the Christian Church was in but not of, the decaying Roman Empire : and its freedom and power began with the utter destruction of the Empire. M. de Champagny agrees with all other historians in regarding this period as one of mere decay. He divides the history of the Empire into three. The first period, that of the Cæsars, ending with Nero (the last emperor allied by blood to Augustus or Julius) gives us the working out of the system invented and established by Tiberius. Then, (after a few months of civil confusion, in which the purple was worn by three puppets, whom Tacitus compares to those actors who for a few hours present on the stage a royal character), came a succession of wise and good rulers—from Vespasian to Marcus Aurelius, under whom the Roman world, for more than a century, enjoyed a remarkable degree of peace and repose, except during the few years of the tyranny of Domitian. This is the period of which M. de Champagny treated in his last work, 'The Antonines,' to which I have already called the attention of my readers. It is regarded by him as an interval during which the decay of the Empire was suspended but not arrested; during which the wisest and most humane emperor could not help feeling that he might be succeeded by a Nero or a Caligula, but during which, as a matter of fact, the material prosperity of the free portion, at least, of the population of the Empire, was greater than at any other period of heathen history, although not to be compared with that of modern Italy, even at its least prosperous times; a fact which he is careful to prove by details, because the anti-Christian writers of the eighteenth century have delighted to exaggerate the period of the Antonines into a sort of millennium, in order to depreciate, by comparison, the condition of Christian nations. With the death of the Emperor Marcus Aurelius, which took place A.D. 180, this period ended. Many subsequent emperors, indeed, took the name of Antoninus, and some degree of confusion has been introduced by the inscriptions on their monuments bearing the well-remembered name, (for the practice of distinguishing from each other, by numbers, rulers who bore the same name did not exist in the ancient world), but it was disgraced by their monstrous vices and tyranny, and history has refused to accord it to them. Thus each of the emperors who have ever since been known only as Caracalla and Elagabalus styled himself Marcus Aurelius Antoninus.

The three volumes now before me take up the history, where it was left by the last volume of 'The Antonines,' at the death of Marcus Aurelius, and the accession of his son Commodus. This imposed on the author the necessity of devoting all the rest of his work to the most calamitous and ignominious part of

Roman history. This fact was so strongly on my mind when I took up the first volume, that I felt almost disinclined to read it. But so skilfully has M. de Champagny performed his task, that he has given us a work, with regard to which the only difficulty I have found has been to lay it down. It is one, moreover, quite essential to the full enjoyment of the volumes which have preceded it, and without which, indeed, many things in them would have been incomplete. For instance, one main subject of Roman history must ever be that of the relations of the Empire to the Christian Church. Of the blessed influence of the Church upon the Empire I have already spoken. The history of the action of the Empire towards the Church, on the other hand, is little more than the history of the persecutions. It is a subject little attractive to an un-Christian writer, for he has to record, much against his will, that great phenomenon stated by M. de Champagny, in the extract with which I began the present review, that every inch of ground traversed by the Church, in her triumphal progress of victory over the heathen world, was won for her and secured to her by the blood of her martyrs. The subject, however distasteful, could not be avoided even by Gibbon. He was compelled to treat it, whether he would or not, and the result is his well-known sixteenth chapter, in which, professing to tell 'the conduct of the Roman Government towards the Christians from the reign of Nero to that of Constantine,' he labours, as far as possible, to explain away and palliate the persecutions which he could not wholly deny; while he throws as much doubt as possible upon every fact connected with them, lessens as much as possible the number of the martyrs, and especially sets himself to engage the interest and sympathies of his readers on the side of the high-minded, philosophical, enlightened men who, no doubt under a mistaken view of the facts, felt it their painful duty to pronounce sentence, and against the score or two of vulgar, wrongheaded, seditious fanatics, whom he admits to have suffered death as Christians at one time or other, and in different provinces of the vast Empire. It is hardly necessary to say that the subject is treated very differently by M. de Champagny. As a critic and a member of the French Academy we cannot suspect him of any tendency to neglect a scrupulous examination of the evidence by which different martyrdoms are proved. But in each successive persecution he gives us the most striking and well-attested records of the sufferings of those whom he loves and reverences as his own brethren and fathers in the common faith; by whose blood and self-sacrifice it has pleased God to preserve to us those blessings which He originally gave us by the Blood and Sacrifice of His Eternal Son. Thus he begins his notice of the last general persecution :—

It is, indeed, the era of martyrs. They meet us more abundantly than ever. Already, pressed by our space, we have often abridged the narrative of the persecutions, lest we should weary the reader by the constant repetition of the same cruelties and the same heroism. In future we shall be compelled to abridge them still more. The harvest is so abundant that it is impossible to gather it ear by ear, or even sheaf by sheaf. We shall only cast our eyes over the plain on which the executioners are the mowers, and the angels those who gather in the harvest. We shall pass in silence over many names which the Church has recorded in her annals; many of the most celebrated names, and of the most popular records. May we be forgiven by these holy ones, if we see in them only the members of the Holiest of Holies, of Him in whom we are all one.—(Vol. iii. p. 330.)

Here is the true Catholic tone. Among Catholics, thank God, there is little ground for the reproach addressed to his countrymen by a poet contemporary with Gibbon.

> Patriots have toiled, and in their country's cause
> Bled nobly; and their deeds, as they deserve,
> Receive proud recompense . . .
> But martyrs struggle for a brighter prize,
> And win it with more pain. Their blood is shed

In confirmation of our noblest claim—
Our claim to feed upon immortal Truth,
To walk with God, to be divinely free,
To soar and to anticipate the skies.
Yet few remember them. They lived unknown
Till persecution dragged them into fame,
And chased them up to Heaven   Their ashes flew
No marble tells us whither. With their names
No bard embalms and consecrates his song ;
And history, so warm on meaner themes,
Is cold on this.

A most true estimate, alas ! of the general tone of English literature. Nor could there be a more just comparison between the popular feeling of a Protestant and a Catholic people than one between it and that of M. de Champagny. In these volumes he goes through the whole period of the heathen persecutions in the old world. Their character was quite different in the later and in the earlier portion of it. At first Christians for the most part were, like their Lord, reluctantly given over to the fury of a popular cry by judges who even in condemning them could not refrain from asking 'what evil have they done?' Under Nero they were thrown to the populace maddened by the burning of Rome. Under Domitian they were confused with the philosophers who had incurred his jealousy. At a still earlier period they had been involved in a momentary jealousy against the Jews. Pliny reported to Trajan that he could find nothing criminal in them except their obstinacy. Thus, in the periods included in M. de Champagny's former series, persecution, though far from unfrequent, was little more than accidental. The power of the magistrate was so absolute, that no set of men could be safe against whom suspicion was once excited, and in them there was at all times peculiarity enough to excite suspicion. Above all, in times of pestilence, (and no age of the world was more severely afflicted with that scourge than that which began with Marcus Aurelius), or when famine threatened, or even when strange portents in the sky alarmed the people, according to the well-known passage of Tertullian—'If the Tiber rises to the walls, or if the Nile does not rise over the fields; if the heaven hath stood still, or the earth hath moved; if there is any famine, if any pestilence'—the cry was still, 'the Christians to the lion.' Such was persecution down to the beginning of the period of which these volumes treat. The reign of the Emperor Severus, which marked in many other respects a new era in Roman history, is selected by the author as the first in which persecution was a deliberate act of Roman policy.

The persecution of Severus may be called the first which was a solemn, spontaneous, political act of Roman authority. Nero had given the signal for persecution, but chiefly at Rome and from accidental circumstances. Domitian had been led to proscribe the Christians rather for financial motives than as part of a proclaimed policy. Trajan, Hadrian, Marcus Aurelius himself, had permitted persecution rather than persecuted, maintaining, of course, the legal principle which condemned Christianity, but not always urging its execution, and allowing it to be active or inactive, according to the fanaticism or the indifference of the different peoples, the weakness or wisdom of the Proconsuls. Severus was the first of whom we are told that by a formal, public, dated act, he forbade that Christians should exist, thus rendering the persecution not merely legal but obligatory, not merely possible here and there, but necessary everywhere. He first gave the signal for one of those single combats hand to hand, between authority and the Church, which the world was to see many times renewed in the course of this age, always to the disgrace of idolatrous tyranny, and to the glory of Christian patience. This combat was fierce and of long continuance. We have a work of Tertullian, written after the death of Severus, and at least ten years later than the commencement of the persecution, from which it appears that it had not yet been given up. The Church was not in numbers what it was later; and the administration of the Cæsars reconstituted by Severus, had a power of action which afterwards steadily diminished. The struggle, therefore, though not more violent, was of longer duration, than those which followed.—(Vol. i. p. 259.)

It was in this persecution that several of the blessed saints whose names we still daily honour in the canon of the Mass, received their crowns—the slave Felicitas, and the noble lady Perpetua, whose martyrdoms, which no one can weary of reading, are given by M. de Champagny in full detail. How little thought those humble martyrs that, age after age, when the very name of Severus should be known only to students, and when the Empire itself should have passed away, their contest and their names should be watchwords in the Christian fight to millions in every clime, men and women of all nations and all languages, wherever the 'world-encircling sun' looks down upon the habitations of men.

It is impossible to read any of these soul-stirring narratives without being strongly impressed by a sense of the wholly fragmentary character of our knowledge, not only of the history of the martyrs, but of ancient times as a whole. Here and there we have the 'genuine acts' of some martyr whose fame is thus preserved in the Church, while we cannot but feel that there must have been many more, in our judgment quite as well worth preserving, which are known only to God. The saints and martyrs would be, of all men, the first to say, ' Even so, Father, for so it hath seemed good in Thy sight.' What to them the applause even of their brethren in the Church, in comparison with the praise of Him for whom they lived, and fought the good fight, and died. 'Receperunt mercedem suam, vani vanum,' says S. Augustine[1] of the successful candidates for posthumous fame. But so it is; our acquaintance, for instance, with the details of the persecution in Carthage, under Decius and Valerian, we owe merely to what, speaking in human language, we must call the chance which has preserved to us the letters of S. Cyprian; our knowledge of the martyrdoms at Lyons and Vienne, to a similar chance which has preserved the letters in which they were re-

---

[1] Quoted, Champagny, vol. ii. p. 140.

ported to the Christians of the East. Who can doubt that many documents as valuable, many narratives as thrilling, must have been wrecked as they floated down the stream of time, set thick as it was with rocks upon which have been lost so many of the most precious relics of ancient literature, whether sacred or secular?

With regard to the later persecutions, they seem to have partaken, each more decidedly than that which came before it, of the same character of deliberate acts of the central government rather than of popular outbreaks like those of the earlier days. M. de Champagny points out also that in the last and most terrible of all, that under Diocletian, there does not seem to have been any of the old popular demand for deeds of blood and cruelty. Christianity had already become so far known as to make it quite impossible that the mass of the people should any longer believe the calumnies against it, as they did in earlier days.

This persecution had much less than those which went before it the support of popular passion. Very seldom on this occasion did the people interfere to denounce, excite, or complain of the backwardness of the magistrates. Sometimes, on the contrary, it did interfere to express sorrow and pity for the victims, and to demand their pardon. Heathenism had lost ground, not only in the number of its adherents, but in its power over their minds. The heathen populace was no longer that of the preceding century. The Christians had lived in the midst of it in too great numbers, and too publicly not to be better understood. Many minds, indifferent or tolerant, had come to think that the worship of God and the worship of the gods (as Tertullian somewhere expresses it) might live side by side. Their reason inclined to the former, although their corrupt hearts shrank from it. The few sincere heathens there were, were a part of the common people, without much reflection or knowledge, in whose eyes the offence of the Christians (whom in other respects they thought worthy people) was to have too much knowledge and too much reflection. Is not that in truth at this very day the offence of Christians in the eyes of the great mass of people who do not wish to know or to reflect?—(Vol. iii. p. 346.)

The most important change was in the popular estimate of Christian morality. Time was, when strange and horrible stories of monstrous and unutterable impurity practised by the Christians in their secret assemblies were really believed, not merely by the vulgar, but even by educated men. This suspicion could not but be fostered by the care with which Christian reverence compelled them to conceal the real nature of that great act which has at all times formed the principal part of Christian worship. By degrees, however, the popular estimate had become so much modified, that it became the general feeling that Christians, whatever else there might be to say against them, were at least more pure than anyone else. Thus, when a woman named Afra, who was well known to have been a harlot, was brought before the heathen magistrate at Iconium, charged with being a Christian, and admitted the charge, he said, 'You a Christian! you are not worthy of Christ. It is in vain for you to call Him your God, for He will never acknowledge you as His.' A still more remarkable case is given by M. de Champagny.

An immodest woman came into a nursery-garden belonging to one Serenus, at an unbecoming hour, professing that she wished to walk there. He reproached her for her boldness, and turned her out. She had a duped husband, who was a favourite servant of the prince, and she complained of having been insulted, and caused Serenus to be summoned before the magistrate. He related what had happened in a simple manner, exposing the artifice of the wretched woman. She was silenced, and her indignant husband took her out of the court. 'But,' said the judge to Serenus, 'who are you? who but a Christian would have had such a scruple?' 'I am a Christian.' 'How then have you escaped our pursuit? Have not you sacrificed to the gods?' 'As long as it was the will of God, He kept me out of notice. I was like the stone which the builders rejected. Now He is pleased to make use of me, and I am ready.' And the Christian suffered death.
—(Vol. iii. p. 396.)

The disappearance of this old prejudice was the sign that the long era of persecution was drawing to an end. I cannot help thinking that a similar symptom gives us good hope for our own country. No one who knows England now, and can remember what it was fifty years ago, can fail to observe the great change that has taken place. Then, the notion of respectable men was that Catholics were a race morally degraded. Now, they are disliked by many people, but on the whole it is on the ground of needless strictness. God forbid that any who bear the honoured name should give them reason to think that Catholic men and Catholic women are much the same as other men and women of their own class of society, except that on Sundays they hear Mass instead of going to the Established Church. No doubt there is always some danger of this, when the fear of persecution has passed away. If the Dioclesian persecution found Christians so well prepared, it was because the Church had been sifted and purified by those of Decius, Valerian, and Aurelian in the preceding half-century. When the first of these broke out—

At the first moment the triumph of the emperor's will seemed complete. The Christians had been sleeping calmly, for the persecution had been suspended for eight-and-thirty years, and they had come to regard it only as a heroical tradition of times gone by. They had accustomed themselves to a life, easy, soft, and in some cases half heathen. At the sound of the edict of persecution they started up in terror. The faith which they had received from their fathers, and which they had been carelessly holding, did not seem to them a treasure so precious as their property or their life. They flocked in crowds before the Proconsul: those who held public offices (for the Christians had begun to enter into such offices), because their rank exposed them to more notice, and in some sense called on them to make a decision; those who had pagan brothers or kindred, because they were urged to it by their kinsfolk; others because they were cited to appear; others because they were in a shameful hurry to apostatise. They were led before the idols and sacrificed. Some were pale, trembling, distracted between fear of man and fear of God.

These timid souls, who had not courage either for martyrdom or for apostasy, were a little laughed at by the heathen populace. Others, more firm in appearance, with an unabashed forehead and a confident voice, shamelessly denied that they had ever been Christians. They said true: these, says S. Dionysius of Alexandria, were those of whom our Lord foretold that their salvation would be difficult. Some went still further in their ardour for apostasy. They proclaimed that they had sacrificed to the gods—that they had sacrificed without compulsion; they obtained from the judge a written certificate of their baseness; they hastened to their shame with an affected joy; they prevailed on their neighbours to come; they brought their children and got the idol's wine poured over their innocent lips. Sometimes when put off to the next day by a magistrate too busy to receive apostasies, they begged and implored.—(Vol. iii. p. 290.)

What picture would the Catholic Church in England present, if persecution should suddenly return upon us? Doubtless there would be many martyrs. It is from the letters of S. Cyprian, the martyr Archbishop of Carthage, that this description of what he had seen go on before his own eyes is drawn. But would none be found 'asleep'? none 'whom the roar of the edicts would startle up in terror'? none accustomed to a 'life easy and soft,' half Protestant? and if so, might not London as well as Carthage[1] see many 'fallen'?

I have left myself no space to follow M. de Champagny's narrative through what may be called the secular part of his history. In this I feel that I have done him less than justice, because, as I have already said, it is the blending of the two elements together that gives to his volumes their special charm. He has been as conscientiously diligent in one as in the other, and the secular history, although I may not have prepared the reader to expect it, occupies more than two-thirds of the volumes before me. As a French writer living under the Second Empire

---

[1] S. Cyprian says: 'Aspice totum orbem pene vastatum et ubique jacere dejectorum reliquias et ruinas.'

he could hardly refrain himself from following, with especial care, the history of the fall of Rome under the Cæsars, if it were only that he might expose the peculiar corruptions against which his own country had most need to be warned. He is strongly impressed with a truth most certain and momentous, and not less necessary to be urged upon England than upon France; that the ruin of nations is brought on, not by material or even by political, but by social and moral causes. It is, therefore, the social and moral bearing of political changes, which has always the greatest attraction for the author. With this thought before him, he weighs and estimates the new system introduced into the Roman Empire by Severus, which is indeed the beginning of the political history of the three volumes before me, and the effect produced both upon his family and his successors, as well as upon the public interests, by the new supremacy given by him to the soldier. He estimates in the same way the object and effects of the change introduced by Caracalla, when he admitted the whole world to the citizenship of Rome. In another part of the work we have a most interesting account of the growth of the Roman law, and of the circumstances to which it owes its peculiar characteristics. Lastly, he considers the new system introduced by Diocletian. Upon all these things I designed, when I commenced my work, to enter at some length. But my space is filled, and I have not touched them. I regret this the less, because I think the extracts I have given will suffice to direct the attention of my readers to the volumes of M. de Champagny himself. He is a writer whose chief characteristic it is, that it is impossible to read him without being set thinking. In words which, in my notice of his former works, I quoted from a French critic, 'Le plus beau privilége des écrivants qui pensent c'est de faire penser ceux qui les lisent. M. de Champagny fait penser.' The remark is as applicable to this work as to those which preceded it.

I will conclude with a single example of the skill of the author in setting vividly before his readers a picture of the men and manners of times in many respects so unlike our own, as far as decency allows, a qualification which, in striking contrast to Gibbon, he never forgets.

Well, then, let us go into that villa of Laurentum, in which, sick of empire, having signed in a heap twenty edicts, and having written at the foot of a letter the single word *farewell*, the son of Marcus Aurelius is resting himself in the shade of the bays of his garden. What is he to do to-day? We are in the golden age, (the era of Commodus has been officially declared such by a decree of the Senate); it is the eve of the Calends of the Herculian month (for by another decree the calendar has been changed, and six of the twelve months have been decorated with the names or titles of Commodus). But even in the golden age, even in the month Ælius, in the month Amazonius, even when one is master of the world, *ennui* will intrude. Upon some thirty letters or edicts just signed, he has been reading the formula magnificent but in the end tiresome—' The Emperor Cæsar Lucius Ælius Aurelius Commodus Augustus Pius (that title he took on the day when he made one of the lovers of his mother Consul), happy Sarmaticus Maximus Germanicus Britannicus, Pacificator of the world, unconquerable, the Roman Hercules, Pontifex Maximus, eighteen times invested with tribunitial authority, eight times Imperator, Father of his Country, to the Consuls, the Prætors, and the Tribunes of the people, and to the Commodian Senate (for the Senate too had taken this title, the historian says, in derision, but if it laughed you may be sure it was not out loud), to the Senate happy and Commodian, health.' Yes, no doubt one is all this . . . . and yet what matter—*ennui* will intrude. . . . . Marcia comes charged to amuse her terrible husband : ' What will my master be pleased to do ? ' she says. ' Will he have the circus prepared, and put on the habit of the green faction to win new victories ? Or will the Roman Hercules call for his lion-skin and his club ? ' Marcia had given him these fantasies about Hercules. . As he must act she wanted to inspire him with a taste for acting some manly character. ' My master knows that I am an Amazon, and I love the combat. Will he like me to take the helmet and cuirass to go out to the combat on the banks of the River Thermodon? Or will he prefer to be an Amazon himself, and to fight, in a female garb, with the courage of a hero?' 'Yes,' says Commodus, 'I will fight. Take off my shoes. Give me a matron's tunic shot with purple and gold. Get ready my domestic arena. Call my gladiators to come and be killed by the first gladiator in the world. What shall I kill? Men, beasts, elephants, rhinoceros. I have killed at one single time, two elephants, five hippopotamus, some rhinoceros, beasts by the hundred—all with a single blow! And I have pierced the horn of a gazelle with my javelin. No, I should like to spare blood to-day: I won't kill anything to-day, except some cripples and lame men. I am Hercules. Bring me my lion-skin and my club. These poor wretches shall be the Titans; put some serpents [artificial, N.B.] about their limbs. I am Apollo. I will pierce them with my arrows.'

Marcia, perhaps, tries to suggest some less sanguinary employment. She tells of the few amusements, comparatively innocent, by which he has signalised his days of special good humour. She reminds him that one day he had had two deformed dwarfs served up on a huge silver platter smothered in mustard, and, of his unheard of mercy, had been pleased not only not to eat them, but to enrich them and make them prefects; that another day he had caused the most delicate dishes to be mixed with the dung from his stables, and had pretended to eat of them that the company at his table might be caught by them. Happy for the world when Commodus had had only these disgusting amusements. But he remembers jokes which were more enjoyable. How for one man he had dressed his beard and cut off his nose; how he had acted as surgeon for another and cut an artery; how he had pretended to cut the hair of another and had cut off his ear; how he had had one enormously fat man embowelled that he might satisfy himself what there could be inside. He remembers how many men he had had deprived of one eye and one leg; how many he had had killed because they were too handsome; how many because he had met them dressed in the style of the barbarians. For so it was that in his private life and in the retirement of his home he had his little private cruelties quite unconnected with politics.

Marcia would try to change these sanguinary instincts. She talks to Commodus of prayers and sacrifices. She hopes to excite some fear of the gods. He replies, 'I have not sacrificed to Isis for a long time. My hair has grown again since I shaved, in order to carry the divine Anubis. Do you remember how, as I held the image in my hand and offered it to be kissed by the servants of Isis, I knocked it violently against their jaws? And when the poor wretches beat their breasts with the consecrated pine comb, how I made them strike hard; and the priests of Bellona, when it was their duty to wound their arms with knives, how I made them do it till the blood ran well? And how I made a serious matter of the trials which precede the initiation to the mysteries of Mithras, trying the courage of the postulants by the sight of bloodshed in real earnest?' Do what they may, talk to him of his religious rites, of his orgies, of his amusements, of his politics, it is always the man of blood that comes foremost.—(Vol. i. p. 35.)

IV.

THE GALLICAN ASSEMBLY OF 1682.[1]

Who can despair of the vitality of truth, when the real history of the struggle between the Holy See and Gallicanism, under Lewis XIV., after lying buried for two centuries, under a vast mountain of falsehood, has at last come to light? And yet this is by no means an overstatement of the fact. The labours of M. Gérin have dealt a fatal blow to the traditions on this subject, which have hitherto been quietly received alike by Protestants and by Catholics. But a long cherished tradition is not at once dispelled from men's minds, even by the publication of clear and unanswerable facts which disprove it. It would be a failure in duty, if Catholics should leave off insisting upon them until the truth has got itself so firmly implanted in men's minds that it will need the courage of a Cumming, a Newdegate, or a Whalley to enable any man to stand forward and talk gravely about Gallican principles; and if I may in any degree judge from experience this will not be until many a confident writer has been called to account for assuming as admitted facts all the monstrous fictions which M. Gérin has exposed. This may be a somewhat weary task, but I feel no doubt of ultimate success; nay, I have a good hope that after a few years the 'Times' itself

[1] 'Recherches Historiques sur l'Assemblée du Clergé de France de 1682.' Par Charles Gérin, Juge au tribunal civil de la Seine. Paris: Lecoffre, 1868.

will not only take it for granted that what used to be called the 'Liberties of the Gallican Church' were really nothing more than maxims forced upon reluctant, but time-serving Catholics, by shameless tyranny on the part of Lewis XIV. and his ministers; but also that such has always been the view taken of the matter by all educated men, and especially by the writers in the Thunderer.

It would not be easy, at any period, to exaggerate the importance of establishing the truth on this subject. But, if I am not mistaken, the present crisis of the history of the world, and most especially of England, gives it a new importance. The European world is still in the middle of that great series of earthquake shocks to which future ages will look back as 'the revolution,' which began with the overthrow of the throne of the Bourbons in France, and as to which no one can as yet form any conjecture when it is to end. In England, especially, it is impossible that the relation of the State to religion should not be seriously altered by the great change which Mr. Disraeli has introduced into our secular institutions. That change is not really less great and momentous, because like other great changes in England, it was brought about by constitutional means, not after the French custom, by force; and we may calculate on seeing it result in a total change of the maxims of our Government. For myself I strongly think that one of its effects is likely to be to diminish the feeling which has long prevailed among English Liberals in favour of religious liberty, and to bring future English Governments into collisions with the Catholic Church, different, perhaps, in form, but not less serious than those which it has experienced with rulers of very different sorts in centuries gone by, and from which it has risen triumphant. If this expectation is well-founded, it is clearly important that, before those collisions are even threatened, the old illusion about the Gallican liberties should be effectually swept away: for the experience of Napoleon I. shows, what indeed common-sense would have sufficed to teach, that there is nothing so welcome to men who, under a new order of things, are setting themselves to assail the Church, as, when they are able to attack it from behind the shelter of great Catholic names of former times.

No man was less tempted to appeal to precedents in the past history of France than Napoleon I., for it was his boast to be the founder of a new order of things. It was only against the Church that he ever thought of urging precedents drawn from the maxims and policy of Lewis XIV. But he was never tired of appealing to the 'declaration of the clergy of France,' in May 1682; and to the great name of Bossuet. M. d'Haussonville shows that on March 6, 1810, when railing at the Belgian clergy who remained faithful to Pius VII., he said, 'You idiots. If I had not found principles like my own in the teaching of Bossuet, and in the maxims of the Gallican Church, I would have turned Protestant!'

He was wont to repeat that 'the second alone of the four articles contained in the declaration of 1682 would have been enough to enable him to get rid of the Pope.' Accordingly, those articles were incorporated in the 'organic articles,' which, with almost incredible cynicism, he added to the Concordat with Pius VII. after it was signed, and after he had, in vain, used all means of fraud, as well as of force, to get them included in it. Nay, when he seized the States of the Church, his servile Senate passed, at his dictation, a new enactment, which he published as a law of the French empire, requiring all future Popes on taking possession of their office to swear to observe the four articles of 1682. M. Gérin tells us that this law was quoted by the Count de Montalembert in the French Chamber of Peers (May 20, 1847), and the Assembly received it with something of incredulous surprise. 'Yes, gentlemen,' said the Count, 'so it stands in the *Bulletin des lois*. And it is well that these monuments of human

The Gallican Assembly of 1682.

folly should, from time to time, be brought forward that men may know how glory itself can be debased by passion.' (P. vi. note.)

The same lesson unquestionably is taught by the volume before me. The glory of Lewis XIV. is disgraced by the tyranny and trickery which it records in so many instances: and, alas, the far higher glory of Bossuet himself is dimmed by his unworthy concessions.

As far as Bossuet has, in times past, been under suspicion as disaffected towards the Holy See, M. Gérin clears his reputation. Bossuet, beyond all doubt, was in heart as good an Ultramontane as anyone else. So far as he is to blame, it is not for being hostile to the authority of the Holy See, but for unwillingly allowing himself to be made, to a certain extent, a tool in the hands of those who desired to assail it.

This, I think, no one can doubt, who has read the documents collected by M. Gérin. And it is a fact of great importance. The weight of any man's testimony is destroyed in the judgment of all sober men, if it turns out to have been obtained either by torture, or by the dread of it. Much more is the value of a great man's opinion upon a theological question tainted, if he has delivered it under secular inducements. It becomes, in fact, not the sentence of a judge, but the pleading of a hired advocate. Bossuet, highly gifted as he ever was, used his gifts in 1682 merely as the advocate of Lewis XIV., or rather, it should be said, of Colbert.

Nothing throws more light upon this than his own conduct, when Lewis, on a former occasion, condescended to use the clergy of France as his tool against Alexander VII.

The outlines of this disgraceful history have been given by all historians. Life and property were in those times insecure in Rome, because the ambassadors of the Catholic powers claimed privileges utterly destructive of all government. Lord Macaulay says:—

'It had long been the rule at Rome, that no officer of justice or finance could enter the dwelling inhabited by the minister who represented a Catholic state. In process of time, not only the dwelling, but a large precinct round it, was held inviolable. It was a point of honour with every ambassador to extend as widely as possible the limits of the region which was under his protection. At length half the city consisted of privileged districts, within which the Papal government had no more power than within the Louvre or the Escurial. Every asylum was thronged with contraband traders, fraudulent bankrupts, thieves, and assassins. In every asylum were collected magazines of stolen or smuggled goods. From every asylum ruffians sallied forth nightly, to plunder and stab. In no town in Christendom, consequently, was law so impotent, and wickedness so atrocious, as in the ancient capital of religion and civilisation.'

It is truly amazing to find that this monstrous abuse, when loudly complained of by the Popes, was supported through false principles of honour by the monarchs of Europe. At a later period it was put a stop to by Innocent XI., 'who felt on the subject,' says Macaulay, 'as became a Priest and a Prince.' The unequalled outrages which Lewis XIV. then committed, in the endeavour to maintain it, I shall have to mention. I now return to 1662. On the 20th of August in that year the troops, kept on foot by the Duke of Crequi, ambassador of France, attacked some Corsican soldiers in the service of the Pope, and in the fray which followed, two Frenchmen and five Italians were killed. The Pope ascertained that, although the French were the aggressors, his own soldiers afterwards had been to blame, and actually caused two, who were found guilty, to be executed. He also sent an extraordinary minister to Paris, to explain the unfortunate event to Lewis. The King refused to give him an audience, and adopted a line of conduct so exactly similar to that of Napoleon I. towards Pius VII., and also towards the republic of Venice, when it suited his purpose to pick a quarrel with them, that it is difficult to read the narrative without imagining that, by some accident, a page of French history has got out of its place. He gave orders that Avignon should be seized, and sent an army into Italy. That nothing might be wanting to complete his disgrace (and I must add his resemblance to Napoleon), hearing that the Pope was obtaining troops for the defence of Rome from the Catholic Cantons of Switzerland, he sent to assure them that the French troops were marching into Italy only to defend, exalt, and protect the Holy See, 'after the example of his glorious ancestors;' and that the 'eldest son of the Church could never think of an action so culpable as that of employing his arms against her.' The Pope continued to negotiate, but Lewis demanded that, before he would consider any terms, Alexander should give practical proof of his good intentions, by depriving of his hat, Cardinal Imperiali, governor of Rome; by giving up to Lewis his own brother, Don Mario, to be dealt with at the King's discretion; and by causing no less than one hundred of his own soldiers and four officers to be hanged, half in the Piazza Farnese, half in the Piazza Navona. Beside all this, the Pope was to engage to send any person whom Lewis might be pleased to name as Legate, to apologise to the King. When the Pope, said the French Ambassador, shall have taken these preliminary steps, it will become possible to believe that he is in good faith desirous to place himself in a position to give satisfaction to the King, my master. 'No account of this wretched affair,' says M. Gérin, 'is more miserable than those given by apologists of the Court of France—for instance, by the Abbé Régnier-Desmarais, attaché to the Duke of Crequi's embassy. These monstrous demands were of course rejected by the Pope, and Lewis continued his threats. After a dispute, the details of which I pass over, the affair was ended by a treaty studiously insulting to the Pope, who was compelled to erect in his capital a pyramid, on which were inscribed its conditions; one of which was, that the whole Corsican nation was disqualified from taking service under the Roman government. 'What,' says a writer in the 'Month,' 'if some one had foretold to Lewis that a Corsican dynasty would one day occupy the throne of his descendants, and a Nuncio of the Chigi family,' which was that of Alexander VII., 'should be accredited by the Holy See to the representative of that dynasty?'

I have said more than enough to prove that the quarrel of Lewis XIV. with Alexander VII. in 1662 was merely one of those outrages by which it was his delight to insult the other European sovereigns, such, for instance, as that in which he indulged himself towards Genoa, when, by the threat of bombarding the city, he compelled the Doge to come in person to Versailles to apologise for an imaginary wrong, selecting this particular reparation simply because it was notoriously a fundamental law, that the Doge, during the period of his reign, might never leave the Ducal Palace and its precincts, and therefore no other submission would be equally insulting to Genoa. As a Catholic, of course his offence in directing these acts of insolent aggression against the Supreme Pontiff was far greater than any other. What his motive was may be doubted. In 1662 he was only four-and-twenty, and his arrogance may have been nothing more than the natural intoxication of so young a man who had been bred up from his very childhood [1] upon the grossest flattery as his daily food. But his continuance in the course of insolent aggression during his life suggests the question whether it was not adopted on calculation.

---

[1] The 'Études' of the Paris Jesuits, a few months ago published a curious paper in which it appeared that Lewis XIV., when learning to write, was set as a copy the words—

'Aux Rois hommage est due, ils font ce qu'il leur plait.'

The paper has been preserved on which the little monarch of six or seven had copied this corrupting maxim six times, signing the whole at the bottom 'Louis,' as who should say 'inspected and approved.'

His power really was irresistible, except by a combination of the European states, which was little likely to be maintained even if it were made. He might naturally believe it to be irresistible; and if he deliberately aspired to universal empire, it may have been his object both to accustom surrounding monarchs and states to regard him as set above all law, and entitled to demand from them a degree of submission which no other king would have exacted even from his own subjects, and to show to the world that to be avowedly the subject of the great King was the only condition which gave to any nation, province, or city the least chance of escaping from insult and oppression.

Be this as it may, it is certain that from the autumn of 1662 to the year 1664 it was the unconcealed object of Lewis to heap all conceivable insults upon the Pope and his government. With this view he assailed his spiritual power, exactly as with the same view he seized Avignon.

He selected as his weapon in this unholy war the Faculty of Theology at Paris, which before the Revolution was a corporate body,[1] composed of the doctors of theology in several colleges of secular and regular clergy, of which the world-famed Sorbonne was by far the most important; to which colleges 'the Faculty' bore a relation analogous to that of the University to the several colleges in Oxford. The liberties of this body had already been tampered with, but it was still possessed of greater privileges and, above all, animated by more of a spirit of liberty than any other institution left in France. Thus remaining a solitary monument of ancient freedom in the midst of the arrogance and servility bred by habitual despotism, the Faculty of Theology in some measure occupied the position which, as it is confessed even by the inveterate and bigoted hatred of Gibbon, was occupied by the Catholic Church in the Roman Empire.

---

[1] There were four other Catholic 'faculties' of theology in France; those of Aix, Bordeaux, Lyons, and Rouen.

The Faculty of Theology then received orders from the King to make a declaration upon the same subjects upon which that of 1682 was afterwards made—those of the power of the Pope in temporal matters beyond his own dominions, and especially in France ; and his infallibility.

It is important to observe that neither this declaration nor the much more celebrated one made in 1682 was the spontaneous expression of the sentiments of the French clergy. Neither again were they or any decree called forth, as modern writers have usually assumed, by any 'Papal aggression' upon the liberty of the French Church and the independent authority of the King. There was no conceivable reason why a declaration against the 'deposing power' should have been made by the faculty or demanded by the King in 1663 any more than at any moment in the last three centuries. The motive was transparent. The King had quarrelled with the Pope. There were two ways in which he could strike at him. He might attack his temporal dominions, and accordingly he seized Avignon and invaded Italy. He might shake his spiritual power, and to do this he turned to the Parliament of Paris and the Faculty of Theology as naturally as in the other case to his troops and their commanders.

Accordingly six articles, in their contents much the same as those of the declaration of 1682, were drawn up and presented to the King by the representatives of the Faculty, headed by the Archbishop of Paris, as head of the Sorbonne. The secret history of this affair is disclosed by M. Gérin in his 'Introduction.'

It must not be supposed that the King was urged merely by his own pride and ambition ; he was surrounded by dangerous counsellors, who, says M. Gérin, were deeply imbued with animosity against the Church, and especially against the Holy See, and who had their head-quarters in the Parliament of Paris, among that class of legists who, to use the expression of M. Guizot, were at all times 'a terrible and fatal instrument of tyranny in France.'

It is needless to say anything of the history of this famous body, its supreme judicial authority, the influence which it gradually assumed in legislation owing to the custom which required that the King's edicts should be registered on the books of the Parliament before they became law, its struggles to extend its own power, in which it naturally failed, because a body, however respectable, can hardly be a true check upon the master of twenty legions unless it has behind it a real constituency, and the Parliament of Paris was merely a corporation of lawyers, not a representative body. One thing, however, is certain ; it was always steadily opposed to the liberty of the Church and the authority of the Supreme Pontiff. Nothing else could have been expected, for of all things that which lawyers as such hate by the strongest instinct is an 'imperium in imperio,'—any body exercising an authority not derived from the law of the land, nor revocable by it. No individual lawyer was ever really hearty in supporting the authority of the Church, unless he was a man personally religious, and viewing the subject in a supernatural light. And such men are little likely to be the rulers in any great legal corporation. We may, then, take it for granted that any body such as the Parliament of Paris will always be hostile to the independence of the Church.

On this occasion M. Gérin shows, from the manuscript journal of a contemporary, that the Procureur-Général (an officer in many respects answering to the Attorney-General in England) taking advantage of the quarrel between Lewis and the Pope, waited on the King and asked him 'whether he wished that the Pope should have the power, whenever he pleased, of taking the crown from his head,' and upon this read him the Bull, *Unam Sanctam*, the novelty of which made the King open his eyes wide. Upon this M. Gérin adds, ' Now this same *Unam Sanctam* was published by Boniface VIII. (1302).'

The Advocate-General Talon then moved the Parliament, and

obtained an order, addressed to the Faculty, forbidding it to allow any thesis to be defended similar to one which had been complained of, in which a bachelor had maintained, in very moderate terms, the authority of the Holy See. This decree the Parliament required should be read in the 'general assembly, before the Doctors, and also the Bachelors who had received their first licence, and then formally entered on the Registers of the Faculty.' Two great lawyers, Talon and de Harlay, then went to the meeting of the Faculty, and required obedience in a speech of much insolence towards the Church, but which declared of the King—

The favours which we daily receive from our incomparable King ought to bind us to our duty as strongly as the indispensable necessity which Jesus Christ has imposed upon all the faithful of honouring kings.

The Church, which has just received from his piety the important place of Dunkirk, which his prudence and the necessity of his affairs had obliged him to take from her for some time, reveres him, not only as the living image of the Godhead—as a man into whose hands God has committed absolute power, but as her benefactor, her support, and her protector.

For our part we have no words to express our gratitude for his continual labours for our good, but we redouble our prayers for his exaltation. We ask of God to give him everything he can wish for the glory of his government, and for his private and domestic satisfaction; if, indeed, his kingly soul is capable of feeling any in which his subjects do not bear a part. We shall regard him as a mighty conqueror in war—as a good and tender father to his people in peace, and shall ask of God to cut short our own years in order to add them to those of his life.

And that these his public and private wishes may not be frustrated, we require that the decree of the Court be now read aloud, and that the registers of the faculty be brought, that it may be transcribed and registered in them[1] (p. 22).

---

[1] This curious passage M. Gérin publishes from one of the manuscripts in the collection of the minister Colbert.

Colbert, Controller of Finance and Secretary of State under Lewis, who was his own Prime Minister, had his tools among the members of the Faculty, and received from them reports of all that passed in the private meetings. These reports have been preserved, but their existence has not hitherto been known. M. Gérin gives them at full length. It appears that the Faculty refused the demand of the crown lawyers for the immediate registration of the decree of the Parliament, and only promised to discuss the matter. The discussion was private, and the report of it is now published for the first time. This report is followed by a list of the doctors who 'have acted amiss, or are liable to suspicion in the matter of the decree of the Parliament;' and another of 'those who have done well, and who have specially distinguished themselves, on the same occasion.' It is worth the notice of those who suppose that the opposition to the Pope came from the Gallican Church, that (notwithstanding the open and undisguised use of threats and promises by a despotic government) the former list contains six-and-twenty names, the last only eight. Another important fact, until now quite unknown, is that the name of Bossuet figures among the opponents of the so-called Gallican party. His character is also specially reported upon among those of its opponents. The private report also contains a list of 'communities to be feared on this matter.' It contains, among others, all houses of the regular clergy, and S. Sulpice, 'in which ecclesiastics are trained in a spirit of perfect regularity; but it is confidently asserted that everything there is extreme for the authority of the Pope.' Among the individuals who are reported against as 'strong supporters of the work which all good Frenchmen and true subjects of the King are labouring to oppose,' we find M. de la Motte Fénelon.

At last under open compulsion the decree was registered, April 4; but the same day a thesis, similar to that which it forbade, was maintained with the approbation of the Syndic of the Faculty,

M. Grandin. Talon was enraged ; the Syndic and several others were called before the Parliament, and Talon having declared that the Syndic, 'far from asking pardon and apologising for his offence, made himself more guilty by the terms in which he defended it,' the Parliament immediately suspended him.

A decree [says M. Gérin] no more legal than if the Council of State nowadays should pass a decree suspending a bishop as a president of the Court of Appeal. This act of violence alarmed the timid, and some days afterwards the Court obtained the passing of the ambiguous six articles, signed by only sixty-six doctors, which the Parliament caused to be solemnly registered in all the universities, while it was secretly admitted with disgust that the maxims of the Parliament were condemned by the Faculty. In 1682, when it again became necessary to break the resistance of the Sorbonne which refused to register the Four Articles, De Harlay, the Procureur-General, with satisfaction, reminded the Chancellor, De Tellier, of the severities suffered in 1663 by the doctors, and advised him to employ the same means to subdue them again. His manuscript (now first published) says that 'the example of these will make the doctors anxious to avoid the same by taking some step which may atone for their offence against the King, as they drew up their articles in 1663, in consequence of the trouble you took about it after the interdiction of M. Grandin ' (p. 33).

Obtained as they were, these six articles, whatever they might have been, could have had no weight. But it is worth while to observe that they bore evident marks of being reluctantly drawn up ; for, instead of speaking clearly and definitely, as men do who are expressing their own cherished opinions, the writers made them as ambiguous as they could ; and this was noticed by all parties, Parliamentary as well as ecclesiastical, at the time.

It is important to observe that the moment Lewis XIV. had made up his quarrel with Alexander VII., these demonstrations against the Pope suddenly ceased. Not that the lawyers would not willingly have carried them on ; but in truth, as things then were, few men dared to do anything in France, unless they had good reason to know that what they did would be acceptable to the King; and, much as the lawyers of the Parliament hated the Pope, they loved their own interest far more than they hated him.

They had to wait near seventeen years, when the next quarrel between Lewis and the Pope became serious. That quarrel was even more disgraceful to Lewis than the former, for it originated not in the wanton insolence of a youth intoxicated with the early possession of absolute power, but in a gross act of rapacious tyranny on the part of a man already in middle age.

The kings of France had long exercised a right called the *Regale*, with regard to the temporalities of certain French sees. They received the revenues and exercised the patronage of those sees during vacancies, and the vacancy was held to continue until the incoming bishop had sworn the oath of allegiance, on taking possession. M. Gérin shows that officers of the crown, at different times, had attempted to extend the claim to other sees, and that this had been expressly prohibited, by royal edicts of Lewis XII. and Henry IV., which last had been registered by the Parliament. The extension of the claim to any diocese not already subject to it had been expressly forbidden by a General Council (the second of Lyons), in 1275. In 1673 and 1675, two declarations were published by Lewis XIV., extending the Regale to all the archbishoprics and bishoprics of France. This was an act of sheer tyranny, besides being avowedly sacrilegious; and the bishops might well scruple even in submitting to it, as they were forbidden to do so by a decree of a General Council.

It is to be remarked that, to say nothing more, it was clearly as much an illegal act of taxation, and a violation of private right, as anything complained of, for instance, under Charles I., yet writers and speakers both in France and England, who profess to be advocates of liberty as well as justice, have taken the side of the King, only because the Pope was against him. M. Gérin shows that even in our own day, 1861, M. Jules Favre declared, unchecked, in the Legislative Assembly, that the contest on the Pope's side was for money. This is simply false. The Pope claimed nothing. He had nothing to gain. He was maintaining merely the unquestionable rights not of the Holy See, but of the French bishops.

Not content with extending the Regale to every diocese in France, Lewis applied it to sees which had been long filled up, requiring their holders (some of whom had been in possession for thirty years and more) to 'close the Regale' by a formal act, by which they would of course admit that their successors were liable to it. So general was the fear of the royal tyranny that resistance was made only by two bishops out of those in a large number of provinces unquestionably free from it. These were Caulet, Bishop of Pamiers, and Pavillon, Bishop of Alet. Pavillon died a year later, so that Caulet was left alone. He had been bishop above thirty years; but not having 'closed the Regale,' the King treated him as never having taken possession, and proceeded to fill up all vacancies which he had filled in that long period. The Archbishop of Toulouse, his metropolitan, was a creature of the Court, and took entirely against him. Caulet—a man revered for his piety and the strictness of his life—wrote to the King, and explained that it was impossible to apply the Regale to his see and chapter, because, by an ancient custom confirmed by the Pope and by Lewis XIV. himself, the cathedral was served by canons regular, who practised strict poverty and community of goods, and the see had no property except tithes. The persons appointed to canonries under the Regale had submitted to no novitiate, and were in every way disqualified to hold the offices. The King made no answer; and the whole property of the Bishop was seized by the Intendant of Montauban, a man afterwards conspicuous in the persecution of the Protestants, and a creature of Colbert's. So rigorously was the seizure executed, that the Bishop lived only upon alms. He wrote a second letter to Lewis, complaining that 'the bare necessaries of life, which are always left to the greatest criminals, had in his case been seized.'

Not content with depriving me of all, it has been made a crime in some persons to have assisted me in my necessity; and a man in good position at Paris has been forced to hide himself, in order to avoid prison or exile, because it was reported to M. de Chateauneux that he had sent alms to the Bishop of Pamiers, who, as well as the greater part of his curés, was at the time in absolute want of everything.

This statement is confirmed by another contemporary manuscript, which shows that Lewis XIV. was, as usual, more just and more merciful than his advisers. The King had been pressed by some persons to send a man of quality to the Bastille for having sent an alms of 2,000 crowns to the Bishop of Pamiers. He checked them by this good answer: 'It shall never be said that I have put any man into the Bastille for giving alms.'

The clergy of the diocese remained firm to their chief, and suffered with him (p. 46).

The Bishop protected his authority by canonical proceedings, but these were annulled by the metropolitan and the Parliament. He wrote again to the King and to the procureur-général. As the last resource, obtaining no redress in France, not one of the 130 bishops moving in his defence, he wrote to the Pope, Innocent XI., since declared Venerable. The Pope showed great caution and moderation. He wrote to the King, March 12, 1678, and received no answer. In the January following he sent a second brief, written as early as September, probably because he wished the King before receiving it to have private knowledge of its contents. Receiving no answer, he formally annulled the acts of the Archbishop of Toulouse. He then waited another year, after which he wrote a third time to the King.

Once more we entreat and conjure your Majesty that, remembering the words of our Lord addressed to the prelates of His Church, 'He that heareth you heareth Me,' you would rather hear me (me who have towards you the bowels of a father, and who give you true and salutary counsel), than those children of unbelief, whose views and affections are only of the earth, and who, by suggestions expedient in appearance, pernicious in fact, are shaking the foundations of your monarchy, which rests upon veneration for things holy, and on the defence of the rights and authority of the Church (p. 50).

He ended by expressing his fear that the judgment of God would light upon the King, and added that he should not again have recourse to letters, but should use the power which God had placed in his hands, fearing, if he omitted to do so, to be guilty of a criminal neglect in the administration of his apostolic office.

Lewis XIV. was keenly moved by language which no man on earth, except the Pope, had ever had the courage to address to him. The Gallican legists wished to go to farther measures, but they were held back by the King; and although resolved not to satisfy the desires of the Pope, he temporised (p. 51).

It was proposed to call a national council, but it was feared that if this were done some of the bishops would openly oppose the Regale; for some were known to speak publicly against it, and others to have protested privately. If nothing was done, it was feared that the King might be excommunicated. Another proposal was to enter into a negotiation, which might be spun out till the Pope should die. The deputies of the clergy met every fifth year to vote subsidies to the King. The King caused them to make 'what is called in the jargon of our times' a *manifestation* against the Holy See, regretting the conduct of the Pope. Public opinion, however, was against them. Madame de Sévigné wrote to her daughter: 'Is it possible that you have not seen the Pope's letter? I wish you could. You will see a strange Pope. Why, he speaks with authority. You would say that he is the father of Christians. He does not tremble, he does not flatter, he threatens. It would really seem that he implies some blame against the Archbishop of Paris. What a strange man! I cannot get Pope Sixtus out of my head.' Madame de Grignan greatly amused her by comparing the French bishops to the wife in Molière, who 'liked to be beaten.' M. Gérin says that he has found many contemporary writings condemning the French bishops, not one in their favour.

While things were in this state, a new cause of quarrel arose. Lewis had appointed a secular superior to a house of Augustinian nuns at Charonne, near Paris, in open violation of the Concordat. The Archbishop, an unworthy creature of the King, took his side. The nuns appealed to the Pope; Innocent quashed the Archbishop's proceedings, and ordered that a superior for three years should be elected out of the community. The King's council and the Parliament declared the Pope's proceedings null, and the legal authorities spoke with a tone of indignant virtue of the resistance they would always offer to the Court of Rome if it thus infringed 'their liberties.' On the very day on which this happened, the Bishop of Pamiers died. There was a formal schism. The canons in legal and ecclesiastical possession appointed vicars-general to administer the diocese *sede vacante*; the canons appointed under the Regale appointed another. The vicars-general, legally appointed, were arrested and imprisoned. Another was elected in their place, who was condemned to death; he escaped, and was executed in effigy. 'Religious men feared, not without reason,' says M. Gérin, 'that the chastisements of God would fall upon the state.' The executioner fled, and was brought back by force, saying that, though poor and miserable, he was a Catholic, that he was sure the late bishop was a saint, and had always retained his charity towards himself.

At Paris the defenders of 'liberty' took no notice of these things, but were proceeding against the Pope's briefs. At last it was resolved to try, not a national council, but what might look like it. It was from this state of things that the assemblies of the clergy in 1681 and 1682 originated. The first was called at the time the *petite assemblée*. It consisted of the bishops who happened to be in Paris. An epigram of Racine said that it made one thing, and one only, quite clear, that we have fifty-two prelates who are not residing in their dioceses. These prelates had before them, no doubt, a task of some difficulty. As to the affair of Pamiers, for instance, it was one about which it was plainly unsafe to say much. They contented themselves with complaining of the form of the Pope's briefs as inconsistent with the 'Gallican liberties.' Whether the proceedings of the Government were consistent with any liberties or any justice whatever they did not say. They seemed totally ignorant of all that had passed, except that certain briefs had arrived from Rome the form of which offended their sensitive feelings about liberty. In the same way as to the affair of the nuns of Charonne, nothing was said as to the rights of the case, only the form of the Pope's brief was complained of. The result was that the assembly petitioned the King to call 'a national council, or general assembly of the clergy,' to be composed of two deputies of the first order, and two of the second order, from each province; the latter to have only a consultative voice, that is, in fact not a national council, but an assembly which it would be easy for the King to pack. The acts of this *petite assemblée* were printed by the King's orders, and dispersed over France and Italy.

M. Gérin shows that upon all the points in dispute all the names held in the highest authority as Gallicans, especially Bossuet and Fleury, expressed the strongest sense that right was on the side of the Pope and against the King.

On June 16, 1681, the King addressed letters requiring the archbishops of all the provinces subject to his Majesty to hold provincial assemblies, for the purpose of deputing two of the first and two of the second order as deputies to the General Assembly called at Paris for the 1st of October, 1681.

The elections took place; how—M. Gérin tells us at length in his third chapter. It were needless and weary to go as he does through the provinces one after another, and show that in each the choice of the representatives was really with the King, or rather with Colbert. The object of the choice was to find unworthy men, and no doubt it too generally succeeded. If I desired to make any man a revolutionist, I can hardly imagine anything so likely to effect that object as a careful study of this chapter and of the two which follow, in which the members of the Assembly are gone through one by one, and of that on the state of ecclesiastical property under Lewis XIV. But it would be a mistake, as well as wrong, to suppose that the state of things exposed in these chapters was a fair sample of the Church of France under Lewis XIV. In justice, it must be remembered that the King, all-powerful as he was, dared not call a national council of the French clergy. Whether if he had, he might have obtained a majority in it no one can now tell. But one thing is certain, that the opposition to his acts would have been so decided, and would have come from quarters so highly and so justly respected, that the moral victory would have been wholly against him. It was to avoid this that he had recourse to an assembly which he, as well as everyone else, well knew could not by possibility have any real authority. Councils (as M. Gérin points out) are either general, national, provincial, or diocesan. The Assembly of 1682 could have no pretension to be either diocesan, provincial, or general. Was it a national council? Such a council consists of all the bishops of a nation, and among Catholics its decrees have no authority until they are confirmed by the Pope. Curiously enough, it was the want of this last qualification which has obtained for the Assembly of 1682 whatever respect it has obtained. Protestants and disaffected Catholics have spoken of it with reverence, because it was assembled to oppose the Pope, and because its proceedings were declared by him null and void. Had it wanted this recommendation; had it been gathered to condemn any heresy, Jansenism, for instance; and had its decrees been approved by the Holy See, they would have protested, with great truth, that it was a mere packed assembly, and represented no one except the King.

Even as it actually was, the King by no means avoided opposition among the bishops. M. Gérin publishes a very curious report addressed by M. Morant, Intendant of Aix, detailing his interview with Cardinal Grimaldi, Archbishop of Aix. The Cardinal was a man near eighty, and except on business of an indispensable nature, had never left his diocese since his appointment to it. The Intendant's report is, at least in one respect, honourable to the Government of Lewis XIV. It shows that its agents were not afraid to let the real state of things be known to their employers. M. Morant shows himself to have been by no means scrupulous about truth. But at least he did not fear to report to the minister the least pleasant things which the Cardinal said to him, 'the miseries which had always fallen upon kingdoms in which the ecclesiastical authority had been confused with the temporal'—'that most of the present difficulties must be attributed to the maxims of the Parliament of Paris'—'that the council called for October the first would not be legitimate, and could not be so without the authority of the Pope'—'that it would never be regarded as anything more than a *conciliabulum*, which the best bishops of France took good care not to attend; and that the deputies to be chosen in the different provinces had been nominated by *lettres de cachet*.' 'This,' says the Intendant, 'he repeated several times in order to make out whether I had not received such a letter touching his own province.' The Cardinal also pointed out that the 'procuration (the instructions which each province was to give to its representatives), required them beforehand to condemn the Holy See without hearing what had been done.' He particularly called attention to the 'evils which had ensued in a neighbouring country, without expressly naming England,' in which, the reader will remember, the Protestant king had thirty years before been brought to the scaffold by his Protestant subjects. The Intendant then gives his own answer at length; after which he says the Cardinal 'returned to the fact that the deputies had been named beforehand, as a thing utterly odious, and which showed plainly that what was really wanted was the election of men of a complacent character. I did not think that the time had come for me to be open as to the orders I had received upon this subject; for which I waited until the assembly of the province should meet.' ... 'At last he did me the honour to read me his letter to the Chancellor, at the end of which, observing that the Chancellor had told the Cardinal that his Holiness had expressed his wish that there should be an assembly of the clergy rather than a national council, I took advantage of this information (as to the truth of which I assured his Eminence that he must not doubt) to reply to what he said about the necessity of the Pope's authority for the calling of a national council.' Considering that both the Intendant, and the minister to whom he was writing, knew equally well that the statement was wholly without foundation, the gravity of this last sentence is amusing. When this report reached Colbert, he wrote, in the King's name, to ask the advice of the Archbishop of Paris under the circumstances. The Archbishop's answer is not preserved, but anyone acquainted with his abject character can imagine it. The result was, that on August 23 a letter in due form, beginning *Mon cousin*, and signed by the King himself, was despatched by a special courier to Cardinal Grimaldi, ordering him in very imperious terms to convene the Provincial Assembly for the election of deputies, who were to be empowered by a 'valid commission' to represent the province. But neither the King nor his minister at all reckoned on the Cardinal's submission, and therefore the same day orders were sent to each of his suffragans, the Bishops of Riez, Sisteron, Gap,

Apt, and Frejus, commanding them to meet, with the senior among them as their president, and to act without their archbishop. The same day orders were sent to the Intendant, directing him to go to the Cardinal and assure him of his Majesty's intention to leave to the Provincial Assembly 'absolute liberty both as to the nomination of the deputies, and as to powers and instructions to be given to them.' In case the Cardinal Archbishop still refused to obey, the Intendant was to deliver the letters to the suffragans, and to command the Bishop of Riez, in his Majesty's name, to hold the assembly, sending further instructions as to the bishop's conduct in the matter, which the Intendant was to give 'as from himself.' The instructions end, 'If Cardinal Grimaldi convokes the Assembly you must say nothing *to him* either as to the nomination of the deputies nor as to the draft of the instructions and powers to be given to them. You must communicate on these subjects with the bishops of the province, and engage them to do what you know to be his Majesty's intentions on the subject.'

The documents do not enable me fully to trace out all the steps which followed. At Carpentras, however, have been found the instructions given by the Provincial Assembly of Aix to their deputies. These direct them to adhere to the rule laid down by the General Council of Lyons, forbidding the further extension of the Regale; to protest that its extension to the Churches not hitherto subject to it would be 'contrary to law natural, divine, and canonical;' to declare that the Regale, where it existed, was a spiritual right, conceded to the Crown by competent ecclesiastical authority, not a temporal right attached inseparably to the Crown; to declare that the charge against the Pope in the matter of Charonne was unreasonable; lastly, to defend the prerogatives of the Holy See in the matter of the excommunication issued against the Archbishop of Toulouse in case he should persist in interfering with the administration of the diocese of Pamiers.

But all these efforts were fruitless. In the name of the liberties of the Gallican Church the seal of slavery was once more placed upon the lips of the clergy. The Assembly of Aix was unable either to choose freely its own representatives or to give them its own instructions. On the refusal of Cardinal Grimaldi, the Intendant Morant took upon himself the management of the affair, in union with Valavoin, bishop of Riez, who had been pointed out for this office by Colbert in his despatch of August 23, and who caused himself to be named as representative of the first order, together with Luke Daquin, bishop of Frejus, and brother to the king's physician.

In all the provinces the king showed the same resolution to make himself master of the elections. The candidates excluded by him were either set aside by their colleagues, or set themselves aside in order not to engage in a contest both unequal and useless. The rigours exhibited in the diocese of Pamiers proved that the ministers had made up their minds not to shrink from any violence in putting down all opposition to the orders of Lewis XIV. (p. 150).

The proofs given of this by M. Gérin in one diocese and province after another, fully establish his statement, but would fill a chapter by themselves. He observes that Bossuet himself bears testimony to the fact that he himself was really deputed not by the province of Paris, by which he was nominally elected, but by the Court; nay, that long before the elections were held the ministers had settled that he was not only to be a menber of the Assembly, but to preach the sermon at the opening. This appears from a letter written by him from the Court at Fontainebleau, before the Provincial Assembly met at Paris, in which he announces that both points were already settled.

So far, then, was the Assembly of 1682 from being a 'National Council,' that it in no sense represented anyone except Lewis and his ministers, by whom its members were selected and chosen. In the province of Rouen Colbert wrote to say that the Bishop of Lisieux was to be elected with the archbishop. Elected he was. But an accident made it impossible for him to attend at Paris, on which Colbert wrote to the Bishop of Avranches to say that in consequence of this accident 'His Majesty has made choice of you to supply the place of M. de Lisieux, who had been named; and he has caused his intentions upon this subject to be signified to the Archbishop of Rouen. I doubt not that he will do all that is in his power, and that the choice his Majesty has made of you will be carried out.' Accordingly the Bishop of Avranches sat in the Assembly. Whether any form of election beyond Lewis's nomination was thought necessary does not appear; M. Gérin supposes that it was not.

As to what was called the 'procuration,' *i. e.* the powers and instructions to be given by each Provincial Assembly to its representatives, to which, as we have seen, Cardinal Grimaldi so strongly objected (as it required the bishops elected to condemn the Pope's proceedings before hearing anything about them), this was so little left to the provincial bishops that it was drawn up beforehand by the king's creature, de Harlay, Archbishop of Paris, and orders were sent in a circular to all the Intendants throughout the kingdom, that it was to be adopted in each province 'without the least change.' It is given in full by M. Gérin. It required the deputies 'to take measures to set right the contraventions of the provisions of the Concordat, as to frivolous appeals, which had been committed by the Court of Rome in the matters of Charonne, Pamiers, Toulouse, and others.'

It had been settled by Lewis before the assembly was summoned, that this same de Harlay was to preside. Custom, however, if not any actual rule, required that the senior archbishop present should be president. It was, therefore, determined that he should be the senior, and accordingly, although as a general rule the archbishop and one of his suffragans were chosen to represent each province, yet in every case in which the archbishop was senior to the Archbishop of Paris he was excluded. In every instance what was thus determined beforehand was, either by force or influence, carried out.

It really seems impossible after this signal exposure, that anyone should claim any ecclesiastical authority for this assembly. With Catholics of course it could have had none, even if it had been a free national council, inasmuch as its proceedings were at once declared null and void by the Sovereign Pontiff. It is, however, important to show that it was absolutely without any moral weight, and this M. Gérin's work has far more than proved. Henceforth no reasonable man can believe that the decisions decreed by this assembly proved anything, except the tyranny of Lewis XIV. and the abject servility of too many of the French prelates in his reign. Still, as I have already said, I do not expect that this exposure will prevent its being appealed to by men whose only notion of liberty is the absolute power of the State in things sacred. M. Gérin shows that M. Dupin breaks out into an access of admiration about Lewis's instructions to the provincial councils. They were to choose 'men distinguished for piety, learning, and experience, and whose merit was most known throughout all the provinces.' ' *Quelle belle loi electorale!*' exclaims M. Dupin. Gérin shows that the real meaning of this was that the Provincial Assemblies should select as the priests to represent them, not men known to the clergy of the province, but strangers chiefly in Paris and mere tools of the Court, and that this was actually done.

In fact, there remains but one thing which can give any weight to the assembly of 1682—the great name of Bossuet, who is always represented as its soul (in Carlyle's language, its king), and who actually drew up the declaration and afterwards wrote a formal defence of what had been done, which he continued to retouch till his death, and which has since been published. But I am sure that any man who reads with tolerable fairness M. Gérin's seventh chapter, will feel that this event of his life, so far as it does anything at all, only diminishes the credit of Bossuet instead of increasing that of the Assembly. It is a necessity of human nature to long to be able to make a hero of a man we admire;

and I quite understand many persons wishing to be able to believe that Bossuet was altogether a hero. But it is impossible to think so. Those who knew him best felt that his great qualities were tainted by a sad want of firmness and independence. In 1663, the keen-sighted spies of Colbert, while they mentioned him as taking warmly the ultramontane side in the discussions of the 'Faculty,' saw the weakness of his purpose, which they thought might yet make him a useful tool to the minister. One writes,—

M. Bossuet is beyond all question a man of high talent, learned for his years, as much so as a young man who devotes himself to preaching could be, but what has made him go wrong on this occasion is perhaps chiefly his consideration for M. Cornet (whose creature he is), and his example.

Another said,—

M. Bossuet is adroit, complacent, bent upon pleasing all with whom he is, and adopting their sentiments when he knows them. He has no mind to get himself into trouble [*ne veux point se faire des affaires*]; nor to risk the success of his own projects which he thinks sure to succeed. He thinks it impossible that this [*i.e.* the quarrel between the king and the Pope] can last. Thus he steers with extraordinary caution, and in the Faculty looks out for some middle course, some shift, when he is not on the other side, and hence he has many followers. Besides, he speaks Latin elegantly and agreeably, and has, in fact, a considerable knowledge of these subjects, because he studied before he devoted himself to preaching, and hence he has weight in the Faculty. Attached to the Jesuits and to those who have the means of making his fortune, more from interest than from inclination, for by nature he is free, keen, satirical, and looks upon many matters quite as a superior [*se mettant fort au-dessus de beaucoup de choses*]. Hence, whenever he shall see a line which leads to fortune, he will throw himself into it, be it what it may, and will be able to make himself useful to it. He manages peaceably the Dean of S. Thomas, and is followed very willingly by Le Plessis-Gesté and by Thomassin.

These life-like sketches have been till now quite unknown.

But other contemporary judges, who knew nothing of them, arrived independently at the same conclusion. Forty years later, in 1703, when his fame already filled France and even Europe, the writer of a manuscript entitled 'Characters of the Royal Family of France, the Ministers of State, and the Principal Persons of the Court,' says of the great Bossuet, 'He is one of the most learned ecclesiastics and one of the keenest courtiers. An indefatigable defender of the sentiments of the Court—this circumstance taints his works. He would be more esteemed if he were more impartial.'

M. Gérin quotes from a manuscript in the Imperial Library some lines of Arnauld's, which he supposes to have referred to Bossuet, in which he quotes the saying of S. Augustine about the hireling shepherd, who flies when the flock is in danger from the wolf, *fugisti quia tacuisti.* 'The prelates were assembled, and none of them opened his mouth to undeceive the king' as to the severities which were going on at Pamiers. In another letter Arnauld says—

The king would have done himself more honour if he had named M. Bossuet to the cardinalate. And yet there is a *verumtamen*, as to which I fear he will have to give much account to God, and that is, that he had not the courage to represent anything to the king. This is the temper of the times, even in those who in other respects have very great qualities—abundance of light but little nobleness. Of the same bishop M. de Treville said, 'he had no bone.'

Before, therefore, the great name of Bossuet can really be urged in favour of the Assembly of 1682 and its proceedings, we must at least ask whether or not he took it as an opportunity of expressing what he really felt, or whether he was reluctantly following the wishes of the Court. And this point he answers for himself. Ledieu records that he

asked Bossuet who had inspired him with the plan of the propositions of the clergy upon the power of the Church. He replied that M.

Colbert, then Minister and Secretary of State, was the real author of them, and the only person who determined the king in the matter. M. Colbert maintained that the quarrel with Rome about the Regale was the best opportunity for renewing the doctrine of France on the use of the power of the Popes. . . . . He brought the king over to his opinion against the advice of M. de Tellier, also Minister and Secretary of State. . . . . Besides, M. de Paris (Harlay de Champvallon), did nothing else in the matter than flatter the Court, catch up the words of the Ministers, and blindly follow their will like a valet (p. 385).

This is by no means the language of a man who felt that the Assembly had given him an opportunity of bearing testimony to a truth for which he cared. It appears, indeed, that he was so far from feeling this, that he himself persuaded De Tellier and his son (Archbishop of Rheims) from doing what was afterwards done, and told them ' you will have the glory of having brought to a conclusion the affair of the Regale, but that glory will be dimmed by *these odious propositions.*' 'Even when the king, pressed by Colbert, La Chaise, and Harlay, had given his express orders, Bossuet still proposed that an investigation of the tradition on the subject should be made, which was nothing more than a pretext for an endless discussion '—in fact, much like what leads, among ourselves, to the appointment of a ' committee' of inquiry, on many subjects upon which honourable members do not wish to come to a vote.

Those contemporaries who disliked what was done did not impute it to Bossuet. Fénelon 'wrote in his celebrated letter to Lewis XIV.: "Your Archbishop and your Confessor involved you in the difficulties of the affair of the Regale, and in the troubles with Rome"' (p. 287).

The whole of M. Gérin's chapter on 'Bossuet and the Assembly of 1682' is well worth study. He clearly shows that whenever Bossuet ventured to express his real feelings and opinions, he spoke against the side of which he is generally supposed to have been the soul. He afterwards made an apology himself that Protestant kings might be more willing to become Catholics if they saw the power of the Pope limited. But M. Gérin shows that the Protestant Leibnitz took the side of the Pope, and that the strong Gallicans, so far from attracting Protestants, put difficulties in the way of reunion.

The flattery of Lewis XIV., by the Assembly, was, I presume, too gross for Bossuet's taste, but it passed without protest from him :—

The deputies of the clergy re-echoed what the contemporary legists were writing ; ' in France it has always been held that kings are not purely laymen, but in a sort of mixed condition.' From the first day to the last they vied with each other to paraphrase the language of the 'Promoteur' Chéron, in the sitting of November 24, who having said that Lewis XIV. surpassed David in sweetness, Solomon in wisdom, Alexander in valour, in power all the Cæsars and all the kings of the earth, applied to him this Byzantine text :—' In the army more than king, in the field more than soldier, in the kingdom more than emperor, in civil justice more than prætor, in consistory more than judge, *in the Church more than bishop*' (*from the procès verbal of the Assembly*). The Pope in his brief of April 11 reproves this base flattery, and asks, ' Which of you came into the arena to stand as a bulwark for the House of Israel ? Who dared to expose himself to ill-will ? Who uttered so much as one voice in memory of the ancient liberty ?'

It is sad to write that Bossuet, who, when speaking freely condemned the Archbishop of Paris as making himself 'the valet' of the ministers, was the man who moved that he should be President of the Assembly. This was the same upon whose death Madame de Coulanges wrote to Madame de Sévigné that there were only two difficulties in the way of the person who was to be selected to preach his funeral oration, one was 'his life,' the other 'his death.'

It is at least pleasing to see that Bossuet was aware of this great infirmity, and asked the superior of a convent to pray for him, 'that I may not have complacence for the world' (p. 305).

We must not infer that the 'declaration' expressed Bossuet's real feelings because it was by him that it was drawn up. It is proved that he took this upon himself only to prevent its sense being expressed with much greater violence by men who knew much less than he what they were doing. It is recorded by Fleury that the Bishop of Tournai had drawn it up ' very ill.''

His propositions maintained that the Holy See as well as the Pope could fall into heresy, and thus overthrew the indefectibility of the Holy See. M. Bousset, shocked at this doctrine, strongly opposed it. The Bishop of Tournai warmly defended it. .... The dispute lasted long. It finished by M. de Tournai refusing to draw up the articles, and on his refusal M. Bossuet was charged with it. This anecdote is attested and given in detail by M. de Fénelon, in a Latin treatise upon the infallibility of the Pope, still in manuscript. He received it from the mouth of M. Bossuet (p. 295).

Bossuet, long afterwards, declared that he undertook the office only to serve Rome by ' preventing things from being pushed to a dangerous extreme.'

There is no doubt that this really was his object, and that he managed it with great skill. His conduct was that of a man who was bent upon satisfying an imperious monarch; and exercising all his ingenuity to do so at the least possible sacrifice of principle. And this intention is evident on the face of the 'declaration.' The articles are full of ambiguities. They were evidently intended to look violent enough to satisfy the Court and yet to be capable of an innocent interpretation. But Bossuet ought to have remembered that his words were sure to be interpreted, not merely by theologians in the schools, but by kings, and the ministers of kings intent upon depriving the Church of her most necessary liberties, and anxious to oppress her under the specious cloak of his authority. The disgrace of having his great name perpetually invoked by Napoleon I., when perpetrating his worst outrages (outrages which Bossuet would have rejected with indignation) was but too just a retribution.

M. Gérin sums up his character—

Happily Bossuet united to this infirmity of character, besides the genius which shines forth in his 'Funeral Orations,' in his 'Discourse on Universal History,' in the 'Variations,' a gift more admirable and more precious still—the deep piety which breathes in his 'Sermons,' in 'Letters to La Sœur Cornuau,' and in the 'Meditations upon the Gospel.' But whatever homage is his due, an upright judge will ever repeat with Arnauld, 'There is nevertheless a VERUMTAMEN, for which I fear that he had to render a great account to God' (p. 331).

It is the fashion to say that the 'declaration' was unopposed in France. There would have been small cause for wonder if it had. It was voted by the Assembly, March 19th, 1682, and on March 20th a decree was issued by the king, commanding that the four articles of the declaration should be registered by every university of his kingdom, and taught by all their Professors. No man could have been surprised if such a decree from such a master had been immediately and universally obeyed. The fact, however, was far otherwise. A general opposition arose, and was only put down by sheer force. Upon this subject I would refer my readers to the very interesting chapter in M. Gérin's book entitled 'Opposition to the Four Articles.' It was most energetic immediately under the eye of the king and his ministers in Paris itself and in the Sorbonne. M. Gérin quotes Le Gendre, 'an unsuspected witness,' to prove that the opposition was almost general, and that de Harlay was specially attacked as the supposed author of the declaration. He adds, 'the common and convenient assertion that it was generally received will have to be given up, and it must be admitted that the doctors opposed to the Gallican maxims were the most pious, the most learned, and the most numerous.' The Gallican Fleury says they included

almost all the regular clergy, not only the religious orders but also the communities of priests, although without privileges and subject to the bishops. They leant to that side as most favourable to piety.

The Regulars, almost the only persons who preserve the tradition of the practices of devotion, have united their opinion to this, and have promoted it by their writings, their conversation, and in the direction of consciences. The ancient [*i.e.* the Gallican] doctrine has remained among the doctors often less pious and less exemplary in their lives than those who teach the other. Sometimes those who have resisted the novelties (*i.e.*, the doctrine opposed to Gallicanism) have been lawyers and politicians, profane and libertine, by whom the truths they teach have been exaggerated and made odious (p. 340).

This is confirmed by the secret reports sent to Colbert. His agents gave him lists of theologians *for Rome* and *against Rome*. These lists were drawn up by declared Gallicans, and therefore the praises they give to the characters of those whom they class as 'for Rome' are the less to be suspected. M. Gérin goes in detail through the different colleges of theology. I have not space to follow him at length. But he much more than makes good his assertion. The Sorbonne had 169 doctors, of whom, 'all but six or seven' were opposed to the declaration; at the college of Navarre all but one; at St. Sulpice and the Missions Etrangères 'all but four or five;' among the orders all. As to learning and piety, he shows that the superiority of those opposed to the declaration was strongly and unanimously testified by Colbert's reports.

On the 1st of May, 1682, a deputation of the Parliament was sent to the Sorbonne where the 'Faculty' had its meetings, to require the registration of the 'declaration.' So much opposition did this meet that it was not registered until after a long struggle. The feeling in the 'Faculty' was so strong that the Procureur-General de Harlay reported to Colbert, June 15th, that the debate in the Faculty was adjourned till the next day, and that he judged it necessary to prevent the conclusion of this deliberation 'by whatever means the king judged would be least mischievous,' concluding by saying that he himself 'was neither wise enough nor indiscreet enough to propose any means to be adopted, but awaited the king's cómmands.' So great was the alarm produced at Court by this report, that—

The king sent the Marquis de 'Seignelay (Colbert's son) to Paris the same night, to arrange with the archbishop and the heads of the Parliament a *coup d'état* on a small scale, to be put in execution the next day.' So early was the Parliament acting, that at six o'clock the next morning, June 16, an usher arrived from it, signifying to the dean of the faculty a decree already passed by the Parliament the same morning, which declared that as the doctors had presumed to debate upon the articles instead of registering the decree, their further meetings were absolutely forbidden, and the dean and six professors of the Sorbonne, the grand master, and four professors of the college o.' Navarre, and all others who should be indicated by the Procureur-Général, were required to attend at the bar of the Parliament at seven the same morning (p. 357).

The declaration was then registered by force, the books having been sent for to the Parliament, and all future meetings of the Faculty were forbidden. Eight doctors of theology were immediately sent into exile, by 'lettres de cachet.'

But violence of this kind was very reluctantly adopted by the Court because it was plain that, if reported, it would make known to all the world, and especially at Rome, that the 'declaration' had been imposed upon the French clergy only by force.

It was just at this moment that the king suddenly dissolved the Assembly in a manner which his creatures in it felt to be cruelly contemptuous. The Archbishop of Paris went so far as to remonstrate with Colbert, requesting that the letter dissolving it might be couched in more respectful language, and he received a very curt reply from the minister. The professed reason for this sudden step which M. Gérin finds in the memoirs of de Cosnac (a member of the Assembly) was, that it was necessary that the bishops should return to their dioceses; the real reason, that matters were arranging themselves at Rome, and as the Assembly had been from the beginning merely a weapon in the hands of the king to attack the Pope, it was contemptuously thrown away when no longer needed. The opposition of the clergy of Paris to the declaration no doubt made the king more anxious to have done with it. It was on June 21 that the decree of exile was signed against the eight doctors, and on June 29 the Assembly was suddenly dismissed. The king even refused to allow its proceedings to be entered on the archives of the clergy; nor were they entered until long afterwards, in 1710. The king and his ministers no doubt heartily despised the men who had degraded themselves to gain their favour. A month before, June 2, Colbert had written that the greater part of the Assembly would willingly have changed their doctrine the next day if they had been allowed to do so (p. 355).

The Procureur-Général laboured to make use of this incident to get the Faculty of Theology more absolutely into the hands of the king. Its meetings were now suspended and could not be restored without royal permission. In order to save appearances it was resolved to get up among the doctors a petition to be allowed to hold their meetings. 'If the petition had promised adhesion, obedience, submission to the four articles, it would have obtained no signatures. It spoke only of reverence for the king's edict and for the declaration of the clergy.' M. Gérin details some curious instances of the intrigues used to obtain signatures. At last it only obtained those of 150 out of 750 doctors. The Procureur-Général de Harlay urged Colbert to use much greater severity, to deprive a very large number of their seats in the Faculty, to remove all the old professors of theology, and that instead of allowing their successors to be elected by the Faculty they should be nominated by the king, and to limit henceforth the number of the Faculty to 100. Especially he desired to punish the Sorbonne, for which he proposes several measures. M. Gérin gives many interesting particulars on this subject, upon which I must not enter.

Meanwhile, it is pretty certain that the opposition of the other universities less immediately under the eye of the Government was even more energetic than it was at Paris. With regard to the University of Douai, which had been newly annexed to France, M. Gérin has found evidences of this fact. It addresses Lewis himself, expresses the strong and unanimous dislike of his new subjects in Flanders to the doctrine of the declaration, and declares 'the great majority of us are ready to abandon our colleges and to renounce all promotion and dignity rather than submit to opinions repugnant to our consciences.'

Nor was this a temporary opposition. M. Gérin shows that it continued and was general among the French clergy down to the time of the Revolution. As late as 1760, the Abbé Chauvelin spoke of those who were attached to what he called true [*i.e.* Gallican] maxims as ' some bishops and some doctors,' and the ultramontanes as ' the great multitude,' and declared it necessary to have recourse to authority to compel the Faculty of Theology to obedience.

In fact, after the publication of M. Gérin's invaluable labours, I do not see how any man can in future speak of the French Church in the seventeenth and eighteenth centuries as having been Gallican in opinion.

And yet it cannot be denied that there was at least one part thoroughly rotten in that great body. The Assembly of 1682 was only too miserable a proof of it. The king was able to collect by his mere will a meeting of two and thirty bishops, the majority of whom, there is reason to fear, were ready to vote whatever he pleased. In this is most strongly marked the contrast with the existing French Church. 'Out of the ashes of the ancient Church of France has sprung a new hierarchy, worthy of the name and the history of that great nation, as fervent as their S. Bernard, as tender as their S. Francis, as enterprising as their S Lewis, as loyal to the Holy See as their Charlemagne.'[1] But in truth,

[1] Newman's Lectures on Anglican Difficulties.

when we look at the abuses which the French kings had introduced and established as to the disposal of church property, the real wonder is not that a portion of the French Church was corrupt, but that it had any part sound. Count Montalembert has expressed in language not more eloquent than true, the horrors of this system: 'The most ancient abbeys, the most illustrious in the history of the Church and of our country, were made the appanage of the bastards of kings or of their still more unworthy favourites, sometimes the price of the foul favours of a royal favourite.' Yet bad as this is, the real state of the case as laid bare by M. Gérin was worse still. For the corruption would have been much less fatal had it been confined to the circle immediately surrounding the monarch. In fact, the revenues of the Church were systematically employed as a means of bribing the whole of the upper classes. This was effected first by granting abbeys, both of men and women, *in commendam*, to persons who were not only not religious, but in very many cases were in no sense ecclesiastics, and had often not the least intention of ever being so. Henry IV. carried the matter even farther. Not content with the abbeys, he heaped bishoprics upon his lay favourites. Crillon, for instance, held the temporalities of two archbishoprics, three bishoprics, and an abbey. But I am not sure that the plan followed by Lewis XIV. was not even more mischievous. For he systematically granted large pensions, payable out of the revenues, both of bishoprics and abbeys. For instance, the Bishop of Mende wrote to Colbert, in 1668, that he had to pay one pension of 2,300 livres, three others of 1,500 each, two of 1,200, two of 1,000; altogether, 11,200 livres. His object was not to obtain relief from these payments, but to petition the king to give him some additional preferment, to enable him to meet them. Thus a bishop was never really independent in his circumstances. His proper revenues were charged with enormous payments, and he was continually a suitor to the minister, either for abbeys *in commendam*, or for similar pensions payable out of some abbey or see held by some one else. No means could have been devised so sure to combine all the evils of an endowed and a disendowed Church, of wealth and of poverty. For the property of the Church being known to be great, the people felt, of course, no obligation to support their pastors, and yet these in their turn could only obtain an income by perpetual petitions to the minister. I have no room to copy instances of this; the chapter to which I have referred is full of them, all in minute detail.

No wonder that courtiers, accustomed to consider rich abbeys and bishoprics merely as funds to be given by the king to whom he would, lost all sense of anything sacred in the property of the Church. There were not wanting men logical enough to draw the legitimate conclusion from the recognised practice, and M. Gérin shows that several writers, who might fairly be taken as representatives of the Court, avowed the principle that the property of the Church belonged to the king, and that he might do with it whatever he pleased. This was the principle which Burke denounced with equal eloquence and logic.[1] But he was certainly mistaken in supposing that, in France at least, it was first introduced by the Revolution. The author says:—

It is a commonplace of our day to deplore, in the interests of royalty itself, that Lewis XIV. gave way so miserably to the spirit of his age by degrading all orders of the state under the feet of royalty.

---

[1] It can hardly be necessary to explain that Catholics, in supporting Mr. Gladstone's measure on the Irish Establishment, did not for a moment accept these principles. That body was merely a creation of the State, and the property it held had been taken by the State from its rightful owners, and given by it to its own creatures. The right of the Establishment could never rise higher than its source. That Mr. Gladstone and his Ministry felt that their measure was really defensible only on this ground is plain by the fact that they respected all private endowments. Had the same reserve been observed in France the whole property of the Church would have been secure.

How comes it that our historians, so sensitive about the humiliation of the nobles, the parliaments, the communes, the provincial assemblies, are so little attentive to relate or blame, nay, so much disposed to praise, the incessant encroachments of the crown upon the power of the Church? Jansenistic and revolutionary prejudices, and the unpopularity with which they have surrounded the Church, are the only explanation of this injustice, against which, thank God, eloquent voices have before now protested.

The crown desired to make the Church a slave like everything else. The French clergy did not resist with sufficient courage. It belonged to the Holy See alone to recall them to their duties, and to defend their rights. . . . .

According to the theories of the French legists the Church obtained the right of holding property only by the concession of the sovereign, who had the power to withdraw it, and the maxims applied to the property of the clergy by the Constituent Assembly, the Convention, and Napoleon, were known, accepted, and favoured by the counsellors of Lewis XIV.

In 1650 Antoine Estienne, first printer and bookseller in ordinary to the king, published, with privilege, at Paris, under the pseudonym of Francis Paumier, a Remonstrance to His Majesty as to his authority over the temporalities of the Church. He said :—'The kings of France have a supreme right over the temporalities of all the Churches in the realm, with full power to use them in the necessities of the State for the benefit of their subjects, as their Council may advise. . . . . One of the principal reasons why the dispensation and permission to acquire property, contrary to the ancient statutes of the kingdom, has been given to the clergy by the piety of our kings, is that they and their successors may have a resource always at hand, ready and powerful at all times, in any measure that the public necessities may suggest.'

At the very period of which I am treating, a very able legist of whom Colbert had made use to attack the prerogatives of the Church, the *maître des requêtes*, De Fayer de Boutigny, composed his famous treatise on 'The Authority of Kings in the Administration of the Church,' in which he attributes to the king of France a supremacy over the Church both temporal and even spiritual, which made both Popes and Councils superfluous. The absolute sovereignty of the monarch as political magistrate extends over everything which is done, and over everything which exists in his kingdom, over things as well as persons ecclesiastical; and if it be objected that the objects of the Faith, dogmas and sacraments, are not subject to him, Le Vayer boldly replies that he has both the right and the duty of taking cognisance of them in his character of Most Christian King and Protector of the Canons.

This celebrated theory, which sums up in a learned and well-connected form all the pretensions of lay Gallicanism, does not sensibly differ from the Anglican doctrine—the religious supremacy of Henry VIII. or Queen Victoria. It may well be supposed that in taking such liberties with the spiritual, the legists, Colbert's hirelings, did not spare the temporal domain of the Church (p. 80).

He shows by several quotations that they claimed for the king the most absolute power to take whatever Church property he pleased, when, as, and for what purposes he pleased.

The author remarks that Innocent XI. not only felt it his duty to defend the temporal possessions of the Church, but that living when he did, between the so-called Reformation and the French Revolution, history gave him no example of a revolution seizing the temporalities of the Church which did not also set up a new religion, so that he felt that he was defending the teaching of the Church as well as its possessions.

As to Lewis himself, great as were his offences, I cannot but wonder that they were not more heinous when I calmly consider that he came to the throne at four years of age, and was trained to believe that kings might do whatever they pleased, that as to morals especially, the sixth commandment did not apply to them, and also, that while the lives and properties of all their subjects were absolutely at their disposal, the Church, and all it had, belonged to them by a special and peculiar right. Contemporaries said most truly that the Gallican view was to substitute the infallibility of the king of France for the infallibility of the Pope (p. 469). Feydeau, a doctor of the Sorbonne, has left among his private papers a memorandum dated January 27, 1688 :—' I find that the infallibility of the Court is not to be traced to Mazarin, who was willing enough to change, but to Colbert, who suggested it to the king.' It is greatly to the honour of Lewis XIV. that instead of requiring to be restrained by his advisers, he was, as M. Gérin (and indeed all other historians) has often occasion to point out, always less unjust, less tyrannical, less rapacious than they wished him to be. I cannot help bearing this in mind in reading the history of his later years, of the reformation of his moral life, and especially of the succession of severe sorrows and humiliations, both in his kingdom and in his family, with which it pleased Him who chastises all whom He loves, to visit him in his declining years.

It is the signal punishment of kings who pollute the sanctuary of God, by lavishing upon worthless minions the property and the sacred offices of the Church, that their own minds are of necessity degraded and corrupted by finding themselves always surrounded by men of the one class most hateful and contemptible in the sight not of man alone, but of God—servile, cringing, flattering, covetous, profligate ecclesiastics. Surely out of hell itself no man could possibly be surrounded by creatures more vile. Lewis was far too able and keen-sighted not to esteem his flatterers as they deserved. It is terrible to think of the contempt with which they must have been regarded by a politician such as Colbert, before whom they were never weary of ostentatiously exposing the foulest deformities of their base characters. Hideous, indeed, are the records of this sort which M. Gérin has found preserved among the minister's papers—for instance the letters written by Bourlemont, Bishop of Castres, to Bonzy, Bishop of Beziers, and to Colbert himself, on the occasion of the quarrel of Lewis against Alexander VII. about the Corsicans,—letters which, as M. Gérin says, lay open to us the heart of a Gallican Bishop under Lewis XIV. In reading these letters one's first feeling is, that nothing could add to the baseness they make a parade of. Yet, surely, it does add something even to it, to find that one of them, addressed by one bishop to his friend another bishop, must have been sent by him to Colbert. He no doubt felt that he was doing his friend good service. Colbert evidently felt that the French Church was useful only because its property enabled the king to make slaves of all the nobility of his kingdom, and because it provided magnificent appanages for all his own kindred—sons, brothers, nephews, cousins. He would probably have felt it an act of virtuous and patriotic disinterestedness to have swept away it and its possessions at a stroke.

What Alexander VIII. felt of these men, he expressed to Cardinal de Boullon:—

'What the king wished was the only thing that signified; what the bishops who were nominated might do, made no difference. He knew the system of France, and the extent to which the authority of the king had been carried, well enough to be sure that the bishops would have no other sentiments and no other religion than those of the king; that if the king wished the bishops of France to make a schism with the Holy See they would hardly hesitate to obey him; that if, on the contrary, the king's intention were that they should declare the Pope infallible in right and in fact, the same bishops would make whatever declaration was required of them on that subject. That was his opinion of the Church of France (p. 434).

Lewis himself said of his bishops, 'no thanks to these gentlemen that I have not assumed the turban. I have only three bishops in my dominions' (page 260). These were exactly those who had refused to fall in with his plans—Cardinal Grimaldi, Archbishop of Aix; Lavardin, Bishop of Rennes; and the Bishop of Grenoble. Fénelon was not yet a bishop. When the Abbé de Polignac had been sent to him by Alexander VIII., and had had a long conversation with him, he said, 'I have been talking with a man, and that a young man, who has always contradicted me without my ever being able to be angry with him for a single moment.'

No doubt it is most likely that, if Lewis had thought fit to have made himself Head of the Church in France, he would have encountered no serious opposition from such men as de Harlay or Bourlemont. Yet I can hardly doubt that, even among the least promising of his ecclesiastics, some would have been found, who would have stopped short when they saw before them the abyss into which they were required to plunge. There were some among that noble army of martyrs and confessors who threw new glory upon the Church of France a century later, from whom little would have been expected beforehand. One, at least, of the Court Prelates of the Assembly of 1682, and at that time one of the least respected of them all, Chavigny, Bishop of Troyes, sixteen years later resigned his bishopric to retire into a life of strict penance and solitude. One of our own most glorious martyrs under Henry VIII. had in earlier life expressed himself in a manner, to say the least, very unsatisfactory upon the supremacy of the Holy See, in defence of which he gained his crown. I by no means believe that Lewis XIV., despotic as he was, could have renewed the work of Henry VIII. and Elizabeth, and have made France a Protestant nation. They were assisted by a combination of circumstances which had gone by before his time, and which, in the nature of things, can never return. Protestantism, in their day, was just rushing out from the open gate of hell (like the winds from the cavern of Æolus) a living energetic power of Satan. Such is the nature of all heresies. But not less is it their nature very soon to sink into indifference and languor, and from thence to utter death. Protestantism, which is now dead, and only dangerous by the pestilence engendered by its corrupting corpse, was already sick to death at the end of the seventeenth century. Lewis might have done much mischief, but it would have required power far greater than his, greater than all the power of earth and hell, to put new life into that dying heresy.

Neither are we to think that the wretched flatterers of

Lewis XIV. were really what they called themselves, the Church of France. M. Gérin says, after going through the members of the Assembly one by one—

> Is there one among these priests and bishops whose name can be mentioned as that of a man who lived and saved souls like S. Francis of Sales, S. Charles Borromeo, S. Vincent of Paul, Berolle, Olier, Cæsar de Bus? Is there one whose name has been attached to any great Christian institution—to any important reform of discipline and manners? Which of them exercised a salutary influence on his contemporaries? Which of them whose memory is still blessed by generations who, kneeling before the altars, call him their spiritual father? (p. 259).

And then he mentions several men living at the time whose names are not to be found on the list. Lavardin, Bishop of Rennes, to whom Lewis gave the testimony I have just quoted. The Abbé Aligre, and the great preachers and theologians of that age, Mascaron, Fléchier, Bourdaloue, Fénelon, Huet, Mabillon, Thomassin, Rancé, Tronson, Brisacier, Tiberge, La Salle, La Chetardie, and many more. There is but one man whose name I regret to see among the list of such a council, if it were to be held—that one is Bossuet.

I have left myself no room to dwell upon M. Gérin's two last chapters. The ninth details the contest between the king and the Pope. It is better known than other parts of this history, because its nature has attracted the attention of secular historians. But upon this he has thrown much new light. Innocent XI. refused to accept any man who had taken part in the Assembly of 1682, when offered for a bishopric. Lewis nominated two. Their Bulls were refused, and the king forbade any other of his nominees to receive his Bulls as long as theirs were refused. This went on for years, until there were more than thirty sees vacant in France. The king and his flatterers threw the blame on the Pope. The Pope published his declaration that he was ready to grant

Bulls to any nominee of the king who had not been a member of
the Assembly, or who, having been so, would make a fitting retractation. The dispute was further embittered by the question of
the 'franchises,' which I have already mentioned. Innocent
declared that he would receive no ambassador who did not engage
to give up the claim which was destructive of the peace and moral
order of Rome. Every other European king agreed to resign so
odious a privilege. Lewis alone refused. The Pope sent an
embassy to entreat him. The Nuncio mentioned that the Emperor
and all other monarchs in Europe had acceded to the desire of
the Pope, but Lewis haughtily replied that God had placed him
in a position to set the example to others, and to follow that of
no man. He refused to surrender the franchises. Innocent declared that he would receive no ambassador by whom they were
claimed. Lewis resolved to send an ambassador to Rome, in spite
of the Pope's refusal, and to support him by an overwhelming military force. He selected expressly for the purpose the most haughty
and overbearing man he could find, who entered Rome by force,
attended with a military array. Upon this Innocent excommunicated him. The ambassador, in despite of the excommunication, went to the midnight mass at the Church of S. Lewis of
France, and the Pope placed the Church under an interdict.
There were not wanting men among the advisers of Lewis who
urged him to make a direct schism by directing his nominations
to bishoprics to the archbishop of the province, and those to
archbishoprics to the provincial bishops. But unscrupulous as
he was, Lewis refused to be guilty of a crime which would have
placed him by the side of Henry VIII. To any length short of
that he was prepared to go. He seized Avignon, and arrested a
bishop living peaceably in the Pope's dominions, and by an act
worthy of Napoleon himself, committed him to prison at Ré, giving
instructions that he should be made uncomfortable on his journey,
and should be told that he was to be transported to Canada—

which in those days was not unlike being banished to another planet. He even instructed his ministers to appeal in his name to a future general council. This appeal was made in the presence of the Archbishop of Paris and of the Père La Chaise.

But he would not quite take the step which would have consummated the schism. The Pope was firm, and at last the king gave way. When Innocent XI. died he sent an ambassador to the new Pope, Alexander VIII., authorising him to give up the claim to the 'franchise.' At last he allowed the men nominated to bishoprics to sue for their Bulls, and those who had been members of the Assembly made their recantation in the terms demanded by the Pope. Lewis XIV. himself wrote a letter to the Pope promising that his edict enforcing the four articles should be without force or effect. It is characteristic that care was taken to conceal this submission, and it was never known in France for a century. M. Gérin in fact gives many details about it never published until now.

I attach great importance to the publication of this work, and feel that M. Gérin has done the Church great service. Some men may be inclined to regard the question as merely historical. But in truth it is far more. It is important that the world should know that it is a mere error to suppose that Gallican principles ever were received by the Church of France; that they were merely put forward by a handful of the flatterers of Lewis XIV., not less to the disgust of the true Church of France in their own days than in ours. And this M. Gérin has made so plain that nothing but ignorance or disingenuousness can in future deny it.

V.

THE CHURCH AND NAPOLEON I.[1]

THE three volumes before me are a reprint of the part which has already appeared of a series of articles in the 'Revue des deux Mondes.' We have still to expect the continuation, which will fill at least one, if not more additional volumes, and the three now published leave us (as is so often the case with the second volume of a novel) exactly in the most exciting crisis of the narrative. Still, although I feel an eagerness for the remainder of the work, which could hardly be much greater if the conclusion of the struggle it relates were not already known to all the world, I am not disposed to wait for it before introducing my readers to the portion which has already appeared. The fact is, that a very large part of the details of the narrative are new, not only to English but even to French readers. I must confess that I was quite unprepared to suspect the existence of so many hitherto unpublished sources of information as the diligence of M. D'Haussonville has discovered. Looking at the volumes of M. Thiers, as multitudinous and massive as they are eloquent and lively, and still more at the one-and-twenty vast tomes of the Napoleon correspondence, published by order of the present emperor, which contain the portion of his uncle's letters written before 1811, I supposed that diligence, fairness, skill, and judgment in working quarries in these great mountains of facts, was all that could be required of him who should give, in a

---

[1] 'L'Église Romaine et le Premier Empire 1800-1814.' Par M. le Comte D'Haussonville. 3 vols. 8vo. Paris, Lévy, 1868.

separate form, the history of Napoleon's dealings with the Church. Such, however, was not the case. M. Thiers, although, as a matter of course, he relates what may be called the public and external events, apparently does not understand, and certainly does not state or explain, the principles and motives which, on the side of the Pope, were the real causes of these events. The Napoleon correspondence, if it were complete, would of course give all that could be desired on the side of the emperor. Unfortunately, it is not complete. What other documents are omitted intentionally or not, I cannot say. That those which throw most light upon the conduct of Napoleon towards the Pope have been omitted, not because their importance was not appreciated, but expressly because they revealed facts which the authorities of the second Empire think it most prudent to conceal—M. D'Haussonville proves to demonstration. It appears that the charge of publishing the invaluable documents preserved in the different official registers of Paris and elsewhere, was committed, by Napoleon III., to a commission, at the head of which was placed his cousin, Prince Jerome Napoleon. This commission were to publish the documents entire, and M. D'Haussonville bears testimony to the fidelity with which they performed their task. But, after fifteen volumes had appeared, the old commission was cancelled and a new one issued. What change was made in the members of the commission we are not told. Prince Napoleon was still President. But a more important change was made. In the Preface to the sixteenth volume of the correspondence they declare that, in future, it will be their object to publish only those documents which present such a picture of Napoleon as the commissioners believe that he himself would have wished to have presented to posterity, if he could have survived to see the publication. Perhaps no man ever lived who would have wished that such a disclosure of his conduct and motives should be wholly complete and fair. However that may be, it is most certain that Napoleon I. was not that man. All the world knew before, what certainly no reader of the volumes before me could fail to learn if he had not already known it, that at every period of his life, whether in war or peace, falsehood of the grossest and most outrageous character, was the instrument which he used most freely, naturally, and spontaneously. In war, we have been told, all stratagems are allowed. This military maxim, it seems, had so completely occupied the whole soul of Napoleon I. that he applied it not merely to military affairs, but to all in which he took any part. It is truly surprising that although his vast genius enabled him to perceive, by a happy instinct, almost every other propriety of the exalted rank to which he had raised himself, yet never at any period of his greatness, not even when he was, and loved to call himself, Emperor, not of France, but of the West; when kings and queens, the representatives of the proudest dynasties, accounted themselves honoured by being allowed to follow him at the most deferential distance; never, even then, did he consider it beneath his dignity to practise, in his own person, the most humiliating frauds, and solemnly to utter in his own person falsehoods which, if he wished them to be told, he might at least have left to some subordinate agent. The sovereign who had the absolute command of such a tool as Fouché was clearly under no necessity to take this portion at least of his dirty work into his own hands. Yet, immediately after the peace of Tilsit, when every European power, except England, was at his feet; and when he had attained a greatness quite without example since the reign of Charlemagne, we find Napoleon condescending to write a letter to his adopted son, Eugene Beauharnais, his viceroy in Italy, in which he attempted, by the most violent threats, to shake the resolution of Pius VII. This letter to the viceroy he was to copy, and to enclose it in another addressed in his own name to the Pope. But Napoleon would not trust him to compose it. He wrote every word of the letter from Eugene to the Pope, with his own hand.

Eugene was only to copy and sign it. It began, 'I enclose to your Holiness an extract from a long letter which I have received from my most honoured father and Sovereign at Dresden. Your Holiness will permit me to say, that the disputes raised at Rome are calculated to provoke a great Monarch, who is deeply penetrated with religious sentiments, and who feels the immense services which he has rendered to religion in France, in Italy, in Germany, in Poland, and in Saxony. He is well aware that the world regards him as the column of the Christian faith, and the enemies of religion as a prince who has restored to the Catholic religion in Europe the supremacy she had lost.' After some more language of this sort was to come the Emperor's letter to the Prince, and then Eugene, once more in his own name, was to write; 'Holy Father, *this letter was not intended to be sent to the eyes of your Holiness!*' Napoleon ended the whole in his own name to his adopted son, 'You will send this letter to the Pope, and write to me at Paris.'

It is plain enough that Napoleon was the last man to scruple about giving a false impression of his conduct and motives, and that no rule could less conduce to historical truth than that of publishing only what he would wish to have been published had he still survived. But this applies specially to his correspondence with Pius VII. and his ministers. Upon this point I am not left to conjecture, for I find that [1] 'Napoleon thought fit to cause a great number of papers relating to his dealings with the Holy See to be burned; no doubt because he considered them injurious to his reputation. This was executed at Rome by General Miollis, at Paris by the chief of the archives of the late office of Secretary of State. But authentic copies of these curious documents have escaped destruction.' Of these copies large use is made in the volumes before me, and page after page there are letters painting most graphically the scenes going on at Rome,

[1] Vol. ii. p. 298.

and in particular the orders and wishes of Napoleon himself. But to almost every one of these extracts is a footnote : 'Not included in the Napoleon correspondence.'

Hence it is that to almost every one of the most curious events of which he gives us the details, M. D'Haussonville adds that it has been hitherto quite unknown in France. In many instances the facts most clearly proved by these documents are among those most exactly contrary to the positive statements of Napoleon in the reminiscences which he dictated to his companions in exile in St. Helena. As a striking example, I may mention his statement that 'at no time were more than fifty-three priests under restraint (*retenus*), in consequence of the dispute with Rome, and in their case the restraint was exceedingly slight.' Upon this assertion M. D'Haussonville says :—

> Following my constant custom, I undertake to make Napoleon refute himself, and that by his own letters, the authentic copies of which lie before me. True, they are not included in the official correspondence of Napoleon; but I am sure that the persons who have not thought it expedient to publish them (no doubt because they exhibit the Emperor in a different light from that in which he would have wished to be represented to posterity) will feel it even less expedient to contradict them. When the Emperor put down this exact number of fifty-three priests, who were the only ecclesiastics 'put under restraint' (*retenus*), in consequence of the dispute with Rome, he had no doubt forgotten (such things are easily forgotten) that, without counting any of those who may have been '*put under restraint*,' in virtue of his general orders, he had, with his own hand, given orders to put under restraint, in Italy alone, a number infinitely greater. I suppose it was a similar failure of memory, less easily explained in that case, which induced the editors of the official correspondence to omit these orders, so numerous and so ruthless.

He then shows that in a single year Napoleon himself gave express orders by which, in the Roman States only, thirteen cardinals, nineteen bishops, and 'a multitude of canons and grand vicars, the number of which it is difficult to ascertain,' were sent from Rome to France, and placed under restraint, under the surveillance of the imperial police in different provincial towns, and, moreover, above two hundred priests were transported to Corsica. (Napoleon by no means considered the island where he was born a paradise.) The number arbitrarily arrested in France itself, and thrown without trial into different prisons, no one can now estimate. Of this last practice also the author gives numerous examples from letters 'not published in the correspondence of Napoleon I.'

I have said enough to show that M. D'Haussonville is no indiscriminate admirer of all that was said and done by Napoleon I. The fact that his work has appeared in the 'Revue des deux Mondes,' that its publication has not been interrupted, and that he is now allowed to republish it in a separate form, is the strongest illustration of the immense difference between the present system, which places the press of France under the control of law, (although of law which in England would be accounted most oppressive,) and that which subjected it to 'avertissements.' I am very sure that a very few years ago no journal would have dared to publish this work. That such a work should have obtained any degree of popularity in France illustrates another fact hardly less important—how much the popularity of the name of Napoleon I. has been diminished (at least among the more educated classes) within the last few years. Under the restoration he came to be looked back upon only as the conqueror who had so often led the armies of France to victory.

All the suffering which in every country affects many classes after the close of a long war, and which was so severely felt in England in 1816, 1817, &c., was naturally laid to the score of the Bourbons. They were accused of having lowered France from the pinnacle of glory to which he had raised it. It was the name of Napoleon that carried the election of the present Emperor, first as President then as Emperor. As Frenchmen have become weary of a rule which they connect with that of Napoleon I., they have become more willing to examine how far his 'glory' was a real benefit to France. I suspect this feeling has not to any very considerable degree spread among the peasantry; that it has become general in the higher classes I am sure.

If France at all resembles England, it is quite possible that this reaction against the blind idolatry of Napoleon which formerly prevailed, may, at least for a time, go farther than reason warrants. For, assuredly, however we may feel the deep moral degradation of his character, his genius will ever be more and more highly appreciated as we more minutely study his life. M. D'Haussonville is far from underrating it. His whole narrative brings Napoleon before us in the strongest relief, as a man able with almost equal ease to grasp every subject to which it was his interest to turn his attention; who detected with an unerring instinct the peculiar gifts and character of every man with whom he had any dealings, and saw with the eye of genius whom he could employ, and for what purpose; and about whom it may be much doubted whether, in any one instance, he was mistaken. Until his head had been turned by a prosperity and glory such as, perhaps, no other man ever attained, he was, alike in every relation of war, politics, legislation, and diplomacy, as wary as he was daring. That he had to do with the weakest opponent never seems to have appeared to him a reason for neglecting any one precaution which could have been necessary against the strongest. When he had made up his mind to seize Rome, although the Pope was without any means of resistance, although he was himself distant from it by half a continent, and although he had brave, able, and trustworthy servants on the spot, he thought it necessary exactly to prescribe in writing all the most minute particulars of the combinations desirable for the purpose; to arrange exactly the number of men to be despatched from the north of Italy, and the number from Naples, the days on which they were to arrive at the different points, and how they were to combine. With characteristic disregard of truth and honour, he detailed the falsehoods to be communicated at different parts of the proceeding to the Government of the Holy Father, and gave especial orders that, as soon as his troops had entered Rome, supposing the people to submit in quiet, the French Minister was to give a ball, to which the chief ladies of Rome and the French officers were to be invited; and that meanwhile all measures were to be taken, by placing French soldiers in the post-office and every other public office, to accustom the Romans to see the administration of their city in the hands of the French. Should any resistance arise, it was at once and sternly to be put down by grape-shot. All this time he continued to assure the Pope's Government, first that his troops were merely passing through the States of the Church on their way to Naples, and were not to enter Rome; and when they had entered it, that they had come merely to seize some brigands, who were devastating the Neapolitan States, and who found refuge under the Pope's Government. Those who have read the similar complaints against the administration of Pius IX. which have been so loudly made by the Roman correspondents of London newspapers for the last few years, will not be surprised to hear, that when Rome had been occupied on this pretence, not so much as one person there was even charged with being a brigand. The pretence had served its purpose, and was quietly laid aside. In short, it is impossible to read M. D'Haussonville's narrative without feeling that, for the purpose of silently occupying Rome, the great Emperor thought it worth while to lavish all his genius and all his treachery, as freely as when, nearly at the same time, he allured the royal family of Spain into his trap at Bourdeaux.

No doubt, the circumstances of the revolutionary era afforded him a matchless opportunity of action, but never was there a man whose success, and I may also say whose fall, was more wholly his own.

Almost every real mistake that he ever made may be traced to a moral, not an intellectual defect. There was one exception to the penetrating power with which his eagle eye penetrated and appreciated the character of all with whom he had to do. When he had to do with men to whom conscience and the fear and love of God were not mere specious words, but realities by which their lives were governed, his penetration failed him, for he was morally incapable of realising the existence of such a character. No reader of the volumes before me can doubt that this moral incapacity was the one cause of every serious mistake into which he fell. In dealing, for instance, with Pius VII. and with Consalvi, he overreached himself: because he could not find it possible to believe that in their minds their own interests, however serious, so far from being the leading consideration, actually had no place at all when their duty to God and the Church was in question. It was only this incapacity to conceive of conscience as a real governing principle, which led him to commit himself to a contest with the Church, from which, when it had once begun, his pride, and his interest alike forbade him to draw back. He had never imagined that he was bringing himself into collision with men who could not be moved either by munificent bribes or by tremendous threats; and that he should really be compelled either to give up that to which he had publicly committed himself, or else to push matters to the last extremities of violence and open tyranny. And thus he found himself involved unawares in a struggle, in which it was simply impossible that he should prevail, and yet in which he was afraid, as well as ashamed, to be defeated. It was this moral defect alone which blinded him to a danger, of which thousands of poor peasants in his dominions could have warned him. For they were conscious of what he, with all his genius, did not know —the truth expressed by Pius IX. in words which have echoed through the world, NON POSSUMUS, and which Pius VII. stated to the diplomatist, a real though unavowed agent of Napoleon, sent to sound him in his prison at Savona:—'When opinions are founded on the voice of conscience and the sense of duty, they become unalterable. Believe me, there is in the world no physical force which can, in the long-run, contend with a moral force of this nature.' Napoleon had hoped to find the purpose of the gentle, aged monk altered by long imprisonment and separation from his friends and counsellors. His agent, on bringing him back this answer, added that 'he had found the Pope a little aged, but not unwell, calm, unruffled as ever, and without a tinge of bitterness in his remarks, even when speaking of the subjects which it was impossible that he should fail to feel most acutely.' It is exactly against moral force such as this that physical force is utterly powerless.

This is, in truth, the one subject of the volumes before me. It is the history of a physical force utterly irresistible, breaking itself in the vain effort to overcome the force of conscience and the power of grace; that is, to conquer Him who lives in the Christian's heart. It divides itself naturally into two parts, separate in the main, although one sometimes runs into the other—Napoleon's relations to Rome, and to the Catholics of France. His relations to Rome have the unity of an epic. They begin with the election of Pius VII. to the Chair of S. Peter in the conclave at Venice in the beginning of the year 1800, and end only with his own downfall. The present volumes, as I have said, continue the narrative only to January, 1811. Eleven years seem to a man who looks back after he has passed middle life but as a few days. But in those years were developed a series of events the most wonderful in modern history. When the history commences, the House of Austria, in full possession of the dignity and prestige of the Holy Roman Empire, was mistress of Italy, and in actual possession of the greater part of the States of the Church. Naples, virtually her vassal, held the remainder; and neither power made any secret of its resolution to keep permanently what it had got. The

Austrian intrigues at the Conclave were aimed expressly at this object; and when, by a remarkable series of events, very well related by the author, the election fell, against the will of Austria, upon Pius VII., the resolution was at once shown to make him a mere tool of the Empire, and especially to refuse to give up the Legations. The whole position both of Austria and Naples towards the Pope was changed by one event—the battle of Marengo. France, not Austria, became once more mistress of Italy; and for fourteen years it was from France, and France alone, that the Holy See had anything to fear. Napoleon's first measures were intended to gain the confidence of the Catholics of Italy, and they succeeded. He assured the clergy of the Milanese that when he had come into Italy two years before as a General under the Directory, he had been unable to adopt a policy of his own—that as First Consul he was now master.

All the changes then made, chiefly in discipline, were opposed to my views and wishes. As the mere instrument of a government which cared nothing for the Catholic religion, I was then unable to prevent the disorders which it was bent on stirring up, cost what they might, with the view of overthrowing it. Now I have full powers. I have resolved to employ every instrument which seems to me calculated to give security and confidence to that religion. France has been educated by her sufferings. Her eyes are at length opened; she perceives that the Catholic religion is the only anchor which can keep her steady on the troubled waves, and save her from the tempest. She has invited it again to her bosom. In this good work I cannot conceal the fact that I have had a great share. I can assure you that the churches of France have been re-opened, that the Catholic religion is resuming its ancient dignity, and that the people look with reverence upon the consecrated pastors who are returning full of zeal to the midst of their abandoned flocks. As soon as I have an opportunity of communicating with the new Pope, I hope to have the happiness of removing every obstacle which could possibly stand in the way of the entire reconciliation of France with the Head of the Church. I shall be glad that the public should be informed, through the press, of the sentiments by which I am animated, that it may be known, not only in Italy and France, but in all Europe, what my dispositions are.

No wonder that Catholic Italy threw itself with delight into the arms of a young hero who, in the moment of his most brilliant triumph, reversed without delay thus publicly, the fatal policy on which France had been acting for more than eight years. Hitherto, wherever the French troops took possession, the clergy had been driven out and persecuted. Foreign nations had seen the most venerable of the French clergy seeking in exile a precarious maintenance from the charity of surrounding nations, and had heard from them that they were themselves but the remnant which had escaped the guillotine. What a consolation such words as these from the mouth of the man who, almost at the same moment, had made himself master of France, and France mistress of Italy! Nor had the Italian clergy any reason to doubt that Bonaparte was a sincere Catholic. He was of a family Italian, Catholic, and religious. It is difficult for us to divest ourselves of the memory of his subsequent actions sufficiently to judge of him as Italian Catholics in 1800 necessarily judged. They did not, like us, know even the past—for instance, that he had made a profession of belief in Islamism equally satisfactory to the ulemas of Egypt only the year before.

The next measure of the First Consul was to bring about the 'Concordat.' M. D'Haussonville relates, very graphically, all the steps towards it—the negotiations, first at Rome, and afterwards at Paris. It was to his first negotiator at Rome, M. Cacault, that Napoleon gave the celebrated injunction, 'Remember to treat the Pope as if he had two hundred thousand men at his command.' Unfortunately, with him was joined another negotiator, a priest whose antecedents led men to trust him, for he had been among the most influential leaders of the royalist peasantry in La Vendée but who was undeserving of their confidence. This is the same person who, being made Bishop of Orleans on the conclusion of the Concordat, distinguished himself by the basest subserviency to Napoleon, and whose disgrace, if I remember rightly, has been noted by the pen of the distinguished prelate who now sits in his seat. The unworthy conduct of this man, and of Cardinal Caprara, who was long Legate at Paris, no doubt contributed to confirm Napoleon in the fatal opinion that 'every man has his price,' and to lead him into his worst errors. I cannot follow M. D'Haussonville through these negotiations. When Napoleon found that he did not get his own way, he threatened to invade the States of the Church, and found that the threat produced no effect. He then threatened to lead France into schism, and even to make it Protestant. In his calmer moments, disposed as he always was to reckon on his power, he felt that this exceeded it. 'To his most trusted counsellor,' he said that—

> It would be a folly to join himself to the constitutional bishops and priests. Their influence was gone. They could lend him no force; still, they do very well to threaten Consalvi with. To put himself at the head of a separate Church, to make himself Pope, for him a man of war in his sword and spurs, would be simply impossible. Would they have him make himself hated like Robespierre, or laughed at like Laréveillère Lepeaux? To make France Protestant! Easily said, no doubt. But everything cannot be done in France, say what they may; even he could do nothing except by going with real feelings. The Catholic was the ancient religion of the land. Half France at least would remain Catholic, and there would be no end of disputes and divisions. The people must have a religion, and that religion must be in the hands of the Government (vol. i. p. 107).

Still, neither to the Pope nor his minister did he confess even so much as this, and it would be a serious responsibility to push him, by insisting upon anything which could lawfully be conceded, into a renewal of the persecution which had hardly ceased, or even into a schism like that of the constitutional clergy. A powerful monarch, quite reckless of the welfare of souls, is, no doubt, always at a great advantage in dealing with a Pontiff with whom the good of souls is a primary consideration.

One point upon which there was much difficulty, but which the Pope ultimately conceded, was whether the Concordat should declare Catholicism the religion of the State, or only that of the vast majority of the French people. At last, after long debates and many delays, the terms of the Concordat were settled, and Napoleon agreed to withdraw the articles in which he had embodied the Gallican doctrines. Nothing, therefore, remained except to sign : and a meeting was held for that purpose. It had been expressly declared that it was a mere formality, 'which would hardly occupy a quarter of an hour.' I need hardly tell, what all the world knows, how, at the moment when he was about to put his hand to the document as the representative of the Holy Father, Cardinal Consalvi discovered that Napoleon had attempted a fraud upon him, by substituting for the document to which he had agreed, another containing the obnoxious articles. I must refer to the author for the vivid description of scenes which followed, which are too long to be extracted here.

Napoleon throughout kept up the character of one who united with the highest genius the lowest and most paltry meanness and falsehood. It is universally known that when the Concordat was at last signed, he published it with the rejected articles added to it as if they had been agreed upon. At the same time he attempted another fraud, not so generally known, for, having always given Consalvi to understand that if the Concordat were concluded, he would have nothing to do with the schismatical clergy, except on condition of their making due submission to the Pope ; he had no sooner obtained the signature, than he caused one of his agents to mention to the legate, as a matter of course, that as many as possible of 'both clergies' (*i.e.* the Catholic and the schismatical) would attend at the *Te Deum* sung for the conclusion at Notre Dame. At the same time he condescended to another trick of the same sort. There had been a dispute whether the legate should take an oath which had formally been required from legates *à latere* in France. The First Consul had promised that it should not be required, and in fact it was not. But, to satisfy the Gallicans, a formal notice was officially inserted in the 'Moniteur,' asserting that Cardinal Consalvi had taken the oath, which, for greater effect, was printed at full length.

The manner in which the difficulty about the constitutional clergy was got over, was also characteristic of Napoleon. There were two ecclesiastics wholly free from the taint of the schism, and of unblemished reputation, upon whom, however, Napoleon, with his usual knowledge of character, felt sure that he might rely for any service, however unworthy. These were the Abbés Bernier and Pancemont. They were named by the First Consul for the sees of Orleans and Vannes. The legate, in the name of the Pope, gladly gave them canonical authority and episcopal consecration, and congratulated his Holiness upon the character of these appointments. The bishops who had compromised themselves in the constitutional schism, and whom the First Consul, against the wishes of the legate and against his own promises, had nominated to other sees, had of course been required 'explicitly to confess their schism and to abjure their past errors.' The bishops of Orleans and Vannes attested that they had made this declaration before themselves, but no sooner had the constitutional bishops obtained canonical investiture than they boasted that they had done nothing of the sort, and that they had even torn into a thousand scraps the letter which had been proposed for their signature in the name of the Holy Father. 'Between such opposite assertions,' asks the author, 'which are we to trust?' Then, after adding that facts are now notorious against the uprightness of M. Bernier, but that nothing was ever alleged to the discredit of M. de Pancemont, he adds:—

In such a case there are, in fact, no positive proofs. Still it is with surprise and pain that, in searching among the contemporary documents for the means of forming my own judgment, I found, in the correspondence of Napoleon I., two letters which may perhaps throw an unexpected light upon the conduct of the two prelates. One is a request to M. de Talleyrand to give to the Abbé Bernier a sum of thirty thousand francs (£1,200) out of the secret service money, to assist him in negotiating suitably with the Legate; the other an order to Citizen Portalis to hold at the disposition of M. de Pancemont, Bishop of Vannes (without any publicity), the sum of fifty thousand francs (£2,000).

I have mentioned merely a few instances of the affair of the Concordat because they illustrate the character of Napoleon, who certainly was, of all great men in history, the most willing to descend to any littleness, any meanness, any falsehood, any treachery, if it seemed likely to accomplish his ends. The whole course of a matter complicated by many strange intrigues, and extending over many months, is related in a lucid narrative by M. D'Haussonville. The publication of the Concordat was long delayed by Napoleon after it was formally signed, partly in consequence of the disputes to which I have alluded, partly for a reason highly characteristic of him. No man ever thought more of what Englishmen would laugh at as theatrical effects. If he wished to publish a decree against British commerce, it was no mere coincidence which occasioned him to sign it in his head-quarters, at the palace of the King of Prussia, at Berlin; the decree regulating the Opera at Paris was dated from Moscow. In this case, he had set his heart upon publishing the Concordat on the anniversary of the *coup d'état* by which he had placed himself at the head of the State—the 18th Brumaire (Nov. 9). As soon as this was gone by, instead of pressing the matter forward as he had done all along, he intentionally delayed it. His reason was, that he thought the next best thing would be to publish the Concordat at such a moment that the *Te Deum* at Notre Dame might be sung on Easter day. For that day, he caused the state carriages of the unfortunate Louis XVI., which had lain by in dust and neglect for ten years, to be regilt for his use. In the same spirit, he selected as preacher on the occasion, the Cardinal de Boisgelin, an exemplary prelate, but whom he no doubt selected because he had preached five and twenty years before in the same pulpit at the coronation of Louis XVI. What a deluge had swept over France since that day! But who shall say that in matters such as this, a man so keen-sighted, did not rightly estimate the effect to be produced upon the minds of the people whom he so thoroughly understood?

In the negotiations which went on while the publication of the Concordat was delayed, as well as in those which followed, it was the misfortune of the Holy See that the Legate at Paris, though by no means a hypocrite or indifferent to duty, was yet not to be trusted. This was Cardinal Caprara, a man of illustrious birth, and who had already been employed in high positions. Napoleon insisted on his being appointed to the office, practically refusing to receive anyone else. Although he was not the man whom Pius VII. would have selected, no definite cause could be alleged for refusing him, and he was appointed. He retained the office until, after the extreme outrages of the Emperor upon the Holy See, the Pope recalled his powers, and appointed no successor. In that time it is not too much to say that, although there is no reason to suppose he intended to betray the cause of the Church, yet he conducted himself on numerous occasions rather as the minister of the Emperor than of the Pope. More than once he acted in direct disobedience to the positive commands and instructions of the Holy See, and at last so entirely lost the confidence of the Holy Father, that, instead of instructing him to say what he had too good reason to believe would not be said, he used to send letters written in full, which his nuncio was only to sign and deliver. M. D'Haussonville finds that Caprara, on several occasions, allowed himself to be under pecuniary obligations to Napoleon.

The next affair of importance between Napoleon and the Holy Father was the coronation in Notre Dame. M. D'Haussonville tells excellently all the circumstances which led to this event—the Emperor's notion of the extreme importance of the religious sanction it would give his title, especially as tending to remove the ill effects of the recent murder of the Duke d'Enghien; the consternation of Cardinal Caprara when first sounded upon it by Napoleon; his pressing importunities to the Holy Father not to refuse; the promises so made as to give the Pope to understand more than Napoleon had any intention of fulfilling; the Pope's enthusiastic reception by the French people, and the jealousy which it excited in the mind of Napoleon.

For all this, and much more, I must refer my readers to his pages. It is, however, important to notice that Napoleon's uncle, Cardinal Fesch, earnestly pressed Pius VII. to make the restitution of the Legations (still held by the French) and a compensation for Avignon and Carpentras a condition of his consent, and that the Pope (although hoping this from the Emperor's generosity) steadily refused to mix the temporal question with the spiritual points upon which he felt bound in conscience to insist. One of these was the form of the coronation oath which the Pope was to tender to the Emperor. As drawn up by the Emperor, it bound him to 'respect and make others respect the laws of the Concordat.' This the Pope refused, because it might be taken to include the 'organic articles,' which, though not really part of the Concordat, had been published as such by Napoleon. A still more important question arose upon the words 'to respect and cause to be respected the liberty of worships' [*la liberté des cultes*]. To this Cardinal Consalvi, in the name of the Pope, objected: 'This implies an engagement, not to tolerate and allow, but to support and protect; and it extends, not only to the persons but to the things, that is to all worships [*à tous les cultes*]. But a Catholic cannot protect the error of false worships.'[1] Caprara replies to this, that the terms of the oath meant nothing. But Consalvi rejoins :—

The formula is such as a Catholic ought not to take, and a Pope cannot authorise by his presence. It is of the essence of the Catholic religion to be intolerant. No one must be quieted with any hope that this difficulty about the oath in the Pope's presence may be evaded (*l'espoir de tourner cette difficulté*). Pius VII. will not be a party to it. He has declared to Cardinal Fesch that, if the attempt is made, he will not hesitate to rise from his seat the same instant, let what may come of it (vol. i. p. 334).

One curious fact, the explanation of which has been hitherto unknown, and has been discovered by M. D'Haussonville, is that while the newspapers of all Europe were filled with circumstantial descriptions of this remarkable scene, the 'Moniteur' alone—so minute as to all that magnified the Emperor—gave no account of it. This was because Napoleon's act in putting the Imperial crown upon his own head instead of receiving it from the Holy Father, was a breach of an engagement expressly made upon this very point. Consalvi had pointed out that in every instance the Monarch had received the crown from the Prelate, from whom he received the anointing, and made it a condition of the Holy Father's coming that this custom should be observed. With his usual perfidy the Emperor gave and broke the promise. Pius declared that if any authorised report was published which showed that things had not been done as had been arranged beforehand, he would make a public protest stating the breach of engagement. To avoid this the 'Moniteur' suppressed all report of the proceedings. Every act of Napoleon's life seems full of the same strange mixture of dignity and meanness.

Pius VII. returned to Rome—the fact is remarkable—so much fascinated by that wonderful power which Napoleon acquired over

[1] Vol. i. p. 330.

all who personally approached him, that no future events, no lapse of time, no outrages, no crimes, were ever able to destroy the affection with which the Holy Father regarded him. From that day began the series of those outrages and crimes which culminated in the prison at Savona, and the scenes at Fontainebleau. Every condition upon which he had insisted, every hope which had been held out to him, had been violated ; but even to the last Pius seems to have found a difficulty in forcing himself to believe that Napoleon himself could be personally guilty of the perfidy and impiety which marked his public measures. Almost as soon as he had reached Rome, a question arose, in consequence of Napoleon's introducing into his Italian kingdom, in which the whole people were Catholics, the rules adopted in France. While Consalvi wrote in strong terms to the Legate, Pius VII. wrote (I may say affectionately) to Napoleon. He received an answer, accompanied by one to the French Minister of Rome (Cardinal Fesch), in which he was directed to arrange with the Holy See modifications of the decree.[1] To this he replied :—

> The proofs which your Majesty gives me of your attachment to religion and your opposition to the false spirit of philosophy of the age, have filled me with consolation. Everything which comes directly from your Majesty always shows the greatness and uprightness of your character. I thank you from the bottom of my heart for the feelings to which you may be fully assured that my own most fully and most sincerely answer. Be equally convinced that, so far as I am concerned, I am guided by no policy. My only guides are the maxims of the Gospel and the laws of the Church. You may, therefore, be sure beforehand that I shall always proceed in perfect simplicity of heart, and with all possible spirit of conciliation and moderation (vol. ii. p. 22).

Well would it have been for Napoleon if he could have believed what the Holy Father here said in simple sincerity of

---

[1] The author adds, these modifications were never really made.

heart, as to the motives of his own conduct; it would have saved him from his greatest and most fatal mistakes as well as crimes. But, as I have already said, this was exactly what the moral defect of his own character made impossible to him. That men should profess sentiments of exalted generosity, of noble self-sacrifice, of simple devotion to the cause of duty; this seemed to him perfectly natural. He felt, as strongly as anyone else, that there are occasions on which such professions are highly becoming, just as it was fit that, on the day of his coronation, he should dress himself in sweeping robes of the richest crimson velvet, spangled with golden bees. Such things were excellent in their place, and so were professions of high principle. In their place he used them himself, and approved of their use by others. What he could not imagine, what he never brought himself to believe was— that any man should really be guided by such principles in the practical business of life. As soon would he have thought of riding into a fierce and bloody battle in his coronation robes. And hence, he never really understood the conduct of the Holy See. Being sure that the reasons alleged for it could not be possibly true, he had to look about for others, and fixed upon some, not in themselves unlikely or irrational, but which quite misled him, because the real reason was that which he had begun by setting aside, without examination, as simply impossible. The first instance of this immediately followed. Jerome Bonaparte had married a Protestant lady in the United States. It was manifestly convenient that the marriage should be dissolved that he might take a wife from one of the royal families of Catholic Germany. At once, and without doubt of a favourable result, the Emperor applied to the Pope. He felt sure that Pius could feel no objection, for it was evidently for the interest of the Church that the Emperor should be surrounded with Catholics rather than Protestants. The Holy Father replied, by a letter in his own hand, assuring him of his wish to declare the marriage null if he could, and explaining why, on the evidence as yet before him, he could not do so without violating the laws of God and the Church. He concluded :—

It is therefore out of my power in the present state of things to pronounce the marriage null. If I should usurp a power which I have not, I should render myself guilty of an abuse abominable before the judgment-seat of God; and your Majesty yourself, in your justice, would blame me for pronouncing a sentence opposite to the testimony of my conscience and to the invariable principles of the Church. Hence I confidently hope that your Majesty will feel certain that it is only by an absolute want of power that the desire I have always felt to second, as far as lies in me, all your designs, and particularly in a matter which so closely touches your august person, has in this instance been made inefficacious. And I entreat you to accept this sincere declaration as an evidence of my truly fatherly affection.

Every Catholic who has paid any attention to the subject well knows that the facts set forth by Pius VII. in this letter, and not disputed on the other side, made it, not merely inexpedient or unbecoming, but simply impossible, that he should, without monstrous wickedness, declare Jerome's marriage null and void.[1] His reply was merely an example of the *Non possumus*. This letter put Napoleon beside himself with rage. The Pope refuse to take, at his request, a step so obviously expedient and beneficial for all parties! What could be his motive? That which he alleged, of course, could have nothing to do with it. What had

---

[1] Prince Jerome Napoleon thought fit to publish in the 'Revue des deux Mondes' a letter maintaining the view taken of this affair by Napoleon I., and going on to say that at a later period of his life Pius VII. himself, 'whatever may have been the motives of his first resistance, did not persist in it.' The proofs he gives of this are simply absurd. I direct the attention of my readers to the correspondence which they will find vol. ii. p. 409, *pièces Justificatives*, because it contains in M. D'Haussonville's answer to the Prince some exquisite specimens, peculiarly French, of keen '*malice*' under the forms of profound reverence, which will greatly amuse them, but which I have no room to extract.

conscience and the 'judgment-seat of God' to do with a practical matter such as this? Very good things, no doubt, to talk about on fitting occasions, but quite out of place now. The refusal, therefore, must have been given to spite him; and he had not far to go to find the motive. He knew that he had both robbed and cheated the Pope by keeping the 'Legations.' No doubt this refusal was the Pope's way of showing his anger at the wrong and the insult. Of course, taking this view of the matter, he was sure that he could easily overcome the resistance of so feeble an enemy by making him feel that, however reasonable his indignation might be, he would lose much more than he could possibly gain by indulging it.

From this point, then, began the contest between Napoleon and Pius VII. Almost at the same moment the policy of Napoleon took a turn which made him feel it important to have the practical control, not merely of the Legations (of which he still kept possession), but of the whole States of the Church. A few months before, his whole heart had been fixed upon the invasion of England (and he never varied from his policy of keeping, at all costs, on friendly terms with other powers while he was attacking any one); he therefore intended to keep things quiet on the Continent. The failure of his plan of invasion in the summer of 1805 determined him to attack Austria. In that war it was of great importance not to leave behind him any country in which England might raise the standard of opposition to him, and such a country he believed the States of the Church to be. True, the Sovereign Pontiff professed absolute neutrality; but he had already shown—so judged Napoleon—by the affair of the divorce that he hated Napoleon, and would do him an injury if he could; the Emperor therefore resolved to occupy Ancona, a harbour which in a war with Austria it would not do to leave in hostile hands. To a mild letter of remonstrance from the Holy Father he replied (waiting until after the stupendous victory of Austerlitz) by letters of studied insult addressed both to himself and to the French Minister at Rome (Cardinal Fesch). To the latter, after referring again to the affair of the divorce, he declared—

> To the Pope I am Charlemagne; because, like Charlemagne, I unite the crown of France to that of the Lombards, and because my empire extends to the boundaries of the East. I expect, therefore, that his conduct towards me should be regulated upon this principle. If good conduct is maintained, I shall not change the outward appearance of things; if not, I shall reduce the Pope to be only Bishop of Rome. In truth, nothing can be so unreasonable as the Court of Rome (vol. ii. p. 78).

Here, probably, Napoleon first gave an indication of the principle upon which he intended to act towards the temporal dominions of the Pope. A little later he expressed it more and more plainly. In few words it was, that the Pope should nominally remain an independent sovereign, both in war and peace, on condition of his becoming, in fact, a feudatory of the French Emperor. It is probable that his natural disposition would have led him to say nothing about these intentions, but silently to assume in detail the control of Rome, and to let the fact that he had become sovereign of the Roman States break by degrees upon the minds both of the Pope and his subjects. But it was not open to him to adopt this plan, because it was necessary to his other plans to assume immediate authority. He was at war with England and Russia. It was convenient that the States of the Church should take his side in the war; he resolved, therefore, as he said in the letter I have just quoted, that there must be no delay, that the Pope must either at once join in the war, or be at once deprived of his territory. Six weeks later, February 22nd, 1806, he explained this, in plain words, to the Holy Father himself.

> I share all your Holiness's distress, and can imagine your perplexity. You may avoid it all by going straight forward, and not

entering into a political labyrinth, and into considerations for powers which, in a religious point of view, are heretical and out of the Church, and, in a political, are far removed from your States, unable either to protect or injure you. I shall not touch the independence of the Holy See. I shall even cause it to be repaid for whatever it may lose by the movements of my army. But the condition must be, that your Holiness must be to me, in matters temporal (*aura pour moi dans le temporel, les mêmes égards que je lui porte pour le spirituel*), what I am to you in matters spiritual; that you must cease to have any useless consideration for heretics, enemies of the Church, and for powers which are unable to do you any good. Your Holiness is Sovereign of Rome; *but I am its Emperor. All my enemies must be yours.* It is not fit that any agent of the King of Sardinia, any Englishman, Russian, or Swede, should reside at Rome, or in your States, or that any vessel of those powers should enter your ports (vol. ii. p. 101).

The author remarks, 'It was the Emperor's ordinary calculation, and ever afterwards his habit, when he wished to make a strong impression on anyone, to assume towards him an attitude of complaint and a tone of profound irritation.' The letter before me is an example of this, but I have not room for half of it. But he wrote the same day to his Minister at Rome—

You must demand the expulsion from the States of the Pope of all English, Russians, and Swedes, and all persons attached to the Court of the King of Sardinia. No vessel either Swedish, English, or Russian, must be allowed to enter the States of the Pope, or else I will confiscate them. I do not intend the Court of Rome in future to take any part in politics. I will protect its States against all the world. It is useless that it should have so much consideration for the enemies of religion. Say that I am Charlemagne, the sword of the Church, their Emperor, and that I must be treated as such. I am making known my intentions to the Pope in a few words. If he does not keep to them, I shall reduce him to the same condition he was in before Charlemagne (vol. ii. p. 105).

I grudge to the letters of Napoleon the space I am compelled to give them, because without having them before their eyes my readers could not realise to themselves the position of the Holy Father. Before answering these last letters, he called together the Sacred College, and asked the opinion of its members one by one, reserving his own till the last. The opinion was unanimous, with the single exception of one French Cardinal. The answer was then written :—

March 21, 1806.

I owe it to God, to the Church, and to myself, to the attachment I profess towards your Majesty, to your own glory, which I have as much at heart as yourself, to speak freely and sincerely, as becomes the uprightness of my character and the duty of my ministry. I have had, and always shall have, the greatest consideration for your Majesty; but still I can neither lend myself to anything absolutely contrary to the obligations which inevitably result from my double character of Prince and Pontiff, nor hide the truths of which I am in my conscience intimately convinced, nor accede to demands directly inconsistent with the oath I have taken, before the face of the Almighty, and at His altar, to maintain untouched from age to age the charge of the patrimony of the Roman Church. . . . . Your Majesty desires that I should expel from my States all Russians, English, and Swedes, and all the agents of the King of Sardinia ; and that I should close my ports against the vessels of those three nations. That is to say, you demand that I, renouncing the peace I enjoy, should place myself, with regard to those Powers, in a state of war and open hostility. Permit me to say, with perfect sincerity, that it is not with a view to my temporal interests, but by reason of duties most essential and inseparable from my character, that I find it impossible to accede to this demand. I, the Vicar of the Eternal WORD, who is not the God of discord, but of concord and peace, who, according to the expression of the Apostle, came into the world to put an end to the enmities of the world, how could I possibly discard the precept of my Divine Master, and place myself in opposition to the mission to which He has called me? It is not my will but the will of God that lays down the duty of peace towards all, without distinction of Catholic or heretic, of those near or remote, of those from whom we can hope benefits or fear great evils. If, as your Majesty says, I ought not 'to enter into the labyrinth of politics,' from which, in fact,

I have held, and shall always hold, myself aloof, how much more ought I to abstain from taking part in the evils of a war which has no cause except politics, in which no attack is made upon religion, and in which there is even involved a Catholic Power! Nothing but the necessity of repelling a hostile aggression, or defending religion from peril, has afforded to my predecessors a legitimate motive for giving up the condition of peace. If, through human frailty, any one of them has not been subject to these maxims, his conduct, I declare openly, can never serve as an example to mine.

Then Pius VII. explained with the same gentleness and the same sound reason that to expel from his States the subjects of heretical Powers, who were at war with the Emperor, and to shut his ports against them, would be to provoke an inevitable interruption of the daily communications which existed between the Holy See and the Catholics who lived under the rule of these courts.

The irresistible force of human events has sometimes led to this fatal interruption of communication between the head of the Church and some of its most faithful members. The Church has then deeply grieved at the calamity. But if she became the cause herself, what would be the bitterness of her remorse, and how could she smother the inward voice of conscience, which would eternally reproach her with so unpardonable a fault? The Catholics who live in heretical countries are, moreover, no small number. Can I abandon so many faithful souls, when I am required by the Gospel to do everything in order to seek one? There are millions in the Russian empire; there are millions upon millions in the regions subject to England. They enjoy the free exercise of their religion; they are protected. What a responsibility to have led to the prohibition of religion in these lands, the ruin of holy missions, the stagnation of spiritual affairs! An incalculable evil for religion and for Catholicism; an evil for which I should have to accuse myself, and for which I should have to give a strict account before the judgment-seat of God! (Vol. ii. p. 141.)

The Emperor had complained of many serious evils resulting from dilatory proceedings at Rome. The Pope replies—

Your Majesty would have spared me the pain of your blame if you had considered that such affairs absolutely require mature counsel, and that it is impossible in discussing them to be as rapid as in temporal matters. This accusation your Majesty particularises by applying it to the ecclesiastical affairs of Germany. You say that for the sake of worldly interests, and the vain prerogatives of the tiara, souls are left to perish. I receive as from the hand of the Most High the humiliating bitterness of the reproach which your Majesty has thought fit to make to me. God and the world are my witnesses whether or not my conduct has been guided by worldly interests and vain prerogatives.

The Pope then explained that the ecclesiastical arrangements of Germany had been complicated, and their settlement delayed, by the territorial changes which had resulted from Napoleon's wars. He continued—

Your Majesty lays down the principle that you are Emperor of Rome. I reply, with apostolic frankness, that the Pope, who became Sovereign of Rome so many centuries ago that no other sovereignty on earth can go back to a more remote point in history, does not acknowledge, and never has acknowledged, any power superior to himself in his own dominions. I will add that no Emperor has ever had the least right over Rome. Your Majesty is immensely great; you have been elected, crowned, consecrated, acknowledged, Emperor of the French, but not Emperor of Rome. There exists no Emperor of Rome; there can exist none unless the Sovereign Pontiff shall have been despoiled of the sovereign authority he exercises at Rome. We well know that there exists an Emperor of the Romans; but this is a title elective and merely honorary, acknowledged by all Europe, and by your Majesty yourself, as belonging to the Emperor of Germany, and cannot be borne by two Sovereigns at the same time. Your Majesty tells me that my relations towards yourself ought to be those which existed between my predecessors and Charlemagne. Charlemagne found Rome in the hands of the Popes. He acknowledged and confirmed without reserve their dominion, and augmented it by new donations; but never did he claim to exercise any supremacy over the Popes, even considered as mere temporal Princes. Never did he require from them any dependence or any subjection of any kind. .... Finally, ten centuries have passed since the time of

Charlemagne, which renders it useless to go back to a more ancient origin. I am compelled to point out to your Majesty that the principles you have advanced cannot be sustained. Still less is it possible that I should accept the consequences which you would draw from them. . . . . I cannot admit the maxim by which your Majesty lays down that I ought to be towards you in matters temporal as your Majesty towards me in matters spiritual. The extent given to this proposition entirely alters the character and destroys the very essence of these two powers. Spiritual things, in fact, do not admit of simple relations [*simples égards*]; they come from [*relevent de*] a divine right. Their essence is superior and transcendent, and does not admit of any comparison with temporal objects. A Catholic Sovereign is such, solely because he professes to conform himself to the decisions of the visible head of the Church, and to acknowledge him as the master of truth [*maître de la vérité*] and sole Vicar of God upon earth. There can, therefore, be no identity, no equality between the spiritual relation of a Catholic Sovereign to the Chief of the Hierarchy, and the relations of one temporal Sovereign to another. . . . . The second consequence which your Majesty desires to draw from these principles is to establish the point that your enemies must of necessity become my enemies also. This doctrine is absolutely contrary to the character of my divine mission, which knows no enmity even towards those who are unhappily separated from the centre of unity; and I could not subscribe to it without breaking the bond of common paternity which exists between the Sovereign Pontiffs and all Sovereigns who are within the bosom of the Church. For, according to your Majesty's very proposition, every time a Catholic Power was at war, it would be my duty to treat it as an enemy. (Vol. ii. p. 146.)

Pius VII. then pointed out that Napoleon, who prided himself upon being 'the avenger and defender of the Church,' would be inconsistent with himself if he demanded the adoption of principles 'through which my temporal independence, so advantageous to my spiritual mission, would in the end be entirely destroyed.'

Among so many trials I have no support except the uprightness of my intentions, the confidence inspired into me by the justice of my cause, and, above all, the hope that your Majesty's filial affection will respond to my overflowing fatherly tenderness; but if I am disappointed, if the heart of your Majesty is not touched by my words, I shall suffer whatever may come with evangelical resignation. I shall submit to every kind of calamity, and accept it as coming from God; I shall encounter all the adversities of this life rather than make myself unworthy of my ministry by deviating from the line laid down by my conscience. .... In conclusion, I will believe that you will not wholly forget that, at this moment, when I am at Rome a prey to so many and such terrible troubles, not one year has passed since I quitted Paris. .... I give you with my whole heart my fatherly benediction. (Vol. ii. p. 148.)

I cannot but feel how much the force of this letter is weakened and lost, by the fact that my readers cannot possibly have before their minds a just sense of what Napoleon really was when it was written. Never before had the power of a man been so widely extended and so absolute; for none even of the heathen Emperors of Rome, whose dominions were more extended, at any time held the actual strings by which all the resources and powers of the empire were set in motion so absolutely in his own hands. What is chiefly impressed upon me in reading the volumes of M. D'Haussonville (especially in connection with those of M. Thiers) is, that for many years no one, either within or without his dominions, had presumed to resist the will of Napoleon, or to give a direct refusal even to his most unjust and most unreasonable demands. At Paris, the ambassadors of the most ancient, most powerful, and proudest royal and imperial houses of Europe trembled before him. When he took the field it was only because the most abject submission could not suffice to avert his dreadful wrath from those whom he thought it his interest to crush. He was wont to look around him upon the great Powers of the Continent and consider, not which of them he could subdue, for he was confident that none could resist him, but which he should for the present spare. A little later he balanced in his own mind, in the same spirit, from which of those houses he should accept a successor to the divorced Josephine. In truth, for years past no one within the European Continent had ever presumed to oppose him. England, no doubt, was still out of his reach, but he doubted not that if only he could get within arm's length of her he could break her in pieces, and meanwhile he boasted that he had shut her out of the world by his continental blockade. But that he should be defied, not in the frenzy of despair, but soberly and calmly, by an unarmed old man; that his orders should be not only disobeyed, but argued against and shown to be unreasonable, —it was beyond belief, beyond imagination. The letter of which I have given such copious extracts, 'filled him,' says M. D'Haussonville, 'not with rage only, but with indignation.' And now began the death-struggle between the all-powerful Emperor and the unresisting Pontiff. His anger was increased by Cardinal Fesch, whose conscience would not allow him to go wholly against the Pope (a little later he refused to accept the archbishopric of Paris, when urged by the Emperor to take it without the authority of the Holy Father), but who hated Cardinal Consalvi to such a degree of madness as even to accuse him of having instigated a murder which had been committed at Rome, in order to throw the odium of it on the French. At last Consalvi had been compelled to resign. Fesch himself was recalled because work was to be done upon which Napoleon did not choose to employ his uncle. M. Alquier, his successor, warned the Emperor in very striking language (vol. ii. p. 303) that in matters which touched his conscience Pius was not influenced or controlled by any adviser, but took his own course. If Napoleon believed him, which may be doubted, he perhaps felt it too late to retreat now. My space will not allow me to follow the different measures of aggression by which Napoleon laid his hands inch by inch upon the dominions of the Holy Father. It was highly characteristic that the execution of the final outrages, even when fully determined, was long delayed, and things remained as they were, because Napoleon was engaged in the difficult and somewhat alarming campaign which ended in the battle of Jena; and while he had before him the task of breaking the power of Prussia, he would not subject himself to any increase of his enemies by a new outrage, even on Pius VII. On the 31st of July, 1806, we have another letter of the Pope, addressed nominally to his Nuncio at Paris, at that time an open partisan of the Emperor, for Napoleon (on pretexts characteristically false and little) had now refused to communicate with him directly, but evidently intended for the eye of the Emperor. I wish my space allowed me to give the whole of it.

I have earnestly commended myself to that God, of whom I, unworthy as I am, am Vicar on earth, and to S. Peter the Apostle, of whom I am the successor, to obtain the light of which I have need, in order to give the answer you demand. Here is that answer, written with my own hand, as an additional proof of the importance I attach to matters of such weight, and how sincere and deep are the sentiments by which I am actuated, and which I am obliged to make known to you. My reasons for refusing to make the declaration demanded of me are too strong, too just, too powerful to make possible any change of opinion. They are founded not upon human considerations, as is imagined, but upon the most essential duties imposed upon me both by my character as the common father of the faithful, and by the nature of my ministry of peace. Admit that the English (as his Majesty tells you), will never believe that Rome suffered itself to be destroyed for their sake, and will never be grateful for it, that is not what I have to consider. I have thought only of my own duties, which lay me under the obligation of not causing any injury to religion by the interruption of communications between the head and the members of the Church, in any place where Catholics exist. This interruption I should myself provoke if I were to exercise acts of hostility against any one nation, and make myself a partner in a war against it. If the injuries caused to religion came from the acts of another, like that which may result from the measures which his Majesty may take in consequence of my refusal to agree to his demand, I shall grieve over them in bitterness of heart, and shall adore the judgments of God, who, for the secret designs of His Providence, allows them. But if, betraying my sacred character and the nature of my ministry, I should take part in a war which provoked resentments injurious to the Church, those evils would be my own act; and this it is that I cannot do. I cannot, in order to avoid the evils with which I am threatened, give occasion by my own fault to those evils to the Church which I have mentioned. Those with which I am threatened are not necessary evils, they depend solely on the will of his Majesty, who is free to make them actual or to avoid them. . . . . His Majesty has told you that if Rome and the States of the Church are once in his hands, they will never come out of them. His Majesty may easily believe this, and persuade himself of it, but I reply frankly that if his Majesty has a right to be confident that power is on his side, I, for my part, know that above all monarchs there reigns a God, the avenger of justice and innocence, before whom every human power must bend. You tell me that the Emperor says to you that the affair has now become public, and that therefore he cannot go back. But I must crave his Majesty to consider that he can lose nothing of his greatness and magnanimity, when it is not before an earthly potentate, a rival of his power, that he gives way and bends, but before the representations and entreaties of a priest of Jesus Christ, his father and his friend. If this consideration does not avail to persuade him, I am bound to tell him with apostolic freedom that, if his Majesty is committed in honour before men, I am committed in conscience before God; that the head of the Church will never take part in war; that I assuredly will not be first to give to the Church and the world an example which none of my predecessors, during eighteen centuries, has given, that of uniting myself in a state of war progressive, indefinite, permanent, against any nation whatever; that I cannot accede to the federative system of the French Empire; that my dominions, transmitted to me independent of all federation, must remain so by the nature of my apostolical ministry; and that if this independence is attacked, if the threats which are addressed to me are executed without any regard to my dignity and to the affection which binds me to his Majesty, then I shall see in that the signal of an open persecution, and shall appeal to the judgment of God. My course is irrevocable. Nothing can change it; neither threats, nor the execution of those threats. . . . . These sentiments you may regard as my testament. I am ready, if necessary, to sign it with my blood, fortifying myself, if persecution breaks out, with those words of our Divine Master, 'Blessed are they that suffer persecution for justice sake.' Make known these sentiments to his Majesty in their fullest extent; I expressly command it. But at the same time tell the Emperor that he still has my affection, and that I have every wish to give him every proof of it which is in my power, and to continue to show myself his best friend; but what is demanded is out of my power to do. (Vol. ii. p. 320.)

This letter was indeed the Holy Father's last word. It reminds one of those of Moses when he appeared for the last time before Pharaoh, 'Thou shalt see my face no more;' and of those more solemn words of his Lord and Master when, for the last time He left the Temple, 'Ye shall see Me no more.' It is true that the end was for some months delayed, not by scruples on the part of the Emperor, but by the war with Prussia. And then came the perfidious seizure of the city of Rome itself, of which I have already spoken. At that point my space compels me to close my account of the relations of the Holy Father with Napoleon, although the part of M. D'Haussonville's book already published carries them on for a year later. The seizure of Rome is the most natural conclusion of the first stage of those relations which was ended when Pius VII. was no longer, even nominally, in possession of his dominions. When the work is completed I hope to return to it.

I must, however, notice that the author thinks the Holy Father was inconsistent, because at the last moment he consented to forbid the entry of English and Russian ships to his ports, after having declared it a point of conscience which he could not yield. It is strange that he does not see that things had then come to a point at which the one cause always assigned by Pius VII. for his refusal no longer applied. The French were in full possession of all his ports, especially Ancona and Civita Vecchia; the Customs' revenues were appropriated by them; his soldiers had been incorporated into the French army. It was therefore evident that his conceding this particular point could no longer be regarded by the English Government as an act of war, because the French occupation had already excluded English ships. His concession, therefore, at that particular moment only confirmed what he had always said, that his refusal of it had been an act of duty, and not a mere point of worldly honour. When the duty no longer forbad, the concession was made. In confirmation of this it is to be observed, that in conceding this one point he still absolutely refused to join in the war or to submit his States to the federal authority of the French empire. The concession, therefore, had no effect, beyond proving the sincerity of the Pope's declaration, that he was anxious to concede all he could concede with a safe conscience.

But in truth the wishes of Napoleon had by this time greatly changed. Time had been when he had meant what he said, that he wished the Pope to continue at Rome a nominal sovereign if only he would exercise his sovereignty in that state of subordination to the French Emperor which he required from his brothers and other subordinate kings. But he wished this no longer. On the contrary, he was now eagerly looking for a pretext for removing him into France and establishing him there, in all splendour and state, as one of the great officers of the new Empire. His plan was to give him a revenue of 120,000*l.* sterling per annum, magnificent palaces, &c.; he even went so far as to name Rheims as the place designed for his residence. This was part of his plan for making the Catholic Church as distinctly a tool in the hands of the French Emperor as the Russian schism actually in the hands of the autocrat of the Russias. This is not the inference drawn by others as to his desires and wishes,—it was his own deliberate plan, sketched in letters at the time and fully drawn out in a note dictated by himself at St. Helena. It was, of course, inconsistent with the *quasi* independence of the Pope, and therefore it is plain in the latter communications between Rome and Paris that the Emperor's fear was lest the Pope should concede what he demanded. So strong was this fear, that in transmitting an ultimatum of almost inconceivable insolence, he expressly retained the right of adding to it, if accepted, any new demands; that it might be always in his power to force the Pope into a refusal which would give him an excuse for going to extremities.

It is impossible not to feel that, to human appearance, the Catholic Church was in greater danger in January, 1810, than at any former period. She had to face not a barbarian invasion like that of Attila, but a strongly-compacted empire; and what she had to fear from it was not a persecution like that of Nero, which was sure to purify and unite the Church by the same acts which gave to individual confessors a martyr's tortures and a martyr's crown, but a deliberate and well-devised system by which she was to be pampered, crippled, and enslaved. Against such a system she had to rely, humanly speaking, on the personal qualities of Pius VII., an old, mild, gentle, unresisting monk. All the world now knows that she prevailed; but, before the event, all the world believed her success to be hopeless. And, considering that the greatest danger of all was that of an election to the Papacy under the tyranny of Napoleon, it is impossible not to note the remarkable Providence by which the reign of Pius VII., which began at the moment when the victory of Marengo was about to make Napoleon absolute master of Italy, was continued until his empire and himself had passed away. It is with something like anxiety that one reads, even now, of the precautions taken by the tyrant to have the cardinals always absolutely in his power, that he might at any moment be ready to act in case of a vacancy.

What use Napoleon intended to make of the Catholic Church when he held her, as he already securely reckoned upon doing, as a tool in his hands, we may see by his actual conduct towards the clergy of France. These volumes are full of instances of the combination of a grinding tyranny which dictated the most minute details of the daily ministration, not merely of great prelates, but of village curés, with falsehood and fraud so deliberate, and so shameless, that even after all we know of Napoleon it is hardly credible.

Perhaps the most curious illustration of his dealings in ecclesiastical matters, hitherto unknown even in France, was the manner in which he contrived to impose a new catechism upon all the dioceses of France. All the world knows that it was professedly authorised by the Pope. It has been made a ground of complaint against Pius VII. (and apparently not without reason), that he should have deprived the bishops of their discretion in this matter, for the benefit, not of the Church, but of the Emperor. It has now been shown that, in truth, he did exactly the reverse. All that passed is most graphically related by M. D'Haussonville. In the concordat as published by Napoleon it is declared, 'There shall be only one liturgy and one catechism for all the churches of France.' This, however, was one of his perfidious additions to the real Concordat. The author skilfully brings in, into the midst of his account of Napoleon's strange interference about the catechism, extracts from two letters written just at the same time, which show how little he really cared about doctrine. He wrote to his sister Eliza, his Satrap at Lucca—

'My sister, require no oath of the priests. Nothing will come of that except new difficulties. Go straight on to suppress the convents.'

A few days later he wrote:—

'The Pope's brief is nothing as long as it remains secret in your hands. Lose not an hour—not a minute—in annexing the property o the convents to the State. Do not trouble yourself about any dogma. Lay hands on the property of the monks, that is the really important matter, and let everything else take its chance.' (Vol. ii. p. 254.)

It is curious to find the same man at the same moment so anxious about the exact doctrinal teaching of the children in every French parish. The Nuncio at Paris, Cardinal Caprara, a tool in his hands, wrote a letter, intended to draw a permission from Rome, for the use of a single catechism in all the parishes of France. Consalvi, 'with his usual acuteness,' suspected something behind, and answered:—

'The Holy See has always desired, aimed at uniformity in the manner of teaching and learning Christian doctrine. For this end, Pius V., after the decree of the Council of Trent, ordered that the Roman catechism for parish priests should be published, and Clement VII. that of Bellarmine for children. Yet their liberty of choice has never been taken from the bishops, and especially from those beyond the Alps, except so far as is defined by Benedict XIV., in the constitution *Etsi Minimum*, Chap. xvii. Therefore the Holy Father, following the example of his predecessors, will not interfere with the French bishops in their choice of the catechism which each of them may judge most suitable to the special circumstances of his own flock, provided that the wise directions of Benedict XIV. are observed. . . . . Should the Government wish to give the preference to any one catechism, or perhaps to make a new one, and impose it by authority upon the use of the bishops, His Holiness would be unable not to regard that act as an insult to the whole body of the Episcopate. His Holiness would have it observed that the Divine Legislator has given the right of teaching only to his Apostles, and to the bishops, their successors, and *not to any others*. . . . . It does not belong therefore to the secular power to choose or to prescribe to the bishops the catechism which it prefers. This belongs only to the judgment of the Church. . . . . Should it come to your knowledge that anyone has a plan for taking an advantage of the religion of the Emperor, and obtaining from him the authorisation and promulgation of a catechism of this sort, your Eminence will not hesitate to warn his Majesty upon the subject, and to say to him, in the name of his Holiness, to be on his guard against the authors of such counsels, and that the Holy Father is persuaded that in matters of doctrine, certainly his Imperial Majesty has no thought of arrogating to himself a power which God has confided exclusively to the Church and to the Vicar of Jesus Christ. .... The Holy Father would feel the greatest repugnance to prescribe to the bishops of a whole nation the use of the same catechism in such a manner that the prelates could not vary from it according to the wants of their respective dioceses.' (Vol. ii. p. 280.)

It is a remarkable proof of Consalvi's foresight that he should have suspected a trap so skilfully prepared for him. Never, probably, did he suspect what really happened. Caprara suppressed the letters, and falsely declared that 'he had authority to approve the new catechism; and some days later (February 1806) formally approved it in the name and by the authority of the Pope.' Next appeared an official notice that a catechism 'uniform and obligatory upon all the dioceses of France was about to be published immediately with the official approbation of the Cardinal Legate.' When this 'Moniteur' reached Rome, Consalvi wrote in the name of the Pope a second letter expressing his doubts whether the announcement could be correct; but strictly requiring Caprara to take no step in the matter without referring it to Rome. This letter also Caprara suppressed, and it cannot be imagined that the Emperor did not well know all about these letters, but Caprara took care that he should have no official knowledge of them.

It soon appeared why so much trouble had been taken. The new catechism professed to be that of Bossuet, whose name suffices to throw any Frenchman into an ecstasy of admiration which deprives him of the use of his intellect. In the main it was so; but, in explaining the fourth commandment of God, Bossuet had taught that it requires us 'to respect all superiors, pastors, kings, magistrates, and others.'

'The Prince himself,' says M. D'Haussonville, who was none other than Lewis XIV., 'was familiarly mixed up with the crowd of "superiors."' What was enough for Louis was far from satisfying Napoleon. M. D'Haussonville shows that this part of the catechism was drawn up by himself and his minister. The duties of his subjects towards Napoleon fill three lessons. Napoleon at first wrote, 'Is submission to the Government of France a dogma of the Church?' The answer was his own writing—'Yes, Scripture teaches that he who resists the Powers resists the order of God. Yes; the Church imposes upon us the most special duties towards the Government of France, the protection of religion and of the Church. She requires us to love and cherish it, and to be ready to make any sacrifice in its service.' This was modified at the suit of the theologians at Paris.[1] But as the catechism finally stood it declares—

'Christians owe to the princes by whom they are governed, and in particular we owe to Napoleon I., our Emperor, love, reverence, obedience, fidelity, military service, tributes, &c. &c.'

It then gives the special claim of Napoleon I., as

'raised up by God under circumstances of difficulty to re-establish public worship, and the religion of our fathers, and to be its Protector. By his profound and active wisdom he has restored and preserved public order. By his mighty arm he defends the State. By the consecration he has received from the Sovereign Pontiff, the Head of the Universal Church, he has become the Lord's anointed. *Q.* What must we think of those who fail in their duty towards our Emperor? *A.* According to the Apostle St. Paul, they resist the order established by God Himself, and make themselves worthy of eternal damnation.'

There is a good deal more, but this is enough. One other thing Napoleon wanted to alter in Bossuet's catechism—the declaration, *extra ecclesiam nulla salus.* This, however, M. D'Haussonville

---

[1] I must refer to the author for the circumstances which made it impossible for the Pope formally to denounce this catechism and expose the perfidy by which the sanction of it was obtained.

says he gave up when it was pointed out to him that he had insisted on pronouncing eternal damnation against all who opposed his government, or who even had not sufficient love towards him. This argument *ad hominem*, says the author, prevailed, 'especially as it was only a question of pronouncing the damnation of some souls.' The fact is that Napoleon was enamoured of that style of argument. He was fond of calling together the clergy of a district and giving them a charge in a style of his own. To such an assembly at Breda (March 6, 1810) he delivered a long sermon, ending, 'if you persist in your maxims, you will be wretched here below, and damned in the other world.' It was well that the latter part of the sentence was less in his power than the former. To the clergy of the Department of the Dyle he declared, 'I won't have either the religion or the notions of the Gregory VII.s, the Bonifaces, the Juliuses, who wished to subject kingdoms and kings to their power, and excommunicated emperors to disturb the tranquillity of peoples. I believe, let people say what they may, that they are burning in hell for the disturbance they stirred up by their extravagant pretensions.'

The mainspring of his government in matters ecclesiastical was perpetual imprisonment, authorised by his simple *fiat* communicated in a letter to his Minister of Police. How many hundreds of country priests were left thus to die by inches in state prisons for years together, merely because some one had complained to the Emperor of a sermon delivered on some occasion, I have no means of estimating. The number must have been very large. Lord Shaftesbury's mouth must water when he thinks how the Ritualists would have fared under the great Emperor. First, he would have a check upon all appointments. To effect this he required that for all the high clerical offices a degree in the imperial university should be a *sine quâ non*, and this, as he writes to his Minister of Religion, 'can be refused in the case of any man known to entertain notions ultramontane or dangerous to authority.'[1] He writes to the same Minister to dictate subjects for Episcopal pastorals. It may suggest something to us to find him specially mentioning the wrongs of Ireland as a subject to be insisted upon. But he condescended lower than this. On one occasion, when no one as yet suspected that he was thinking of the divorce of Josephine, he was the guest of the Archbishop of Bordeaux. He was in high good humour and most munificent; even condescending to reprove the Archbishop for not allowing himself greater personal comforts. But the Grand Vicar and a chanoine ventured to state, in answer to some remark of the Emperor, the doctrine of the Church about divorce and the indissolubility of marriage. He was enraged, and had no sooner returned to Paris than he wrote to require the Archbishop to deprive them of their offices. To his Minister he wrote :—

'Make known my displeasure to M. Robert, priest at Bourges. He preached a very bad sermon on the 15th of August.' Sometimes he addressed his Minister of the Interior, to require him to set right ecclesiastics who, in his opinion, erred from their duty. More commonly, however, the orders were given to his Commandant of Gendarmerie, or by preference to his Minister of Police, the Duke of Otranto (Fouché), whom he charges to watch attentively the manner in which the members of the French clergy conducted themselves. The Abbé de Courcy,' he writes to M. Lacépède, 'does me great mischief. He is always corresponding with his parishioners [à ses diocesains]. I desire that that man be arrested and confined in a convent.' But before long convents did not seem to him a place of retreat sufficiently secure. Some days later Napoleon, this time addressing Fouché, wrote, ' It is important that you keep your eyes open upon the diocese of Poitiers. It is really shameful that you have not yet had the Abbé Stewens arrested. They are asleep, for how else could a wretched priest have escaped' (June 30th, 1805). His Minister of Police had generally a more lucky hand, and then his master addressed compliments to him, even from the heart of Poland.

[1] Vol. ii. p. 243.

'I see by your letter of the 12th that you have arrested a curé of la Vendée. You have done quite right. Keep him in prison.' It is needless to say that these arrests were not preceded by any investigation or followed by any trial. In proportion to the difficulty of the relations to the Holy See their number became more considerable, and thus little by little, in France as in Italy, the prisons were peopled by a multitude of obscure priests. They were committed sometimes to the dungeons of Vincennes, sometimes to the Isle of Sainte Marguerite, to Fenestrella, to Ivrée, and to all the places of confinement set apart for political offenders. In many cases there was nothing alleged against them except suspected opinions on matters of religious discipline, some thoughtless act (*propos?*) or insignificant fault into which they had been imprudently led by an excess of Ultramontane zeal. Once imprisoned, these unfortunate men became dangerous to release, for they would have been applauded and made much of as martyrs by the enthusiastic partisans of the Holy Father, who himself was confined as a prisoner at Savona. In prison, therefore, they were kept indefinitely. Of these poor priests, whose plebeian names have never figured in any history, everyone either perished in the dungeons which the Emperor had assigned to them, (if they were old men), or else never left them till after his fall. Many of them never had any means of guessing the particular reasons which led to their arrest. (Vol. ii. p. 246.)

I regret that my space forbids me to call attention to many details of extreme interest, especially with regard to the relations of the Emperor to the French clergy and laity.

NOTE.—I have been disappointed at not finding such clear information as I desired as to the grounds of the sentence of nullity passed upon the marriage of Josephine. The author says there are documents on this subject to which he has been refused access. They seem, although in this I may be mistaken, to have been made accessible to M. Thiers. One important fact he was the first to establish, viz., that a religious marriage between Napoleon and Josephine was celebrated by Cardinal Fesch the night before the Coronation at Notre Dame. The question is whether there were any real grounds for pronouncing that marriage null. The great fact to prove that there must have been such grounds is that M. Émery, a man far above suspicion, delivered his opinion against the validity of the marriage. His reasons he did not state. The author says that Napoleon was so inconceivably shameless as to desire that the sentence of nullity should be grounded upon his having withholden his consent. It is difficult to suppose that other grounds would not be found were all the documents accessible. They may have been connected with a subject at which the author only hints in reference to the marriage of Louis Bonaparte with Hortense Beauharnais, and with the anger of Louis when it was proposed that the eldest son of that marriage should be declared presumptive heir to the Emperor, which he refused to sanction, as it would give colour to reports already existing as to the birth of that child.

VI.

PIUS VII. AND NAPOLEON I.[1]

THE history of the relations between Pius VII. and Napoleon I. naturally divides itself into two periods. The first embraces the years in which Pius was a Sovereign in possession of his dominions, and communicated with Napoleon as one monarch with another. The second includes those in which Pius VII. was a prisoner, in the power of the French Emperor. This may be considered to have commenced on February 2, 1808, the day on which the French took military possession of Rome, because on that day the temporal government of the Pope really came to an end; although the States of the Church were not formally annexed to the French Empire until May 17, 1809. I have already called attention to the portion of M. D'Haussonville's work in which he relates the events of the first period: I now propose to examine his account of the other, which extends from February 2, 1808, to the restoration of Pius VII. to the Vatican, May 24, 1814. In many respects this last is by far the most valuable part of his work. As long as Pius VII. was in fact, as well as right, an independent sovereign, and recognised as such by Napoleon himself, all communications between the two Governments were in their nature to a considerable degree public, and even those which were at the moment secret were in the possession of both parties: it was therefore comparatively difficult to the French Government to give to the world a wholly false account of them. From the day on

---

[1] 'L'Église Romaine et le Premier Empire, 1800–1814. Par M. le Comte D'Haussonville.' Lévy: Paris. Vol. iii.

which the Pope was a prisoner things were in this respect very different. Absolute secrecy as to everything which it did not suit the despot to make public was the universal system of the French Empire. The penalties by which it was enforced were so tremendous, that the attempt to preserve this secrecy actually succeeded to a degree which, to men who, like ourselves, have lived all our lives under a system of which entire publicity is the principal characteristic, seems almost inconceivable. And this secrecy was maintained in order to keep the field open for the free action of a system of lying, so enormous as to be truly portentous. To what extent this system was carried was, I believe, never known or imagined, even by the French themselves, before the publication of the result of M. D'Haussonville's researches. For although secrecy and lying were the characteristics of all Napoleon's dealings, both with the people of the French Empire and with the world around it, there was one department in which he felt it specially necessary to employ them. This was in all that regarded religion. Upon this he expressly wrote to his ministers, —' I do not wish people to talk at all about ecclesiastical affairs ;' and by a system of terror, unscrupulously carried out, he succeeded in making it during almost fourteen years quite impossible for private friends, priests, bishops, and cardinals so much as to speak of them, except with all the secrecy and restraint which marks the councils of men plotting against a strong and unscrupulous Government. The consequence was that what really happened with regard to the Pope, while he was a prisoner in the power of Napoleon, was unknown at the time, in a great measure, even to Napoleon's own ministers, and absolutely to the French clergy and laity, and (it need not be said) to the world at large. It might have been expected that as soon as the First Empire had fallen all would be made public. Many things no doubt were. Private journals, written by men who had taken part in the ecclesiastical events of that Empire, have years ago been published and have thrown light upon many of them. The Memoirs of Cardinal Pacca, for instance, made known a vast number of most valuable and interesting facts. But there was very much of which no record existed, except in the secret correspondence of Napoleon himself with his ministers, and in that which went on between them and their agents, especially those who from time to time were entrusted with the charge of the Pope's person, or who though he regarded them as his friends were in reality placed as spies about him; or, again, who were commissioned to negotiate with him on the part of the Emperor. All these invaluable documents have been carefully preserved, and many of them have already been published in the vast collection of the 'Correspondence of Napoleon I.,' which was published at the expense of the French Government during the Second Empire. That collection is a mine of invaluable historical materials, and it professes to supply the means of writing a true and correct history of the ecclesiastical relations of Napoleon I., and especially of his conduct towards Pius VII., no less than of his military and political acts. In fact, very many of his letters, instructions, memoranda, and other documents bearing on these subjects are actually given. Everything has been done which could possibly suggest to a diligent student of that huge collection, that it is a full and fair account of all that happened while Pius VII. was a prisoner, so far as it was known at the time to the French Government itself. That it is so, has, I believe, always been taken for granted. As a matter of fact, however, the impression given is as false as it could be made by the *suppressio veri*. This has been M. D'Haussonville's great discovery. He has, most carefully and successfully, sought out the letters, reports, and other documents which the commissioners, appointed by Napoleon III. to publish the correspondence of his uncle, have suppressed without giving the least notice of their existence. These suppressed documents supply the materials of the whole of his narrative during several successive years.

It appeared at a fortunate moment, when the extreme severity with which the press was silenced during the earlier years of the Second Empire had been relaxed, but before the overthrow of that Empire. At an earlier period the work would at once have been suppressed, for the picture it presents of Napoleon personally, as well as of his system of government, is most disgraceful—nay, contemptible. Especially it exposes the gross, wilful, and deliberate falsehood of the whole of that portion of the memoirs dictated to his friends by the dethroned tyrant at St. Helena, which refers to the ecclesiastical events of his reign, whether relating to Pius VII. himself, or to the bishops and clergy of the Empire. That this was felt to be the case by the Government of Napoleon III. is proved by the manner in which they dealt with it. A few years earlier it is certain that the serial work in which M. D'Haussonville's labours were first published, the 'Revue des Deux Mondes,' would not have dared to publish it, and that any periodical which had ventured to do so would have been suppressed. When the laws against free publication were relaxed, the Government showed its dislike to the book as well as it could, by giving orders that M. D'Haussonville should be exceptionally refused access to the documents in the 'Archives,' which were open to the public in general. The book may have lost something by this exclusion, but it has gained more, for it proves that the attention of the Emperor and his Government had been turned to it, and that, if they could, they would have denied the authenticity of the very numerous letters and documents of Napoleon I. which the author gives, but which had been suppressed by the commissioners appointed to publish his writings. Again, had the work first appeared after the fall of the Second Empire, some doubt might have been thrown upon it, as has actually been the case with papers of Napoleon III. published under the 'Government of Defence.' All this is now prevented, and M. D'Haussonville's volumes, in which he carefully puts together both all that has before been published, and also all that has hitherto been suppressed, will henceforth be the main authority for historians who undertake to treat of the conduct of Napoleon, either towards the Pope or towards the Church in his empire.

Neither must it be supposed that it is, like the 'Correspondence' itself, so unwieldy as to be without value to any except historians and deep students. The work extends to five volumes. But it is luxuriously printed, and a very large proportion of each volume is composed of 'Pièces Justificatives,' consisting of Napoleon's suppressed letters and other documents, which, though invaluable as authorities for what is stated in the text, need not be read by any ordinary student, who will be satisfied with the account given of them by the author. In the fifth volume, for instance, these documents occupy two hundred and fifteen pages out of five hundred and sixty-seven. The narrative, moreover, is so interesting as to carry the reader on, whether he intends it or not; and it is much easier to take up the book than to lay it down.

The early part of the third volume gives an account of the state of things in Rome during the seventeen months which elapsed between the occupation of the city by Napoleon's troops and the violent carrying away of the Holy Father into France. It is impossible not to be struck with the parallel between the situation of Pius VII. during these months and that of Pius IX. at the present moment. Thus we find that the French took possession of the printing-offices and the post-offices in obedience to positive commands from Napoleon himself, who wrote to his representative at Rome (vol. iii. p. 9) to 'prevent the publication of any printed papers or acts, of whatever kind, opposed to France, which might be put out by the Roman Government, and to make the police and the booksellers of Rome responsible for them.'

The Holy Father, however, had already drawn up a protest against the occupation, which must have been printed before the entrance of the French troops, as it was posted at all the usual places on the day they came in. It is said to have been 'clandestinely printed during the night, and to have made its unexpected appearance on the walls of Rome.' It declared—

His Holiness Pius VII., being unable to fulfil all the demands made upon him on the part of the French Government, because he is forbidden to do so by the voice of conscience and by his sacred duties, feels himself bound to submit to all the disastrous consequences with which he has been threatened in case of refusal, and even to the military occupation of his capital. Resigned in humility of heart to the impenetrable judgments of Heaven, he puts his cause into the hands of God, but he will not fail in the essential obligation of maintaining his sovereign rights, and has therefore commanded us to protest, and he does hereby formally protest, in his own name and in that of his successors, against all usurpation of his dominions: it being his will that the rights of the Holy See should ever be, and remain intact. (Vol. iii. p. 5.)

A protest, in the main similar, was also presented to all the ambassadors of foreign Powers in Rome. After this the Holy Father (like Pius IX. at this moment) remained passive.

Satisfied that he had saved his honour by the protest affixed to the walls of his capital, having made up his mind in spite of the importunities of the *corps diplomatique* not to stir out of the enclosure of the Quirinal, so as to mark the more strongly that he considered himself a prisoner; Pius VII. had laid in a stock of patience. He did not dislike, in his capacity of Sovereign, to shut himself up as long as possible in a resistance purely passive, and there was no saying to what point his resignation would go. (Vol. iii. p. 28.)

Thus, as the author says, the only embarrassment caused by the occupation of Rome was that felt by the usurper.

What was to be the next move? Napoleon had already resolved to annex the States of the Church; but he always liked to make some excuse for every outrage, and the modern custom of *plébiscites*, though 'a Napoleonic idea,' had not yet been applied to such cases. He would have thought himself degraded by such a device as that employed the other day by Victor Emmanuel. Not that he would have felt that there was anything degrading in its falsehood. That was a notion which evidently never presented itself to his imagination. So far, he would have been the last man to have any scruple in professing to have received in a day, twice as many votes as could physically have been taken in the time, by the method of voting adopted ; but he would have felt it unworthy of his dignity to profess that he held Rome merely by the election of a Roman mob. What he did resolve upon was to drive the Holy Father to resistance by further injuries, and he chose them with his usual skill. The Pope had shown that he was ready to submit to any outrage upon his temporal sovereignty, although he would neither do nor omit anything by which he might make himself responsible for it. Napoleon therefore resolved to interfere with his spiritual administration. This could not be carried on without the assistance of a body of ecclesiastics. The Emperor therefore determined, that all the dignitaries of the Church, cardinals, bishops, priests, &c., 'including those who discharged about the Pope's person purely spiritual functions, relating only to the cure of souls,' should be driven or forcibly carried away from Rome. The only exception was to be in the case of natives of the States of the Church. The Pope gave positive commands to each cardinal not to leave Rome, and, should he be carried away by force, not to continue his journey any farther than he was so taken. The Emperor began with the cardinals, and then went on to the bishops and other prelates, born in the kingdom of Naples, many of whom occupied the most important positions in the Pope's spiritual administration. The Neapolitan cardinals were carried away by force, the prelates received orders to follow them. The Pope (against the advice of those around him) recalled his legate from Paris, and having no other means of publicly expressing his feelings, (for the printing-presses had been seized,) he collected the cardinals remaining in Rome and addressed to them in an allocution the strongest protest, ending,—

'We exhort, nay we entreat, we conjure the Emperor and King Napoleon to change his resolution, and to return to the sentiments which he manifested at the beginning of his reign. Let him remember that the Lord God is a King far above all kings, far above himself, all-powerful as he may be; that He accepts no man's person, and respects no grandeur, be it what it may; and that those who command others will themselves be one day most severely judged by Him. We understand that we have now a great persecution to endure, but we are fully prepared for it, being fortified by those words of the Divine Master, "Blessed are they who suffer persecution for the sake of righteousness."'

There was no possibility of delusion; and at Rome especially none was entertained. The recall of the cardinal legate and the allocution pronounced by the Holy Father in the Consistory of March 16th, were acts which could not fail to excite to the extremest point the fury of the Emperor. For several weeks the members of the Sacred College and all the functionaries of the Pontifical Government were in trembling expectation of seeing ruthless orders arrive from France which would bring the fatal dispute to a crisis. (Vol. iii. p. 39.)

Yet the expected thunderbolt was delayed, and the reason of the delay was characteristic. It was a rule with Napoleon never to run the slightest risk of having on his hands two difficult matters at the same time. Daring and unscrupulous as he ever was, never until he had become intoxicated by the long continuance of success and prosperity such as never fell to the lot of any other man of whom history speaks, did he, in a single instance, forget the restraint which this rule imposed. He was at this moment starting to Bayonne, whither he had lured the King of Spain. His whole mind was engrossed with plans, all perfidious and shameless, but each weighed with the calmest and most calculating prudence, as to the future fate of the monarch who had been so unhappy as to trust to his honour, and of the kingdom of which he resolved to deprive him; and no provocation would have moved him to get into any difficulty about the Pope, so long as there was any possibility that the Spanish affair might yet give him trouble. Neither was it his way to threaten when he had made up his mind to strike. As he wrote at this very crisis to his brother Louis, offering him, before it was taken from the head of Ferdinand, the crown of which he intended to dispose (Vol. iii. p. 41), 'A thing should be completed before it is known that we have even thought of it.' As yet therefore, he took no decisive measure, but left it to his ministers to keep the Holy Father in a state of perpetual torment by one act of aggression after another. Thus the Marches and Umbria were formally annexed to his 'Kingdom of Italy,' and formed into three departments. All cardinals, prelates, officers, and other functionaries born in that kingdom were ordered immediately to return to it, on pain of the confiscation of all their property. The French troops (by a disgraceful stratagem) forced their way into the Quirinal and disarmed the Pope's guards. Pius VII. then wrote to the Bishops of Umbria and the Marches to forbid both clergy and laity to take any oath of fidelity to the intrusive Government, or accept any employment under it. The bishops and clergy were not to sing *Te Deum* on its establishment, but an oath of passive obedience, submission, and non-resistance might be taken. Individuals should never disturb the public peace by plots and factions, because this commonly results in still more grave disasters and scandals (p. 52). The French general at Rome replied to this by seizing, in the Quirinal, and carrying off to Sinigaglia (of which he was bishop), the Pope's Secretary of State, Cardinal Gabrielli, successor to Cardinal Doria, who being a Genoese by birth, had already been ordered to return home, Genoa having been annexed to France. When the news of these events reached Napoleon, who was still at

Bayonne, his repeated charge to his agents in Italy was to keep things quiet, to take care that nothing got into print, and that no noise was made.

Cardinal Pacca was now made the Pope's minister. The French general gave him notice that, the Emperor had given him orders to hang or shoot any person in the States of the Church who should oppose his sovereign will. 'General,' replied the Cardinal, 'you ought by this time to have discovered that the ministers of His Holiness do not allow themselves to be intimidated by threats. As far as I am personally concerned, I shall faithfully execute the orders of my sovereign come what may.' There the matter rested for the moment. On September 6th, 1808, two French officers arrested Pacca in his apartment in the Quirinal, and told him that they were to conduct him to Benevento, his native place. He obtained leave to send word to the Pope, and in a few minutes the door was thrown open and Pius VII. entered. He forbad the Cardinal to submit, took him by the hand, and led him to his own apartments, where he kept him. Of this scene we have a most curious description. And thus things went on for several months. Rome was in a strange state.

The Holy Father was still morally obeyed and reverenced by the immense majority of his subjects as if still in possession of his temporal power. The French general on his side allied, by the necessity of his position, against his own will, to the faction of disorder, maintained discipline not only in the ranks of his own army, which was exemplary in its conduct, but also among his compromising allies.' (Vol. iii. p. 81.)

But it became more and more clear that this state of things could not last much longer. Napoleon, though so anxious to keep everything quiet, was not too busy to think of petty annoyances which he thought it possible to offer to the Holy Father, or to write to his agents from the heart of Spain to prescribe them. When the spring of 1809 came he had left Spain and had for a second time made himself master of Vienna, the Austrian Empire having renewed the war: and from Schönbrunn he sent orders for the annexation of Rome to his empire.

On the 10th of June, at two o'clock P.M., the Pontifical flag was pulled down from the castle of S. Angelo and the tricolour hoisted. It was saluted by a discharge of artillery, while the French troops proclaimed through the city, with the sound of trumpets, the Imperial decree, dated from Vienna.

The minister of the Pope shall tell his own tale. 'I rushed,' writes Cardinal Pacca, 'into the apartment of the Holy Father, and as we met, each pronounced the words of our Saviour, *Consummatum est*. It is difficult to describe my feelings, but the sight of the Holy Father, who preserved an unalterable tranquillity, both greatly edified me and restored my courage. A few minutes later my nephew brought me a copy of the Imperial decree. The Pope rose and followed me to the window to hear me read it. I tried to overcome the first pain of the moment, and to read with attention this important document, by which the measures we had to take were to be regulated, but my just and deep indignation at the sacrilege that hour consummated, the presence close to me, before my face, of my unfortunate Sovereign the Vicar of Jesus Christ, waiting to hear from my mouth his sentence of dethronement, the calumnies which at the first glance of my eye I saw in this impious decree, the continual roar of the cannon which announced, with insulting triumph, the most iniquitous sacrilege,—all this so deeply moved me, and so much affected my sight, that I was unable to read, without frequent interruption and a half-choked voice, the principal articles of the decree. Then, attentively watching the Pope, I saw his countenance affected at the first words, and remarked the signs, not of fear or dejection, but of an indignation only too natural. By degrees he recovered himself, and listened to what I read with great calmness and resignation. When it was finished the Holy Father went to the table, and, without saying a word, signed the copies of a protest in Italian which was stuck up in Rome the night following. (Vol. iii. p. 98.)

Two forms of a Bull of Excommunication had already been drawn up by Cardinal Pietro, one to be signed if Napoleon should seize the person of the Pope at the same time that he took possession of Rome; the other if he should (as actually happened) leave him for the moment at liberty. This last was signed the same day and posted at S. Peter's, S. Mary Major, S. John Lateran, and the Market Place. Although posted in the broad day, none of the persons who did it were arrested or even discovered. It is stated by well-informed persons at Rome (but not mentioned by M. D'Haussonville) that this was managed by a man who carried on his back a large barrel like those in which wine is carried at Rome. He leaned his burden against the wall, as if to relieve himself of its weight; while he thus stood a boy who was concealed in the barrel opened a small door which had been prepared in it, and pasted the paper on the wall. When the man moved on, it was left behind, and yet he had not so much as turned his eyes towards the wall.

The publication of this Bull was immediately followed by the seizing of the Pope's person.

Napoleon always declared, he wrote in his memoirs, he repeated several times over to M. de Las Casas in his conversations at St. Helena, that he never gave orders for the arrest of the Pope. When he made this prodigious assertion, Napoleon I. did not suspect that his correspondence would at a later period be officially published by Napoleon III. .... The letter written to his brother-in-law, the King of Naples, leaves no room for evasion. 'If the Pope, contrary to the spirit of his order and of the Gospel, preaches revolt, and tries to make use of the immunity of his house to cause circulars to be printed, *he must be arrested.*' (Vol. iii. p. 102.)

It is remarkable, observes the author, that ' we already possess four accounts of the carrying away of the Holy Father, all written by eye-witnesses, or, to speak more exactly, by actors in the drama.' The Pope ordered the doors to be locked, and no person whatever to be admitted after dark. Sentinels stood where they could see anyone who approached the palace, and the populace continually watched all the movements of the troops, and gave notice of everything to Cardinal Pacca. General Radet wrote to the French Minister of War : 'The horizon gets darker. The Pope governs more effectually by lifting his finger than we do with our bayonets.' It was essential that the violence about to be done to his person should be concealed from the people till it was completed; and this was skilfully managed. The general found that the Pope's sentinel left his post at daybreak. Some French soldiers who had waited till then got in at an upstairs window into an unoccupied room, and opened the door. The general did not know the way to the apartment of the Vicar of Christ; but, that the resemblance to his Lord might be more complete, those who came to seize him were guided by a traitor, a servant, who had been a thief, and who had accepted hire for his treason. It was at daybreak on the 6th of July, 1809; yet, early as it was, Pius VII. was found quietly seated on the sofa opposite the door of his apartment, with the two Cardinals, Pacca and Despuig, sitting on either side; for he had given the most positive orders that he should immediately be awakened in case of any alarm, and, on hurrying to his room, they had found him dressing. 'Now,' he had said, 'I am with my true friends.' Cardinal Despuig had then proposed that he should retire to the private chapel, and there await the soldiers; but the Pope thought there would not be time, and that if he were overtaken going to the chapel, it would look as if he were flying. The French soldiers came on, breaking open the doors of the antechambers :—

To avoid disorder, he gave orders that the door of the room should be opened. Then Radet came in, not yet knowing either where or in whose presence he was; but he soon discovered by the manner of the men who followed him, some of whom (not to mention him who acted as guide) were Romans, to whom the person of the Holy Father was known. Finding that he was in the Presence, Radet took off his hat, and sending back most of his band caused to enter one by one the greater part of the officers of his suite and some non-commissioned officers of gendarmerie, who, silently gliding in at the half-opened door and along the wall of the apartment, ranged themselves in order, with drawn swords and arms grounded, on his right and left. Thus the room was occupied by two groups drawn up facing each other. At the head of the one General Radet, his hat in his hand, booted and spurred, his sword at his side, in the attitude of a military man who has just been taking a place by assault, but perfectly respectful, and at his side a dozen Frenchmen, officers commissioned and non-commissioned, with whom were mixed two or three officers of the Roman civic guard, who were followed by some of the dregs of the people. Opposite to him the Pope, in an ecclesiastical habit as simple as possible, wearing on his finger (says our Italian authority) the Pontifical ring which Pius VI. had worn during his captivity in France, the two Cardinals seated by him, and behind him a group made up of the principal servants of his household. Each party looked at the other, and silence lasted for more than five minutes. It was evident that General Radet was much disconcerted. He could not without difficulty recover his self-control; it seemed that he wished to speak, but the words would not come. At last he came forward a few steps, bowed low, and said to his Holiness that he had to perform a painful mission—a mission imposed on him by his oath and by the sacred duties of his position. At these words the Pope stood up, and looking at him with dignity, said, 'What do you want with me? and why have you come at such an hour to disturb my rest and my house?' 'Most Holy Father,' replied General Radet, 'I come in the name of my Government, to repeat to your Holiness the proposal of giving up your temporal power. If your Holiness consents to this, I have no doubt matters can be arranged, and the Emperor will treat your Holiness with the greatest respect.' Pius VII. replied, 'If you have felt yourself bound to execute such orders of your Emperor because of your oath of fidelity and obedience, consider the duty imposed on us —on us, We say,—to maintain the rights of the Holy See, to which we are bound by oaths so numerous. We have no power either to yield or abandon what is not our own. The Temporalities belong to the Church, and we are merely the administrator. The Emperor may have power to tear us in pieces, but that he will not obtain from us. After all that we have done for him, could we look for treatment such as this?' Radet was more and more disconcerted. 'I know, Holy Father, that the Emperor is under great obligations to you.' Yes; and more than you are aware of. But, to cut this short, what are your orders?' 'Most Holy Father, I regret the commission imposed upon me; but since such is the resolution of your Holiness, I am compelled to say that my orders are to conduct you with me.' At these words the Holy Father, who till then had maintained the most dignified tone, suddenly addressed himself to Radet and said, with an air of tenderness and compassion, 'Indeed, my son, that commission is not one to bring down on you the Divine blessing.' Then, lifting his eyes to heaven, 'This, then, is the return made to me for all that I have done for your Emperor. This is the reward for my great concessions towards himself and towards the Church of France. But perhaps God has seen that I have committed a fault in them. It is His will to punish me, and I submit with all humility.' (Vol. iii. p. 120.)

As Radet was leading him to his bedroom, he suggested to the Pope to commit any valuable property to safe hands. He replied, 'A man who does not care for life, cares less for worldly property.'

He then took only his Breviary, and the Crucifix which he usually carried hanging at his breast. Then, leaning on Radet's arm and followed by Cardinal Pacca, he went down the great staircase of the Quirinal. On reaching the great doors, Pius VII. stood still, and gave his blessing to Rome. The French troops were drawn up in order of battle on the Great Place of Monte-Cavallo. None of the population of Rome were either there or at the windows. It was four in the morning, and profound silence reigned everywhere. General Radet says that the soldiers received with a sacred reverence the blessing of the Pope. He then caused the Pope and Cardinal Pacca to get into a carriage, the blinds of which had been carefully nailed, and the doors of which were then locked by a *gendarme*, took his place on the box with a quartermaster, and gave orders to the postillions to go out of the city by the Porta Pia and go round, outside the wall, to the Porta del Popolo. The carriage was escorted by a detachment of *gendarmerie*.' (Vol. iii. p. 123.)

It was nearly five A.M. when the carriage, with fresh post-horses, started at full speed for Florence. The Pope asked the Cardinal whether he had any money. They found that the Cardinal had about sevenpence halfpenny, the Pope tenpence. 'We are travelling in apostolic fashion,' said Pacca. Pius VII. added with a smile, 'This is all that remains to me of my dominions.' The Cardinal had a secret feeling of uneasiness, because it had been by himself that the publication of the Bull of Excommunication had been advised. He was relieved when the Pope added with an air of satisfaction, 'It is well that we published the Bull of June 10th, for how could we have done it now?'

Pius VII. was aged, and afflicted with a painful disease, which was aggravated by travelling, and he suffered much on his journey. He reached Florence on the 8th, near midnight. It was governed by Napoleon's sister, Eliza. At three A.M. a colonel arrived with orders that the Pope should instantly go farther. He particularly wished to stay to say mass, especially as it was Sunday, but she would hear of no delay. This was not from cruelty, but from absolute terror. Three days brought him in a very suffering state to the immediate neighbourhood of Genoa. This was then called part of France. But the fear of the authorities was as great as it had been in Tuscany. The mountains came so near to the sea, that there was no possibility of sending the august prisoner by land in any way which would avoid the city. But he was hurried by night to the shore, and carried by sea across the Gulf of Genoa. Thus he reached Alessandria on his way towards Turin. But the Prince Borghese, who governed Turin, was far too much alarmed to let him come there, and he was hurried on by Mondovri and Rivoli to Grenoble.

Whence all this fear? It cannot be doubted that each of Napoleon's satraps had at heart a real terror, like that which induced the Philistines to send away the Ark of God—a sincere dread of the Divine judgments upon anyone who should take any part in keeping as a prisoner the Vicar of Christ. But mixed with this was a horrible dread of the tyrant whose instruments they were. They had received no commands from the Emperor.

How was the Pope to be received? If he were treated either with too great or too little severity, who could say into what disgrace they might fall? There he was, an old and ailing man; what if he should die in their hands? The matter was made ten times worse by the enthusiasm of the people. The Holy Father had been hurried from Rome unknown to the inhabitants. But the tidings of his having been carried off soon spread, not by newspapers, for none were allowed to publish anything without the special permission of the authorities, but from mouth to mouth. The farther he went, the longer the news had been spreading, and, therefore, the greater the enthusiasm of the people and the crowds who assembled by the road-side in the country and in the market-places of the towns to kneel for his blessing. 'The journey,' says M. D'Haussonville, 'which at its beginning had been that of a martyr, soon became a procession of triumph.' The farther he went the more decidedly was this the case, and the greater was the fear of the subordinate authorities. The people, naturally enough, could not believe that their religious Emperor could be otherwise than pleased by their expressions of loyalty to the Pope, whom they had so lately greeted with the same enthusiasm as he went to Paris for the coronation.

When news of these things reached Napoleon he was far from pleased. To deny that he had ever authorised the arrest of the Pope was naturally his first instinct, for no lie was too mean for that mighty monarch, that vast genius. As things were, he ordered that he should be sent to Savona on the Riviera, and that Cardinal Pacca should be separated from him, and shut up in the State Prison of Fenestrella. It is a curious instance of the absolute suppression of all news in France under his tyranny, that no journal was allowed to allude to the fact that the Pope had ever come into France. At Grenoble, at the moment when the town was thronged with multitudes from all the country round to kneel for his blessing, the local official journal made no allusion to his having ever been there. Throughout France and in Paris nothing was known about it. Strange to say, there appeared in the 'Moniteur' a letter dated from Grenoble on the very day on which the Pope was hurried away by orders given by Fouché in obedience to those of Napoleon. Those who had heard reports that he had been there, and knew not what to believe, turned eagerly, says the author, expecting some official news on the matter. The letter said: 'All men's minds here are occupied by the passage through the commune of Bornin (which the Pope passed through on approaching Grenoble) of an unknown animal. The marks it left seem to show that it must have been a reptile of extraordinary size.' Then followed half a page of details about this reptile, which, it was added, after having wholly engrossed public attention, disappeared in a torrent. What induced Fouché to publish this one can hardly imagine. Was it an attempt to laugh at the Pope? Napoleon, at least, evidently felt the whole thing to be no laughing matter. Nothing could exceed the precautions taken to keep the Pope's journey from Grenoble to Savona out of public observation. He was not allowed to pass through any town when it could be avoided, and so strictly was he watched, that when the uncle of the Emperor, Cardinal Fesch, who was Archbishop of Lyons, sent his Grand Vicars to pay homage to the Holy Father and present him with some money, they were not allowed access to him. For a long time France was not let to know that the Pope had ever left Rome. At last, when it became necessary to admit that he was at Savona, the only version of the matter which Napoleon allowed to be published was that he had gone thither of his own accord. As late as 1811, when he had been in the most strict imprisonment for nearly two years, the Emperor declared in his official message to the clergy of France assembled by his command in what he called a National Council, 'The Pope had so acted that his presence at Rome became useless; and some of his partisans might, against his own will, make it dangerous. On the 6th of July he left Rome without the knowledge of the Emperor, and came to Savona, where his Majesty caused him to be received, entertained, and established with all the respect due to misfortune.' (Vol. iii. p. 141.)

Pius VII. reached Savona on the 21st of August, 1809. All that passed there until he was carried, still as a prisoner, to Fontainebleau on the 9th of June, 1812, was kept at the time absolutely secret; and M. D'Haussonville says (vol. v. p. 140) that at least the whole of the negotiations carried on with him on the part of Napoleon have been till now wholly unknown, 'no historian, either ecclesiastical or lay, having made any mention of them.' His own account of them, in general very minute, is taken exclusively from the official documents, and although there are expressions here and there which a Catholic could not have used, I cannot but express my astonishment, on the whole, at the tone of fairness maintained by the author, who, it is to be specially observed, is a French Protestant. I must in justice confess that I doubt whether any English Protestant, even if he belonged to the school which most loudly claims to call itself Catholic, would have written in a tone of so much candour, and even reverence towards the Pope. But this I believe to be the natural result of the different position of Protestantism in the two countries. In England Protestantism, as a religion, is in its death-struggle. In France it has long ago been dead and buried; and a French Protestant, even if, like M. Guizot, he presents the strange inconsistency of being still a really religious man, is, in truth, only a 'Christian unattached.' There are, no doubt, plenty of the same class in England, but they are not our religious men, still less are they to be found in the school which cares most about religious questions. Such persons would have written, and I fear will read, the deeply interesting history before me with their minds occupied with the idea of proving that communion with the Pope is not essential to a Catholic position, and other such figments, which to an impartial looker-on like M. D'Haussonville would seem very pitiful nonsense. That he never felt any wish to be a Catholic is only too probable. But that he would feel it childish and absurd to pretend to be a Catholic without being in communion with Pius IX. is most certain and evident. Such nonsense is a growth indigenous in our happy island, and peculiar to it.

When the Pope arrived at Savona, after residing four days in the family of Count Egidio Santone, where he was received with all due reverence, he was moved to the Episcopal Palace, where his apartments were fitted up, by order of the Emperor, in a manner suited 'to a sovereign prince of the first dignity' (vol. iii. p. 395). He was surrounded with servants to whom high salaries were offered in the name of the Emperor. He was using 'a poor copper lamp and a very ordinary desk;' but this was no sooner seen than 'a superb silver lustre and an escritoire magnificently inlaid with gold' were substituted for them. 'Equipages, horses, &c., were supplied, and an income of four thousand pounds monthly promised him.' All this was declined 'with great gentleness and many thanks,' and those around him were requested to receive nothing except actual necessaries. General Cæsar Berthier (brother to the Prince of Wagram) was sent to preside over his household, with orders to keep up a good establishment, and invite habitually the friends of the Holy Father, to whom all possible reverence was to be shown. At the same time the strictest *surveillance* was to be maintained. The general was never to be absent from the Pope's *levées*, or, if absent, was to be represented there by an officer of *gendarmerie*. At the same time there must be nothing which could suggest the idea of captivity. The difficulty of reconciling these orders, says the author, was increased because the Pope would not in any degree lend himself to lessen it. He found pleasure in returning to the simple life he had led as a monk before he rose in the Church

He refused to attend the Cathedral pontifically, and would only say mass in his private chapel. 'There he was often found in tears, praying not only for the oppressed Church, but also for the prince who, after having so decidedly protected it, had suddenly become its most vehement persecutor. His only relaxation was to walk in the walled garden of the Episcopal Palace, where his walk was only about fifty paces backward and forward.' It was difficult for Napoleon to deal with a man of habits like these. Where wealth and splendour were considered no gain, it was hard to discover what would be felt as a loss. Hitherto the Emperor had found that if he began with violence and intimidation his victims were only too glad to accept a reconciliation upon any terms he might be so gracious as to concede. He had calculated without a misgiving that such must be the case with Pius VII. But he found himself wholly mistaken. Unluckily, he could not go on as if nothing had happened, for do what he would, he could not help negotiating with his prisoner. Cardinal Pacca might be left at Fenestrella till he died, and things in France would go on quietly; but without Bulls from the Holy Father no Bishop could take possession of his See, and he could not leave the Sees vacant. Almost from the first, therefore, he discovered that by violence against the Pope instead of smoothing the course of affairs, he had thrown them into a state of embarrassment out of which he himself, all-powerful as he was, was utterly unable to extricate them, and that, however unwillingly, he must negotiate with his unresisting prisoner. This was a position wholly new and eminently distasteful to him.

His first step was to suggest to his uncle, Cardinal Fesch, to the Cardinals Caprara and Maury, on whom he could reckon, and to several of the French bishops, to write, as if of their own will, to the Holy Father, and explain how much the Church was suffering by the want of canonical bishops. The letters would have been delivered to the Pope before he reached Savona, if they had not been intercepted by the zeal of Fouché. When they arrived, there was a remarkable difference between them. 'The letter of Cardinal Fesch was full of expressions of reverence and of a sincere sympathy for the recent sufferings of the Holy Father. That of Cardinal Maury made evident and becoming allusion to them.' Cardinal Caprara, who had been the Legate of Pius VII. at Paris, and M. de Barral, Archbishop of Tours, made no allusion to the subject. The Archbishop seemed to suppose that the refusal of the Pope to institute 'proceeded from some childish caprice, and that he had no motive to assign for it.' The Cardinal did not seem even to have heard, either of the departure of the Pope from Rome or of the seizure of his dominions. The Pope's answer would have made him aware of these facts if he had really been ignorant. It ended by declaring his wish to fill up the Sees, but that he could not do so, consistently with his duty, till he had about him his natural counsellors, the members of the Sacred College. When Napoleon saw this answer, says M. D'Haussonville, he seems for the first time in his life to have felt a doubt as to the wisdom of his own manner of proceeding. He resolved that while the Pope should have no ecclesiastical advisers, he would have some for himself, and he constituted an 'ecclesiastical committee' composed of a few whom he believed he could trust. This committee at least saved him from one inconceivable absurdity which he had so far contemplated as, according to his custom, to make his minister write him a report as to the details of the plan. This was that of calling a general council by his own authority, and presiding in it himself. The committee seem to have convinced him that this would not do, and he took up another idea (which Cardinal Maury says he suggested to him), that the bishops nominated might be sent to administer their dioceses, receiving from the Chapters faculties as Vicars Capitular, a plan from which the unfortunate ecclesiastics shrank with the strongest repulsion.

The fact is that the contest of Napoleon against the Church was in truth a necessary part of his system, and must have come on sooner or later, even if the questions connected with the temporal power of the Pope and the difficulties about the institution of the bishops springing out of it, had never been raised. The real cause of the quarrel was, that he was resolved to be an absolute despot, without control and without limitation. Now the Church is the kingdom of Heaven, and it was even more impossible that a man, who had made up his mind to be absolute master of the civilised world, could be content that the souls of his own subjects and their spiritual relations should be exempted from his dominion, than that he should be content that the neighbouring kingdoms should enjoy a real independence. His attack upon the Pope was as certain to come on as his wars with Austria, Prussia, or Russia. Upon this point M. Thiers and M. D'Haussonville are of one mind.[1] M. Thiers says what he wanted from the Pope was, ' the suppression of the temporal power of the Holy See—the annexation of Rome to the territory of the Empire—the establishment of a Papacy dependent upon the new Emperor of the West, residing at Paris or Avignon, enjoying splendid palaces, a salary of eighty thousand pounds, and many other advantages, but placed under the authority of the Emperor of the French, as the Russian Church is under the authority of the Czars, and Islamism under the authority of the Sultans.' M. D'Haussonville himself says—

> Let us repeat, for upon this point delusion is impossible, the two monstrous chimeras of domination over all Catholic consciences and of the resurrection of a new Empire of the West, entertained at the same time and caressed with the same love by this strange genius, had now become to his disordered imagination substantial realities. In order to put his hand officially to the work, Napoleon, as we shall soon see, was waiting only till he had won a decisive victory over his

---

[1] Thiers, t. xiii. 35, quoted by D'Haussonville, iii. 412.

last adversary on the Continent—the Emperor Alexander. On the morrow of some triumphant treaty, signed at the gates of St. Petersburg or Moscow, a decree like that which after Wagram pronounced the deposition of the Pope from his temporal dominion—a decree all the particulars of which were already long since matured in his own mind—was all of a sudden to proclaim the Pope's subordination in spirituals to the will of the chief of the French Empire. The final catastrophe of the Russian expedition was necessary in order that Europe might be spared the spectacle, not less strange than lamentable, of the two despots reconciled and dividing between themselves the nations like a miserable flock, and each making himself in his own dominion the absolute master not only of the political destinies, but of the religious faith, of his wretched subjects. How would Napoleon have set about the realisation of his universal supremacy with regard to the Catholic faith? By what means would the terrible despot have set himself to overcome the obstacles, moral and material, which would certainly have been opposed to him by the branches of the Roman Church, which, spread over the European Continent, were not subject to his Empire, and those (more numerous still) in England, the United States, South America, the East, and over the whole surface of the globe, which were out of his reach? No man knows, and the world will never know; for the Emperor did not think fit to explain to us in his Memoirs, how he intended to set about a task so extraordinary. He preferred to carry with him to the grave this incomprehensible secret. (Vol. iii. p. 314.)

But, though his Memoirs do not explain how he imagined it possible to set about the undertaking, they leave no doubt that he really intended it, and it need hardly be said that the mere forming of such a design implied the deliberate intention of engaging in a life-and-death struggle with the Catholic Church. And as it was his marriage with an Austrian archduchess, which brought to the highest point the intoxication of his ambition, it was from that moment that he seems to have made up his mind to begin his attack upon the spiritual power of the Pope. On the second Sunday after his marriage, April 15, 1810, he directed his *ministre des cultes* to draw up a paper upon religious affairs, in which he was not only to lay down principles, but to give in detail all the measures which it would be expedient to adopt. It is explained, that this paper is 'not exactly a decree, because it will not be put into execution or published, but is to remain in the hands of the minister,' and that as circumstances arose which made it expedient that one or another part of the arrangements detailed in it should be carried into execution, a decree was to be published embodying them. Thus, writes Napoleon, 'the trouble of successive reports will be saved, and every time there is a measure to be taken the minister will recite both how much of the plan has been carried out and how much remains to be carried out.' 'These general arrangements,' he adds, 'must be divided according to the different territories and according to the order of matters.' This paper therefore, if we had it, which unfortunately is not the case, would show Napoleon's ideal of Church affairs, which he intended to carry out ultimately and by degrees. The order to the minister shows what the ideal was; for he says, 'things are to be laid down as they ought to be, and in an absolute manner, *as if no Pope existed.*' Nothing could more clearly show that he had, at this period, deliberately made up his mind, ultimately to take upon himself the whole power of the Pope throughout the world. In the meantime, however, he must begin by dealing with Pius VII., and how to do that was a matter of difficulty—a difficulty which he had himself created by his own violence and tyranny. By carrying the Pope away as a prisoner he had hoped to compel him to begin negotiations, and to approach Napoleon as a petitioner. That hope had been completely frustrated. It now appeared that he might wait as long as the Pope lived, and that things would remain exactly as they were. This was quite inconsistent with the Emperor's plans, and therefore he found himself compelled, in some way or other, to open negotiations with his prisoner. In order to sound him, he began by allowing an Austrian minister, who had been well known to Pius VII. at

Rome, to have an interview with him, ostensibly merely upon some affairs in Austria, but with secret instructions to introduce the subject of the Pope's relations with Napoleon, and to report what was the state of his mind with regard to them. This unauthorised agent reported, that 'he had found the Pope a little aged, but in good health; calm, serene, as usual, saying not one word of the least bitterness, even when entering on subjects upon which he could not but feel most keenly.' He had asked the Holy Father whether he could do nothing to prevent the dangers to the Church which the present state of things implied, and had been struck to observe the tone of affectionate feeling towards Napoleon with which he spoke, decidedly more so than towards his own master, the Austrian Emperor. But he had said—

For ourselves we ask nothing of the Emperor. We have nothing more to lose. We have sacrificed all to our duty. We are old and without wants. What personal consideration could turn us aside from the line which our conscience prescribes! There is absolutely nothing that we desire. We wish for no income, we wish for no honours. The alms of the faithful will be enough for us. There have been Popes poorer than we, and we form no wishes beyond the narrow enclosure in which you see us. But we do ardently long that we may be restored to free communications with the bishops and with the faithful. (Vol. iii. p. 419.)

Still there was evidently no disposition to give way, for he added—

When opinions are founded on the voice of conscience and on sentiments of duty, they are unchangeable, and be sure that there is in the world no physical force which can long contend with a moral force of this nature. The judgment we have pronounced as to the unhappy events which have taken place in our Apostolic See has been dictated by such sentiments, and therefore cannot vary so long as our duty obliges us to pronounce anything upon them. (Vol. iii. p. 421.)

It was plain enough, from this report, that the time was not come for making overtures to the Holy Father. Napoleon next sent two Cardinals, upon whom he felt that he could depend to act as his creatures, still without any acknowledged mission, but with secret instructions. The Pope, divining why they were come, received them with civility, but still remained purely passive, only saying, in answer to their suggestions, that he would not go to Paris except as a prisoner, nor negotiate with the Emperor, unless he had two cardinals of his own choice for advisers.

The unfavourable report of these new commissioners decided Napoleon to change his policy, and show that he could manage the ecclesiastical affairs of France without the Pope's action. He at once ordered the persons whom he had already nominated to the Sees of Asti, Liége, Poitiers, and St. Flour, but who were waiting for canonical institution, to go to their respective dioceses; his minister had already explained to him their extreme reluctance to do this, and it had hitherto been indulged. At the same time he determined to fill up, without waiting for canonical institution, the See of Paris. It had been vacant for two years, and Napoleon had nominated to it his uncle, Cardinal Fesch, whom the Chapter had at once made Vicar Capitular, glad to have the uncle of the Emperor as their medium of communication with the Government. He was already Archbishop of Lyons, and the excellent Abbé Émery, who was his confessor, had warned him not to assume at the same time the administration of the two most onerous Sees in France. Fesch, however, had the confidence in his own powers which marked the Bonaparte family, and had now for two years acted both as Archbishop of Lyons and Archbishop nominate of Paris. He was now required to act, without the Pope's authority, as Archbishop in full right. He refused. Napoleon insisted. His uncle replied, 'Sire, *potius mori.*' 'Ah ! ah !' replied the Emperor, '*potius mori* ; rather Maury. Well,—be it so. Maury it shall be;' and Cardinal Maury was nominated. He was a man of talent, and especially of eloquence, who had become distinguished under the old *régime*, and had resisted with great eloquence the attacks on the Church in the Constituent Assembly. He had been driven from France, and had been made a cardinal by Pius VI. ; had returned to France after the *concordat*, and unhappily tarnished a great reputation by becoming a mere tool of Napoleon. He now submitted to the terms which Fesch had refused, and acted as Archbishop of Paris. It happened that there was in the Chapter of Paris a certain Abbé d'Astros. ' He was,' says my Protestant author, 'anything but a fanatical priest. He was not only prudent and moderate, but a man penetrated with respect for the public authorities, and naturally inclined to conciliation. His tendencies were moderately Gallican. He had been one of the most decided in the Chapter in favour of conferring upon Cardinal Fesch the provisional administration of his diocese.' He was, however, conscientious, and he had since discovered that, in doing this, he had made a mistake, and acted in opposition to the manifest intentions of the Holy Father. He had therefore voted against giving the same authority to Cardinal Maury, although as President of the Chapter he had spoken in the name of the commission which announced the vote to him. On that occasion the cardinal had declared that 'he would never take his seat on the episcopal throne of Paris except the Pope should take him by the hand to conduct him to it.' The cardinal showed no intention of keeping this engagement, but the Abbé d'Astros watched him closely. One day in society the cardinal introduced him and his colleagues as 'my Grand Vicars.' 'Your Eminence is mistaken,' said the Abbé ; 'not the Grand Vicars of your Eminence, but of the Chapter.' Another day the cardinal, in grand state, was administering ordination, and proceeded to require from a newly-ordained priest the usual oath of obedience to himself as his bishop. 'Monseigneur,' interrupted the Abbé, out loud, 'permit me to observe, for the information of this young priest, that your Eminence has no right to demand from him this promise.' On days of ceremony he had also forbidden the crossbearer to carry before the cardinal the Cross which is the emblem of Episcopal authority, and had bade him take it back to the sanctuary. This brave man wrote to the Pope at Savona to ask of him directions as to his conduct. ' Before he received an answer, he obtained privately a copy of a brief, addressed to the cardinal, forbidding him to exercise any jurisdiction in the Archdiocese of Paris. Of this he could make no public use, but he privately consulted his own first cousin, M. Portalis, a member of Napoleon's Council and 'Director of Publications,' who advised him to keep it secret ' in the interest of religion,' adding that, if it were published, it would be his own official duty to suppress it as ' unauthenticated and dangerous.' A few days later, a brief addressed to the Abbé d'Astros himself, fell into the hands of the Police in which Pius VII. declared that : 'To remove all doubt and for greater security he took away from Cardinal Maury all power and jurisdiction, declaring null and void everything done in opposition hereto, whether knowingly or ignorantly.' This brief the Abbé had not received, it having been intercepted. Napoleon's wrath was gathering.

On New Year's Day it was the custom that all the authorities in Church and State attended the Emperor's reception, and on that day Napoleon I. delighted to make a scene by breaking out into violence against some man who had given him offence. This he did, as we all know, in March 1803, in the case of the English Ambassador, Lord Whitworth, and he was imitated by Napoleon III. in 1859 when he wished to quarrel with Austria. In 1811 the humble Abbé d'Astros was selected as the victim of such an explosion. The Emperor passed by the Senate, the generals, and officers with an angry air, and requiring Cardinal Maury to present his Grand Vicars, made one of his usual speeches to the poor Abbé about Bossuet, Gregory VII., the Gallican liberties, and the like, and that a man should be a Frenchman first, and that that was the way to be a good Christian, ending,—

'I know that you are opposed to the measures which my policy prescribes. In all my empire you are the most suspected man. But I have my sword at my side (putting his hand on the hilt, an action familiar with Napoleon but rather out of place under the circumstances); take care of yourself.' M. d'Astros says, 'Nothing could be more pitiable than these last words and this menace of a sovereign who dominated over all Europe, against a poor priest in rochet and mozetta, armed only with his square cap. I said nothing, but contented myself with looking unaffectedly at the Emperor.' (Vol. iii. p. 465.)

When the reception was over the Cardinal asked M. d'Astros to go with him to the Minister of Police, the Duke of Rovigo, who after questioning and threatening him, and saying that if he did not confess he would never again see his family, 'perhaps never the light,' told him that his cousin M. Portalis had confessed that M. d'Astros had shown him the brief addressed to the Cardinal. This was simply false, but the Abbé fell into the trap and admitted it. Napoleon at once declared that he should be shot. One of his followers remonstrated that this would be a stain on his own glory, and he gave way, saying, 'Let him be thrown into prison for the rest of his life.' He actually was sent the same day to the dungeon of Vincennes, where he was kept utterly without news of anything in the outer world till the fall of the Empire.[1] M. Portalis was publicly rated by the Emperor in the Council of State, deprived of all his offices, and sent into banishment. With regard to the Archbishopric of Florence much the same thing happened, except that the Emperor induced the man whom he had nominated, to undertake the office by personally assuring him that the whole question with the Pope would be arranged in a very few days, and that his Bulls would arrive before he could reach Florence. When he said this, he must have known not only that what he said was false, but that its falsehood would in a

---

[1] He was Archbishop of Toulouse and Cardinal under the restoration.

few days be evident to the man he was deceiving. It does not appear that the idea of there being something undignified in deliberate falsehood ever struck the mind of Napoleon.

I have in general confined myself to the history of the Holy Father, not having space to show in detail the monstrous tyranny of the Emperor toward the French clergy; I have made an exception in the case of the Abbé d'Astros because it did very materially affect the treatment of the Pope. He had hitherto been allowed to correspond with the clergy of the Empire through the instrumentality of the Bishop of Savona. Napoleon had not been unwilling that he should grant marriage dispensations and the like. But that he should direct the conscience of bishops, and that against the will of the Emperor, he considered a monstrous crime. The letters he wrote on this occasion are among those suppressed by the official editors of his correspondence. He at once wrote ordering the Pope's household to be cut down, his carriages and horses (which he had refused to accept) to be taken away, that he should be deprived of books, pen and ink, should not be allowed to communicate with anyone, and that spies should be posted in all the inns at Savona to see that none obtained access to him. He even gave orders that his ring, the *annulus Piscatoris*, should be taken from him and sent to Paris. Pius VII. gave it up, but took care first to break it.

It is painful to read these orders, written with his own hand, by the man who when himself a prisoner at St. Helena complained so bitterly of the sufferings of captivity; and reproached his jailor for treatment, the rudeness of which never approached to that which he cruelly practised towards the prisoner of Savona. The object of the Emperor was to give himself the pleasure of inflicting personal suffering upon the Pope, nor did he attempt to conceal it. He wrote, 'You will make the Prefect and Prince Borghese understand, that it is my intention that the Pope should himself intimately feel my displeasure at his conduct.' His agent, M. de Chabrol, reports, 'that in conformity with his instructions he had markedly treated the Pope as one ignorant of what is due to sovereigns.' (Vol. iii. p. 477.)

The Emperor also gave orders that the director of his archives should publish an historical book against the Popes: and was even thinking of deposing him by his own authority, for he directed his librarian to examine and report, 'whether there were any examples of Emperors who had deposed or suspended Popes.'

The extreme violence of Napoleon's conduct at this period has been supposed to have been caused by passion, and he himself gave this account of the matter at St. Helena. M. D'Haussonville is convinced that it was deliberately adopted, that he believed he had almost completed his military victories, and was resolved to make himself absolute master at home. In civil matters this was already done; the only difficulty foreseen by his 'marvellous sagacity as a despot' was in the Catholic Church; and here he resolved to put down opposition to his absolute will by sheer terror. The evidence that this was the deliberate reason of his demonstrations of passion was, that he took pains to make them known. Thus he wrote a special letter to the Viceroy of Italy to tell him of his disgraceful outbreak of rage against M. Portalis. Just at the same time, by way of increasing the terror, he seized and committed to dungeons, avowedly for life, three cardinals and a very large number of ecclesiastics, accused of no offence except that they were suspected of feeling sympathy with his victims. Two great ladies were seized, detained for a while, and threatened with the same fate. He even thought of imitating Henry VIII. by regulating all the affairs of the Church by a decree of his legislative body, and was dissuaded from this madness only by Cambacérès and other members of his council, who, though themselves unbelievers, saw its extreme wildness. They, no doubt, saw, what his own immense penetration would have made plain to him, if he had not now been intoxicated by his wonderful prosperity, that the same thing cannot be done in states of society widely unlike; and that the period in which an Anglican Church could be created by Act of Parliament was gone by for ever.

But though he gave up this, he did not give up the hope of making himself as absolute in spiritual matters as he already was in temporal. He resolved that no one should even talk of ecclesiastical affairs ; and, carrying out this resolution, made an address to his 'Legislative Body,' in which, while professing to go over all that had happened since its last session, he passed over without a word the carrying away of the Pope from Rome and his imprisonment at Savona. The Minister for Worship had to make a report to the 'ecclesiastical commission,' and though it consisted of his own creatures on whom he could safely depend, Napoleon would not allow the facts to be stated even to them. 'The habit of invariable lying was too strong for him,' adds M. D'Haussonville, and he returned to the minister his proposed address requiring him to leave out of it what he had said about the Holy Father.

It seemed curious that while so anxious to prevent all mention of the Pope, and of what he had done and what he was actually suffering, he allowed the 'Moniteur' day after day for months together to publish addresses from different ecclesiastical bodies which professed the most absolute devotion to his policy, and especially supported his claims, as opposed to those of the Holy Father, as to the vacant bishoprics. The first of these addresses purported to be from the Chapter of Notre Dame at Paris. M. D'Haussonville gives a curious and interesting history in detail of the drawing up of this address, which was dictated by Napoleon himself, received in silence by the mass of the Chapter when read to them, objected to by the saintly Abbé Émery, altered owing to his objection, and then published by Napoleon, not as the Chapter had agreed to it, but as he had drawn it up. It appeared in the 'Moniteur,' and then for months were published addresses echoing it from all the chapters and ecclesiastical bodies, in the empire and in the kingdom of Italy. The space in the official journal formerly occupied by war was now devoted to these declarations of the clergy against the Holy Father. No doubt, what the author says is true, that the servility which he found among them inspired Napoleon with contempt for the clergy in general. He was wont to say that Émery was the only man who inspired him with fear, yet with all this he revered him, and said in his better moments that he should die more happy if he could feel that he left the education of the next generation in hands like his. Yet it was evidently nothing but his opportune death which saved Émery himself from persecution, and his community was actually broken up. It must be remembered, moreover, that although Napoleon found much servility, he did not find that alone. How many hundreds of priests died in his dungeons will never be known till they and he stand together before the judgment-seat of Christ. And as for these addresses, we only know the details of one case, and in that one we know that the canons refused to vote the address which Napoleon dictated, and that he published it declaring they had voted it. How many more of the addresses may have been forgeries we know not.

But what was Napoleon's object in departing from his ordinary policy of entirely suppressing all expression of opinion on religious matters, by publishing in the 'Moniteur' these addresses and a discussion in the Council of State to which the author calls attention, when it professed to make null and void the decree of the Holy Father about the archbishopric of Florence? There can, I think, be no doubt that the author gives the true answer to this question. Pius VII. was now a close prisoner. No friend, no intelligence from the outer world could reach him except by the connivance of his jailor, M. de Chabrol, Prefect of Montenotte. Care was taken that every cardinal and bishop who was admitted to see him repeated to him, however respectfully in manner, that the Church was in a desperate state, and that the only cause of all its miseries was, that he himself refused to make arrangements which might be made without any sacrifice of principle, which were absolutely necessary in the changed state of society, and which the whole Church agreed in desiring. Then as to reading, M. de Chabrol took care to supply him with the 'Moniteur,' and he never saw anything else. No letters, except such as were written in exactly the same spirit, were allowed to penetrate to him. And in the 'Moniteur' he saw addresses from all the ecclesiastical bodies of the Empire and of the Kingdom of Italy, all re-echoing the same statements. There are well-known stories of men who have been convinced of facts opposed to the positive evidence of their own senses by what seemed to them the independent testimony of a number of witnesses all agreeing together.[1] Never was this device tried upon any man so unscrupulously, so ably, so consistently, and for so long a period together as it was upon Pius VII. To add that it was not wholly without success is really to say little more than that he was a man. This great conspiracy was not set in motion with any intention of changing the doctrines which he believed and taught, and of which he would at once have said, 'Though we or an angel from heaven preach any other doctrine, let him be anathema.' All that was desired was to convince him that the good of the Church required that he should agree to certain practical measures, not in themselves desirable, but which had become absolutely necessary in the existing state of the political world. Many of his predecessors had made concessions, more or less important upon similar subjects. Nay, he himself had done the same in the *Concordat* which he had made with Napoleon in 1801. He might very naturally be persuaded, that he was mistaken in refusing to make new concessions of the same class if he found that all Catholics, cardinals, bishops, chapters, priests, theologians, laymen, all the wisest and all the most learned, all the most devoted men, were of one mind in declaring that he was wrong, and that his error was entailing upon the Church the most fatal consequences. This was

[1] My readers will find an instance of this very amusingly described by Macaulay, in his 'Critical and Historical Essays,—Mr. Robert Montgomery.'

the plan which Napoleon determined to carry out, and in which he was unscrupulously seconded by many able French ecclesiastics. They persuaded themselves no doubt that the object was good. But it is difficult to believe that they did not know that multitudes of the ablest, wisest, and best men in the Church believed that the concessions demanded by Napoleon were such as Pius VII. could not make with a safe conscience, or without grievous injury to the Church: and therefore if they had allowed themselves to think fairly on the subject, they would surely have seen, that however good they might consider the end proposed, the means by which it was to be obtained, implied or required that they should practise a very gross deception upon the Holy Father.

How this deception was carried on, and the degree of success it obtained, are related by the author with extraordinary research and great skill in his fourth and fifth volumes. The result, thank God, all who take up the history know beforehand. On the part of the Holy Father, there was great bodily weakness, all the infirmities of age, and a habitual distrust in his own judgment, which made it seem almost impossible that he should stand firm under a trial like that to which he was subjected. But there was a single eye, a fixed resolution to adhere to his duty as far as he could see what it was; and, above all, he had on his side the power of God, and when, humanly speaking, all seemed most certain to go against him, it turned out that the moment was come, the moment of man's extremity and of God's opportunity, in which, with His own right hand and His holy arm, He interfered to get to Himself the victory over every enemy.

VII.

PIUS VII. AT SAVONA AND FONTAINEBLEAU.[1]

IN two former essays on the history of Pius VII. and Napoleon I., I have traced the very able narrative of M. D'Haussonville from the Conclave in which the Pope was elected, in the year 1800, down to the beginning of 1811. Nothing could be more critical than the whole state of things at that moment. Indeed, those who regarded the Catholic Church as a mere human institution, not unnaturally regarded it as hopeless. And yet the oppressor had already begun to feel some of the inconvenience which was the effect of his own violence. The Pope was a prisoner at Savona. Being deprived of freedom, and resolved not to be a tool in the hands of Napoleon, he refused to do anything. The affairs of the Church in France were suddenly brought to a standstill. No bishop could be instituted; the usual course of business was suspended, and Napoleon found it a matter of simple necessity to do something which should put a stop to this paralysis of ecclesiastical affairs. For some time he was in absolute perplexity what could be done, and how he should set about it. I have already shown how he tried to get the Pope to act, by causing the highest ecclesiastic in France to write to him, and by trying to work on him by unaccredited agents; but all was in vain. Then he resolved to cut him off in the most absolute manner from all communication with the external world, and when in this state of solitude to overwhelm him with declarations from the Catholic

---

[1] L'Église Romaine et le Premier Empire, 1800–1814. Tom. IV. et V. Par M. le Comte D'Haussonville. Paris: Michel Lévy.

clergy that they considered the obstinacy of the Pontiff the only obstacle to the peaceful and healthy action of the Church. Care was taken that he should neither see nor hear anything except what was published in the 'Moniteur,' and this official organ was daily loaded with addresses to the Emperor in this sense. For many months,

> To the great astonishment of Parisian readers these ecclesiastical documents usurped the place usually devoted to the bulletins of the 'grand army.' In truth, however, it was not for them that they were intended. The Emperor cared much less what effect they might produce at Paris than at Savona. Pius VII. was deprived of the society of his most confidential servants, and just now also of all his books, and of pen, ink, and paper; no doubt also, of the magnificent inlaid escritoire, which in the first days of his captivity the Count Salmatoris had so zealously caused to be placed in his *cabinet*. The only recreations allowed him were a walk in the very small garden of the Episcopal residence, and the study of the 'Moniteur.' This last M. de Chabrol took especial care that he should never be without, but when the official paper contained any news likely to work on the mind of his prisoner, he managed that his attention should be specially called to it. If he attended at all to the addresses inserted in the 'Moniteur' of January, February, and March, 1811, Pius VII. must have observed that, with the exception of only five chapters, which preserved a significant silence, all the canons of the See not yet suppressed in Italy were eager in conforming to the *mot d'ordre* given from Paris. (Vol. iv. p. 23.)

The fact is that care was taken to get up such addresses everywhere by means of the Prefect. Some persons might be disposed to wonder, that a man so keen-sighted as Napoleon did not see that they would have carried more weight if they had been less exactly like each other. But I imagine that his contempt of anything like liberty, and his resolution to govern men's consciences by absolute terror, made him indifferent to this consideration. All the chapters in Italy expressed themselves in words nearly identical. The inference no doubt would be that their addresses were dictated to them from above. And he was perfectly content that people should see that. *Oderint dum metuant,* was his almost avowed principle in dealing with the clergy. The author remarks that it must have been doubly bitter to the Pope's feelings to see in the 'Moniteur' the addresses of the chapter of Imola, once his own diocese, and of Savona, his actual residence. This last, I suspect, must have been drawn up by M. de Chabrol himself, because it is full of peculiar phrases and expressions, which figure in his daily despatches, and which he took care to borrow from Napoleon's own letters. The Emperor no doubt calculated that the impression made on the mind of the Pope was likely to be all the stronger, if he saw that the whole clergy of Italy, as well as of France, were driven by sheer terror into adopting not merely the general wishes of Napoleon, but his very expressions. At the same time, while intimidation was chiefly relied on, bribery was not neglected. Five days after the appearance of the Savona address, the author finds an order, under Napoleon's hand, for the payment of 240*l.* sterling to the Bishop of Savona, 'who,' he adds, 'is very poor.' But it is well to observe that the subserviency of the majority of the clergy, while it filled him with contempt, so far from inducing him to treat them with favour, only made him resolved to multiply his demands.

From this moment he proclaimed at every opportunity, and more loudly than ever, the maxim of State, that bishops, canons, and *curés,* all owed to him an obedience as entire as that of the other functionaries of his Empire. And what wonder? The authority of a Church is purely moral, and when great characters gradually disappear out of it, —when it shows no *esprit de corps,*—when each of its members is so little occupied with the care of its dignity, that the most considerable among them, instead of feeling its loss as an irreparable disgrace, feel it no merit to stand up for it, the man who has exacted from them these disastrous sacrifices seldom retains any gratitude for them. By a just retribution, it is usually from the hand of the master to whom they have had the weakness to submit, that these unworthy priests receive their punishment. They have exalted his pride until, for his misery and for their own, they have turned him into a mad despot, whose ever-increasing demands they are sooner or later unable to satisfy.

In the commencement of 1811, the man who had made the *Concordat*, had fallen into so strange a state of mind, that at one time he really thought of nothing less than a legislative settlement of the question of the institution of bishops, to be enacted merely by his Senate and his Deputies. (Vol. iv. p. 26.)

From this plan he was dissuaded by the advice of those whom he was wont to call 'the *philosophes* of his Council of State,' among whom Cambacérès was the first. 'Strange inversion of parts—while prelates, sincere believers, deserted from weakness the cause of their Church, its defence was taken in hand, upon principles merely of good sense and moderation, by men who had once been revolutionists, and most of them avowed enemies of the Catholic Faith, or at least utterly indifferent to it.' M. D'Haussonville, who views the matter as a Protestant, is amazed; to a Catholic it is nothing surprising that He in whose hands are all hearts should, when He so pleases, make use even of His enemies to effect His own purposes,—

> 'He moulds the Egyptian's heart of stone
> To do Him honour, and e'en Nero's throne
> Claims as His ordinance; before Him still
> Pride bows unconscious, and the rebel will
> Most does His bidding, following most his own.'

But those who would judge truly of the conduct of the French clergy at this crisis must remember that the number of priests and bishops who, because they refused to submit to the demands of the tyrant, were actually lying in pestilential dungeons or banished to distant isles, can be actually proved to have amounted to many hundreds. Napoleon, indeed, to whom deliberate falsehood never cost even the most passing feeling of shame, dictated to his faithful and deluded followers at St. Helena a statement that the number 'detained' in consequence of his difference with the Church never exceeded fifty-two. By giving an odd number so exactly he evidently wished it to be observed that he was not speaking loosely from memory, but stating the exact number as ascertained by actual calculation. But this was only an instance of what Sir Walter Scott calls 'a lie with circumstance.' M. D'Haussonville prints a number of letters, under his own hand, ordering the imprisonment and transportation of a number many times greater. With the keen polish of French satire, he remarks that these orders must have escaped his memory. 'Such things are so easily forgotten.' In this world it will never be known how great may have been the number of confessors who were seized, in obedience, not to letters from himself referring only to their own particular case, but to his general directions, which were unsparingly severe, for the arrest of all who in any degree opposed his policy. These were the men 'of whom the world was not worthy.' But his system of imposing absolute silence, and concealing even the punishment of his victims from the eyes and ears of all men, while he paraded the submission of those whom he succeeded in intimidating, had the effect of deluding not only his contemporaries, but his historians (many of them willing enough to believe anything base of the priests) into the delusion, that the clergy of France and Italy, like every other class of men, suffered themselves to become his unresisting tools. The truth was, that although he found among them only too much of baseness and servility, he encountered a real resistance which he met nowhere else, and which filled him with a rage which shows itself in a very undignified manner in the letters suppressed in the official edition of his correspondence, and published by M. D'Haussonville.

And thus I venture to say that, even when every other institution and individual was crushed beneath the iron heel of Napoleon I., the Church still retained her liberty. For that liberty varies according to the varying condition of the States among which her sons are sojourners. In a non-Catholic State, in which the private and political rights of every subject are defended by just laws equally administered, the freedom of the Church consists in the freedom of each one of her children to do all that is just and right, without suffering for so doing. Such liberty, thanks be to God, we, to a great extent at least, enjoy in these islands. But when, in the inscrutable Providence of God, nations are afflicted with a tyranny like that which oppressed France and Italy sixty years ago, or that which now afflicts unhappy Poland, the Church is still free, even while her children are enslaved, so long as they continue to do what is just and good and to suffer for it. This liberty she possessed under the persecuting heathen Emperors, and she possessed it under the man who more perhaps than any other that ever lived combined the highest gifts of genius with the vilest baseness of heart and character, the Corsican tyrant under whose yoke Europe groaned in the earlier years of the present century.

It is necessary to keep this steadily before our minds on reading M. D'Haussonville's narrative, which sets vividly before us the unworthy subservience of so many bishops and members of the Sacred College. The Church was still free even when Napoleon felt himself most secure of her submission, and when all external resistance to his will seemed to have been for ever crushed. She was free precisely because Pius was in captivity, because Cardinal Pacca and several others were in the dreary prison of Fenestrella, among the wildest rocks of the Alps, and several more in the dungeons of Vincennes ; because thirteen more were deprived of all their revenues, forbidden to wear the *insignia* of their spiritual rank, and placed under the *surveillance* of the police, in different sequestered towns ; because several of the most eminent French and great numbers of the Italian bishops lay in state prisons ; and because hundreds of priests (how many hundreds is known to God only) were suffering in one or another of these ways, and only suffering more severely because their less elevated rank gave them less claim to the consideration of their jailors. There was not one of these noble confessors but might well echo the words of the great Apostle; they were in bonds, but because they were bound the Truth was free (2 Tim. ii. 9),—'Laboro usque ad vincula, quasi mala operans—sed Verbum Dei non est alligatum.'

It is evident that all this was keenly felt by Napoleon himself, even when he most affected to despise it; and hence, as the author points out, his language about the act by which the Holy Father annulled the assumed authority of Cardinal Maury in the diocese of Paris, was totally different, according to the audience which he was addressing. Of this, as (at an earlier period) of the Bull of excommunication, he spoke privately to the few whom he most trusted as of 'a most dangerous act, plotted on the part of the Holy Father with the most black perfidy.' Terms failed him to express the fury with which it filled him, because that fury was the result of secret fear. Before the clergy he confined himself to vague allusions to it, as to a foolish and impotent manifestation of ill feeling, to which he attached not the slightest importance. In his public acts and official speeches he systematically avoided even the most distant allusion to it.[1] What he really wished was, that no man should know anything about it; he seems almost to have flattered himself that he had succeeded, at a moment when he could hardly help knowing that the acts of violence by which he had wreaked his vengeance on M. de Portalis, the Abbé d'Astros, the cardinals, and the Pope himself, must be talked of in secret by every functionary of the Empire and by every humble *curé* in the most remote village. All he really effected was, that every man who whispered his feelings about the matter felt that he was acting against the Emperor, and thus became more and more decidedly

---

[1] Vol. iv. p. 31.

enlisted as his secret enemy. Still the great monarch kept up his futile attempt at absolute concealment.

The '*Philosophes* of his Council of State' soon convinced Napoleon that his first project, that of regulating the institution of bishops after the example of Henry VIII., would not hold water. It was a matter which required ecclesiastical authority, and it followed that nothing less than a council could deal with it. In preparation for this Napoleon had referred questions (which the reader will find, with the answers given to them, in the author's 54th chapter) to two Commissions, appointed, one in 1809, the other in 1811. The questions proposed to the latter of these Commissions began by assuming it as already a settled point that in future the Pope was to have nothing to do with the institution of bishops in France, and the bishops on the Commission were to report on the steps to be taken to supply his place. Cardinal Fesch was a leading member of these Commissions, and with him the saintly Abbé Émery had great influence. He now wrote to the Cardinal that the time was come for 'resistance to blood.' The Cardinal went to the Emperor and warned him that he 'had now come to a point at which he would be compelled to make martyrs;' but the report of the Commission, though not quite all that Napoleon wished, was elastic enough to comprehend anything. He could not fail to see that if he acted upon it he might wholly dispense with the Pope. What it recommended was the calling of a National Council, and it said plainly enough that, if the Pope still refused to submit, this might take his place. In preparation for the Council the Emperor called together at the Tuileries a great gathering, consisting of the members of his ecclesiastical Commission, and the chief dignitaries of the Imperial Court, Talleyrand, Cambacérès, &c. M. Émery, though a member of the Commission, was unwilling to attend; when specially sent for he retired into his oratory, and, falling on his knees, prayed to be directed how he ought to act, and after a few minutes came calmly out to the bishops who had been sent to bring him. The Emperor opened the meeting with an invective against Pius VII., asking what means the canon law afforded 'for the punishment of a Pope who preaches rebellion and civil war,' and accusing him of doing his best to stir up assassins against the life of the Emperor.

After this discourse (says Cardinal Consalvi), which was nothing but a tissue of erroneous principles, falsehoods, atrocious calumnies, and anti-Catholic maxims, not one cardinal or bishop had the courage to confront force and power in defence of the truth. They all forgot their duties, and maintained a scandalous silence. Even the civil magnates present looked at each other with evident alarm, but in absolute silence. At last the Emperor turned to M. Émery and demanded his opinion on the matter. The simple priest thus questioned looked to the bishops of the Commission, as if asking their permission to express his opinion in their presence; then turning to the Emperor he said, 'Sire, I can have no other opinion than that expressed in the Catechism which is taught by your orders in all the churches of the Empire. There I read—"The Pope is the visible head of the Church." Now a body cannot dispense with its head, with him to whom it owes obedience by Divine right.' The simplicity of this answer and the quotation from his own Catechism seemed to take the Emperor by surprise, and as he made a pause, as if waiting for M. Émery to say something more, he added, 'In France we are compelled to maintain the four articles of the Declaration of 1682. But we must receive what they teach as a whole. The preamble to that Declaration states that the Primacy of S. Peter and of the Roman Pontiffs was instituted by Jesus Christ, and that to it all Christians owe obedience. Moreover it is added that the four articles have been decreed in order to prevent any attack upon that Primacy from being made under pretext of the liberties of the Gallican Church.' M. Émery then went into some developments of the subject, to show 'that the four articles, although they limit the powers of the Pope upon certain points, preserve to him an authority so great and eminent, that without his participation no affair of importance either in doctrine or discipline could be regulated.' From all which he drew the conclusion, that if a council was assembled, as was talked of, such council would have no validity if held without the sanction of the Pope. (Vol. iv. p. 86.)

Nothing so very strong after all, it may be said; he only said what all Catholics know. But it was a strong thing to be laid down by a humble priest, a man invested with no dignity and secured by no diplomatic character, before the face of Napoleon himself, and in the presence of his arch-Chancellor and his grand vice-elector, and of all the highest dignitaries of his Empire specially convened to sanction the purpose he had formed of obtaining the authority of a council to enable him to dispense with the interference of the Holy Father in the institution of bishops; and that, after he had already extorted from his ecclesiastical commission, consisting of cardinals and high prelates (some of them long ago distinguished for having bravely maintained the rights of the Church in the Convention), the concession that 'in case of necessity' (of which necessity he, of course, was to be the judge) such a proceeding would be valid. Everyone present expected a violent outbreak of rage. If as much had been said by Cardinal Fesch, all his dignity as the Emperor's uncle, and as Primate of all the Gauls, and Cardinal, would not have protected him from it. But the Abbé Émery had established over the mind of the tyrant the influence of sanctity, and to the surprise of all present he controlled himself. Again addressing M. Émery, he said:—

'Well I do not dispute the spiritual power of the Pope, since he received it from Jesus Christ. But Jesus Christ did not give him the temporal power. That was given by Charlemagne, and I, as successor of Charlemagne, think fit to take it from him, because he does not know how to use it, and because it interferes with the exercise of his spiritual functions. What have you to say to that, M. Émery?' 'Sire,' replied M. Émery, 'I can only say what Bossuet says, and whose great authority your Majesty justly reverences, and whom you are so often pleased to quote. Now that great prelate, in his "Defence of the Declaration of the French Clergy," expressly maintains that the independence and complete liberty of the Sovereign Pontiff are necessary for the free exercise of his spiritual authority throughout the world, in so great a multiplicity of empires and kingdoms.' And then, without a moment's hesitation, he went on to quote the exact words of Bossuet, for he had them quite ready by heart, having often quoted them in the Commission itself. And he laid special emphasis upon these words of the Bishop of Meaux, 'We rejoice at the temporal power, not only for the sake of the Apostolic See, but still more for that of the Church Universal, and we most ardently hope from the bottom of our hearts, that this Sacred Sovereignty may ever remain safe and entire under all circumstances.' 'Well,' replied Napoleon (who had listened patiently, as he generally did when he met a man who knew how to pronounce a weighty opinion upon a subject which he perfectly understood), 'Well, I do not reject the authority of Bossuet. All that was true in his times, when Europe acknowledged a number of masters. It would then have been unsuitable that the Pope should have been the subject of any one sovereign. But what inconvenience is there in the Pope's being subject to me,—to me, I say, now that Europe knows no master except myself alone?' M. Émery was considerably embarrassed by confronting this unlimited pride of the Emperor: he wished to convince and not to wound it. 'Your Majesty,' he replied, 'is better acquainted than I with the history of revolutions. What exists now may not always exist, and in that case all the inconveniences foreseen by Bossuet might once more make their appearance. Therefore the order of things so wisely established ought not to be changed.' The Emperor made no reply, but passing to the clause which the bishops had proposed as an addition to the *Concordat*, that His Holiness should give institution within a fixed period, in default of which the right of institution should devolve upon the Provincial Council, he again questioned M. Émery, asking him whether he thought the Pope would make this concession. M. Émery replied without hesitation that he thought the Pope would not make it, because it would reduce to nothing his right of institution. The Emperor started, and turning towards the bishops who were on the Commission, said to them, 'Ah, ah, Messieurs, you want to lead me into a *pas de clerc* [an expression for a blunder, in terms contemptuous towards the clergy] by leading me to demand of the Pope a thing which he has no right (*ne doit pas*) to grant to me.' The bishops were much mortified by the apostrophe which M. Émery's reply had drawn upon them. When the Emperor rose to retire, he bowed his head with a gracious salutation to the ex-superior of S. Sulpice, without seeming to take much notice of the other members of the Commission. As he was leaving the room he asked one of the bishops whether the account M. Émery had given of the teaching of the Catechism about the authority of the Pope was correct. The bishops could not help remembering it. For a moment there was a general conversation, and M. Émery's colleagues, who feared that his openness must have offended the Emperor, gathered round him begging forgiveness for the abbé, in consideration of his advanced age. 'Gentlemen,' said the Emperor, 'you are mistaken. I am not in any degree offended with M. Émery. He has spoken like a man who knows his subject, and that is the way I wish people to speak. It is true he does not think with me, but in this place each one ought to have his opinion free.' (Vol. iv. p. 91.)

No other man ever ventured to speak the truth to Napoleon as boldly as did the Abbé Émery. The great men who had been silent witnesses of the scene were struck with amazement. Talleyrand said publicly, 'I was well aware that the Abbé Émery was an able man, but I never believed him to be so much so. He has skill enough to tell the Emperor the truth without offending him.' Napoleon himself showed his feelings by exclaiming to Cardinal Fesch, who tried to speak to him on ecclesiastical affairs a few days later, 'Hold your tongue. You are a dunce (*un ignorant*). Where did you ever learn theology? I must discuss it with M. Émery, who does know it.' But he had refused to be led by this wise counsellor, and he was no longer to possess him. M. Émery had before this been severely punished for his integrity. Napoleon found means of hitting even those who had least to lose. He had already dissolved the different missionary congregations, and had positively forbidden the preaching of missions; because he feared that the missionary priests might let out the truth with regard to his relations with the Holy See. The Sulpicians had been the last; but a year before this he had broken up their congregation, and had specially ordered M. Émery himself to leave S. Sulpice; because, being consulted by Cardinal Somaglia as to whether he could attend the Emperor's marriage with Maria Theresa, he had replied, 'that he himself should have no scruple, but that, if the Cardinal had any, it might be better not to attend, as conscience binds.' It availed nothing to M. Émery that he was unembarrassed by natural ties; that he had refused to be elevated to high dignities in the Church; that he cared nothing either for wealth or worldly honours. To him S. Sulpice was instead of wife and children and houses and lands; within its walls he had spent a long and holy life, had 'feared God in youth and loved Him in age,' and out of it he had sent generation after generation of priests trained in the holiest rules and practices; there was not so much as one of its stones which was not endeared to him by some holy recollection. But because he had, most cautiously and with the greatest moderation, given advice to a friend who sought it, he was turned out laden with the burden of eighty years to seek a new home in which to die, separated from the brethren among whom he had lived, and expressly forbidden to have any communication with them. Years before he had sent one dear friend across the Atlantic to found a Sulpician community at Baltimore, in the United States, and now he began sorrowfully to anticipate that the time was come when his congregation could exist only in a Protestant land under the shelter of political freedom, expelled as it was threatened to be from Catholic Europe by the overmastering power of Despotism.

Pius VII., when discussing with the French minister in 1800 the demands of the First Consul with regard to the *Concordat*, extolled the peaceable and regular working of religious affairs in free countries, even although they were heretical. Pius VII. was destined once again to do the same thing at Savona, during the terrible storms of the council of 1811. In the same spirit the Abbé Émery at this time turned his mournful eyes towards the United States. He wrote to his most intimate friend, the head of the Sulpician Seminary at Baltimore: —'Alas! after the overthrow which has already taken place, and that which is now threatened, it must be admitted to be probable that before long it will be impossible that Sulpician communities should exist in France, and that both the thing and the name will be confined to America. For myself, I cannot think of moving thither. My age does not permit it; but I forewarn you, that if things turn out as I fear they will, many of our members will go where you are, and I shall take measures to secure their being followed by all our property and all the most precious things we possess.' (Vol. iii. p. 300.)

So well pleased, however, did Napoleon profess himself to be with the Abbé Émery at this moment, that Cardinal Fesch even conceived a hope that he might be permitted to return to die among his brothers and children at S. Sulpice, and ventured to intercede with the Emperor for this favour. But that was too much to hope from the magnanimity of the great Napoleon. The favour was refused, and it was the last which the tyrant was able either to concede or to refuse to the aged priest. The day of weary, disappointing toil was over; the evening had come; the sun had set; in the natural world all was shut in by a sky which had never been so dark and lowering; but faith assured him that above the clouds and darkness the Sun of Righteousness was shining in undiminished glory, and that when the right time should come He would dispel every mist that man could raise, and once more shine out upon the world which He had created and redeemed. To Him he was willing to leave the care of the future, and for himself he had nothing to desire except the summons by which he was to be called, without longer waiting, to soar beyond those earth-bred clouds, and plunge into the full effulgence of the True Light. And now that summons was come. The last earthly news which reached him was that the Emperor had convened a national council, to be his tool in getting rid of the Pope. He knew too much both of the character and objects of the tyrant, and of the degradation of the great majority of those with whom he had to deal, not to know that this, according to all human calculations, could hardly fail to issue in a great schism and a relentless persecution. It was his last fear, his last grief, if indeed he could be said to fear or to grieve, knowing, as he did with a sober, calm, infallible assurance, that whatever might come first, 'sooner or later his must be the winning side, and that the victory would be complete, universal, eternal.' He had done his part, and now joyfully left to his Lord the working out of the results. He wrote to an intimate friend, 'It is a good moment to die;' and passed to his rest, April 28, 1811.

But his plain-speaking had not been without its result. Napoleon had learned that his Commission (fearing to tell him the truth) had deceived him into believing that, by calling together a council, he might get the right of institution transferred from the Pope to a provincial synod. He now found that he had no alternative, but must, one way or another, come to terms with the Pope. He pushed on the convocation of the council without consulting him, hoping to intimidate him by the expectation that its object was to pronounce against him a sentence of deposition; and with the same object the letters which summoned it were filled with invectives against the Pope, although, curiously enough, mention of his name was avoided, the complaints being made against 'one of the parties to the *Concordat.*'

And now the Emperor judged that the time was come to bring to bear upon the Pope the arts for which he had been preparing by long imprisonment and entire shutting out of all intelligence as to the events of the outer world. He determined to send some prelates to treat with him. He selected them with his usual penetration. The author remarks that when he had to deal with churchmen his object was not by any means to select men of bad character. On restoring the public recognition of the Church in France at the time of the *Concordat* he had been at pains to select 'before everything else worthy and commendable pastors, but taking care to find men who had the good qualities of private rather than of public life.' His instinct seldom deceived him, and on this occasion it did for him all he wished.

M. de Barral, whom he made Archbishop of Tours, and M. Duvoisin, Bishop of Nantes, had both belonged to the clergy of the *ancien régime*, and before 1789 had even gained a distinguished position in it by their exceptional merit. Both had emigrated during the Reign of Terror, and had returned to France almost at the same moment, shortly after the signing of the *Concordat* and before its publication. The First Consul immediately saw in them the dispositions which at that moment were shared by all the ecclesiastics to whom he had just opened once more the long-closed gates of their country—a sincere gratitude for the interest which he exhibited in the welfare of religion and a warm admiration for his own person. Their tried piety, their exemplary character, the character of their opinions, and (if I must speak out) the partiality and complaisance which they professed towards the authority which had just established itself upon the ruins of our liberties, naturally marked out M. de Barral and M. Duvoisin for the favour of Napoleon.

M. Maury, Bishop of Trèves, was another man of the same class. These three prelates he selected as his emissaries; and in a long personal interview gave them their final instructions. 'They were authorised to sign two conventions—one on the special affairs of the Church of France and the institution of bishops; the other on the affairs of Christendom at large and the person of the Pope.' With regard to the first, the Pope was to engage to institute all bishops named by the Emperor, and that if this was delayed three months, then institution was to be given by the metropolitan, or if his was the vacant see, then by the senior of his suffragans. As to the other, the Pope might return to Rome if he would take the oath to the Emperor in the form laid down for bishops in the *Concordat*; if he refused this, he should not return to Rome, but might fix himself at Avignon, whence he might direct the spiritual affairs of Christendom, and where the ministers of Christian States accredited to him should enjoy the immunities of diplomatic agents, and he should be treated with the honours due to a sovereign, and have free communication with foreign Churches. Eighty thousand pounds sterling per annum should be set apart for his revenue. This sum—

Whether paid by us, or by all Christian princes, shall be raised in whatever manner the Pope prefers out of the benefices of Christendom. As for the spiritual power of the Pope in the interior of our empire, if he goes to Rome and takes the oath, we demand nothing more ; if he does not think fit to take the oath, and goes to Avignon, we shall require him to engage not to do anything in our empire which is inconsistent with the four propositions of the Gallican Church. If these first articles were arranged, the bishops were to assure the Holy Father how much the Emperor desired 'to come to an understanding with him upon all subsequent questions, and to arrange all the different matters relative to the glory and prosperity of the Christian religion.' In their intercourse with Pius VII. they were never to forget that they were sent in order to impress upon him the afflicted condition of Christendom, and the evils which the ignorance and obstinacy of his counsellors (Pius VII. had no counsellor left within his reach) had produced, and were calculated to produce. My intention is (the Emperor expressly added) that you should make no use of your powers, unless you find the Pope in a reasonable state of mind, and unless, enlightened by what you tell him, he abandons the madness by which he has for so many years been guided. (Vol. iv. p. 109.)

At the last moment he seems to have had some misgivings as to his taking the first step towards a reconciliation, and his minister wrote to renew his instructions that ' they were not to acknowledge that they were invested with any powers, until they saw the Pope disposed to treat ;' also, before signing anything, they were to send it for the Emperor's approval. The bishops were ostensibly sent, not by him, but by their brethren the prelates at the moment present in Paris, from whom they bore letters to the Pope which had been dictated by Napoleon himself. The whole was carefully managed to impress on Pius VII. that the French Church was prepared to separate itself from him, if he did not immediately accept the Emperor's terms.

The three prelates reached Savona on May 9, 1811. The Prefect of Montenotte, an adroit man selected by Napoleon as his gaoler, informed Pius VII. that they had arrived, deputed to him by the clergy of France. He reported to the minister, 'I found the Pope as if he had something on his mind, although calm. He said that the bishops could come in whenever they would, alluding apparently to his want of liberty. I then expressed the strong desire and hope of all enlightened men for a conclusion to the ills of the Church. He answered that he wished it, only on condition that nothing should be demanded of him which could wound his conscience.' At the first interview the bishops assured him that they were not sent to judge him or to announce the intention of the bishops of France to do so, and he told them that he could not take any step until he had 'his natural advisers,' his theologians, and the means of obtaining information as to the qualifications of the persons proposed to him, and that he was now separated even from his confessor, who had been refused admission to him, deprived of books, pen, and paper; but, adds M. de Barral, among these complaints he did not insist on the necessity of his return to Rome. He appointed a second interview two days later, as he must have time to read the letters they had brought from different cardinals and bishops, of which there were seventeen or eighteen.

We have two very full and independent accounts of all that went on round the person of the Holy Father at this time—one from the letters which the Archbishop of Tours daily despatched to the minister at Paris, and which gives the particulars of what may be called the official negotiation with the Holy Father. These letters were afterwards published by him, and have therefore long been public. The other is contained in the letters of M. de Chabrol, the Prefect of Montenotte, and, in fact, the Pope's gaoler. These were as regular and far more full than the others, and contain what may be called the secret history of the affair— far more important, I need hardly say, than the other; and this has never been made public until the appearance of M. D'Haussonville's work. It is on these reports that any true narrative of the proceedings at Savona must be founded. As soon as the first interview had taken place he wrote:—

> The Archbishop of Tours gives your Excellency a detailed account of the first interview with the Pope. We have all agreed that it is specially important to work upon the Pope's feelings, and produce an effect upon his heart, in the situation in which he is placed. He seems prepared to stand firm against all argument and discussion, but to be accessible to an impression on his feelings. He reserved yesterday for thinking over the letters which had been sent to him. The day was spent by us in establishing our relations in the interior of the palace, so as to be acquainted with everything the Pope lets drop in familiar conversation, and to have it in our power to bring before him by a channel direct, though not official, whatever it is expedient for the success of the negotiations that he should know.

And what were these secret means of *surveillance* and of operation, the establishment of which was so important, and from which the Prefect of Montenotte hoped so much? Must it be confessed? The Pope's medical attendant had been secretly gained over to the interest of the man who kept his master a prisoner.[1] It is possible that such disgraceful proceedings may not be so rare in history as one would have hoped. But what we think really extraordinary is, to see a sovereign lower himself by taking a direct path in them. However, the affair was important, and the Emperor was not a man to be checked by such scruples. We have already mentioned that Napoleon had written with his own hand to M. Bigot de Préameneu, the *Ministre des Cultes*, to tell him that the Pope was to suffer in his own person from his resentment at his conduct. In consequence, things had been so arranged, that the expenses of the Pope's household had been reduced to two shillings and a halfpenny a day for each individual, the Pope included. But the good offices of the Pope's medical

---

[1] It is to be remembered that Pius VII. was suffering from a painful and dangerous disease, which made surgical assistance indispensable, and had, therefore, a medical man always about him. M. Porta had been about his person in the days of his prosperity at Rome, and everyone must have observed the remarkable influence which an educated man acquires under these circumstances over a person whom he has often relieved from severe pain. It was this influence which Napoleon characteristically turned to his own account.

attendant deserved to be rewarded on a different scale, and Napoleon valued them too highly to subject himself to be blamed for having forgotten them. He wrote to the minister, 'Tell Dr. Porta that you have laid his letter before the Emperor; tell him that His Majesty has written in the margin of his letter from Amsterdam that whatever disputes there may be between the Pope and His Majesty, and although they may be more or less warm, His Majesty will always regard personal services rendered to the Pope as if they had been rendered to himself. Dr. Porta has only to express his wishes, and his salary shall be paid as it was when the Pope was at Rome; therefore a salary of 12,000 francs (£480 sterling) is awarded to him from the time at which he quitted Rome, and this salary shall be continued as long as he stays with the Pope. Add that you are to send him an order for the payment, and that he is to let you know the period at which he ceased to be paid.'

M. de Chabrol's letters say 'M. Porta, the Pope's doctor, is of wonderful use to us.' 'The official communications are thus seconded by insinuations which suit our purpose.' He is able to report every doubt which crossed the mind of his prisoner. A complete cordon of conspirators was drawn round the oppressed Pontiff—prelates whose character invited confidence and who professed (and no doubt believed themselves sincere in professing) nothing but an earnest desire to serve the interests of the Church in a crisis of extreme danger, and those whom he regarded as his private friends, drawing out of him his secret feelings and doubts for the purpose of betraying them day by day and hour by hour to his oppressor. The tyrant, one of whose greatest qualifications was a happy instinct in judging of the characters of those with whom he had to do, had laid his snare with the greatest skill. Cardinal Pacca says :—

The talents of Pius VII. were of no ordinary kind. His character was neither weak nor pusillanimous. On the contrary, he was remarkable for resolution and quickness of wit. Adequately versed in the sacred sciences, he was also endued with that rare practical talent which enables a man to look at matters in their true light, and to see through their difficulties. But to all these fine qualities he united a natural disposition, which some regarded as a virtue, others as a defect. His first impression of a subject, his first view of it, showed admirable discernment and exquisite good sense; but if one of his ministers, or any other person of weight, opposed his opinion in private conversation, and urged him with importunities, this excellent Pontiff would give up his own opinion, and adopt that of the other, which was very often not the better. His enemies attributed this yielding disposition to a great intellectual weakness, an excessive love of repose. Those who were more just regarded it as the effect of a singular modesty, and a want of confidence in his own powers.

Such a man was just the person to be gradually worked upon by assurances day by day repeated, and it seemed to him, by persons quite independent of each other, that the whole of the clergy and bishops of France, and indeed of the whole world, were unanimous in condemning the obstinacy with which he refused the proposals of Napoleon as the sole cause of all the troubles of the Church. It was this which induced Cardinal Pacca to pronounce that in his concessions to Napoleon he 'deserved rather sympathy than blame'; 'and yet,' says M. D'Haussonville, 'even Cardinal Pacca never knew the dramatic scenes of Savona, for Pius VII. himself could not describe them to him, because he did not know them himself, as they stand out for the first time in all their touching misery in the letters of the Prefect of Montenotte.' (Vol. iv. p. 156.)

For the details of the intrigues which followed I must refer to the pages of the author, the first in which they have ever been made public. In the second interview the Pope, referring to what Cardinal Fesch had laid down in his letter as the only possible basis of negotiation, said that he could not in conscience decide such questions without the assistance of suitable advisers. The bishops (who, it will be remembered, were known to him, not as agents of Napoleon, but only as delegates sent by the bishops of France), with what they call some 'round-about expressions of modesty,' proposed themselves as being 'qualified both as bishops and by their sincere attachment to the Holy See and to the person of the Pope' to act in that capacity. He then told them that as to the declaration of 1682 he never had done anything contrary to it, and did not intend to do so, but that it was impossible for him to engage not to do so, it having been condemned and nullified by Alexander VIII. 'The Holy Father's tone,' says the bishops' report, ' was touching, and without the least bitterness.' When the details of the Emperor's demands were discussed, and the bishops enlarged on the number of persons most attached to the Pope, who were suffering by the existing state of things, 'he seemed touched and, lifting his eyes to heaven, said to himself, *Pazienza.*' Still his conscience would not allow him to give way. 'I am without advisers,' he said; 'the Head of the Church is in prison. If he were free, and had his natural counsellors, it is possible that he might find means of reconciling everything. *Plus vident oculi quam oculus.*' The bishops began to despair, and yet they continue to report; 'his kindness, his gentleness, his resignation, and even his friendliness towards us have never varied for a moment. Since our arrival he sleeps little, and frequently complains of his health.' 'They were much more affected,' says the author, 'than Napoleon would have liked by what went on before their eyes.' M. de Chabrol became alarmed. On May 13 he writes : ' I went to the palace this morning to make out the secret motives of so ill-timed a resistance. I had a very long talk with Dr. Porta, and made him well understand the situation in which his master was placing both himself and all those attached to his cause. He is thoroughly imbued with these principles, and seemed disposed to do us indirectly all the service in his power.' Next day M. de Chabrol reports a long interview with the Pope himself, to whom he spoke in 'terms which the bishops would have found it difficult to use,' answering to his complaint that he could not act while deprived of his advisers, that 'no counsellors could be so authoritative as the general agreement of the Churches both of France and Italy'; that 'the Council was about to pronounce against him, and deprive him of the power he still had of making terms'; that the Emperor was making concessions out of pure generosity, as the Council was ready to give him his full demands; that all the Pope's adherents felt that he ought to give way, and that his successor would blame his memory as having uselessly compromised the power of the Holy See. The Pope

replied, with gentleness, that no doubt the opinion of men was something, and that it was possible he might be blamed, but that his opinions had their foundation in his conscience, that upon this he took his stand, and easily forgot the judgment of men to think only of the judgment of God. (Vol. iv. p. 144.)

M. de Chabrol then says that he tried to move him by his feelings, speaking of the sufferings, not of himself alone, but of so many persons on his account.

He was affected, but I had gained no real victory against his inconceivable obstinacy. For himself, he said, he was prepared for everything, and cared little what happened to him. As for the others God would provide, but that he would never purchase the peace of which I spoke, or seek to avoid the reproaches with which I threatened him, by the sacrifices which were proposed to him. He left me, seeming, I repeat, much affected, but resolved. (Vol. iv. p. 145.)

M. de Chabrol continues his reports. He learns from Dr. Porta that the Pope's health is giving way, that his anxiety prevents his sleeping, and that he seems crushed by the fatigue of these discussions, and by his sense of the responsibility resting on him. M. de Chabrol's inference is, that the bishops should see him again, and try what repeated conferences would do, and that 'all other possible means are to be used to work on his feelings.' Then he writes: 'Dr. Porta has served us well. He went out yesterday, and took an opportunity this morning to assure the

Pope, on his own knowledge, that the whole population, both of Savona and Genoa, are looking for his giving way.

The reports continue in the same strain, but, says the author, 'the letters of the bishops suddenly become as short and enigmatic as those of the Prefect are clear and detailed.' May 18th, they say that the Pope told them that 'his head was worn out, and that he should be in a better condition in the evening. The fact was, that the ten days during which he had been subject to this incessant persecution had been too much for his bodily and mental strength.'

Twenty-four hours later, without entering into any further details, the bishops report that, having found the Pope tolerably well disposed, they had taken advantage of it to obtain his agreement to several articles relating to the canonical institution, and the additional clause to the *Concordat* [*i.e.*, the clause authorising the metropolitan to give institution, if not given by the Pope within three months]. The Pope having by degrees become familiarised with this idea, they had even taken the pen and sketched a draught of what they hoped he would agree to. 'This morning we drew out the whole clearly and in French. We presented it to the Pope. He wished for some changes of expression, some additional phrases, some trifling suppressions, and the result is on the whole tolerably good—much better than we flattered ourselves a few days ago that we could obtain.' The note thus hastily corrected by its authors in the Pope's cabinet, and of which we shall later republish the text entire, was with his consent left by the bishops upon the Holy Father's chimney-piece. Next morning, at a very early hour, they all set off together for Paris. (Vol. iv. p. 153.) This memorandum made the Pope promise,—1. That he would grant institution to the persons nominated by the Emperor. 2. That he would extend the same provision to the Churches of Tuscany, Parma, and Placentia by a new *Concordat*. 3. That he would consent to the insertion in the *Concordat* of a clause providing that he would expedite the Bulls for the Emperor's nominees within a time to be fixed, which he thought could not be less than six months, and if they were delayed beyond six months (for any reason except the personal unworthiness of the persons named), authorising the metropolitan of the vacant Church, or in default of him the senior bishop of the ecclesiastical province, to give the Bulls in his name. Finally, the Pope makes these concessions in the hope of obtaining for the Holy See the 'liberty, independence, and dignity which become it.' (Vol. iv. p. 430.)

The fact was, and Dr. Porta's reports fully bear it out, that both the body and the mind of the Holy Father had given way under the stress of perpetual anxiety, agitation of feelings, and loss of sleep, continued without sparing during so many days. For several days past he had 'felt that he was no longer master of himself, and that (in his own words) he had been in a state of intoxication.'

On the night preceding the departure of the bishops the assistant-chamberlain, who slept in the room opening into the Pope's bedroom, heard him for the first time uttering deep sighs, and accusing himself out loud in terms of the strongest self-condemnation. At seven in the morning he caused M. La Gorse, Commandant of the Palace, to be called, and asked with extreme anxiety whether the bishops were gone, and sent to request the immediate attendance of the Prefect of Montenotte. Before M. de Chabrol had arrived Pius VII. sent again to him by M. La Gorse, and immediately explained to him with great agitation that he had not adverted the evening before to the last lines of the note that had been left with him, that the bishops must immediately be informed by courier. Then begging the Commandant of the Palace to sit down while he corrected a postscript written in the margin of the note which he held in his hand, he began to make so many corrections and interlineations, that when M. de Chabrol arrived half an hour later the note had become very difficult to understand. (Vol. iv. p. 158.)

M. de Chabrol saw that the Pope was in a state of mind in which it was useless to oppose or reason with him, he took the note, and, leaving the room, tried to decipher it with Dr. Porta. But he was soon recalled. This time it was, not the last words, but the first clause in which the Holy Father saw the greatest difficulty. He admitted having read it; but he had made an error, and another article must be substituted for it. After trying in vain to calm him, M. de Chabrol left him, promising to return in an hour. When he came back he found Pius VII. in extreme agitation.

He said that he had done wrong (*prévariqué*); that in the last phrase, which treated of the government of the Church, there was a stain of heresy; that he would a hundred times rather die; that he had not adverted to this last article, and that it was necessary that I should send off a courier to the bishops to get it suppressed. For the rest, he would abide by it, but the suppression of this was absolutely necessary. He would rather make a public outburst (*éclat*) in order to make his sentiments known.' Little by little M. de Chabrol succeeded in quieting him, especially by giving him an assurance that he would write to the bishops. 'Next day the Pope was in as great a state of nervous agitation as ever. He assured M. de Chabrol that he had not slept at all in the night, and that his head was quite worn out, and he was in the state of a man half-intoxicated.' Dr. Porta thought his state serious. 'He was led to fear some hypochondriacal affection (*hypochondriaque*). He still hoped, however, that it would not come on. Unhappily the doctor's hopes were not realised. Some days later he was obliged to certify that the Pope's pulse was irregular and his appetite diminished. He observed that the Pope at times broke off what he was saying, remaining wholly absorbed in one thought; and then suddenly woke up from this absorption as if from a dream. In short, he observed every symptom of an hypochondriacal affection, the tendency of which was to destroy the faculties both of the body and of the intellect.'

M. de Chabrol writes that he observes the same symptoms. A few days later he says, 'The Pope is still in the same state; he expresses no opinion on any subject, but preserves a profound silence towards everyone.' When the Prefect attempted to introduce a conversation about the Council, which was already to have met, he made no answer; absorbed in absolute silence, he shut his eyes like a man buried in profound thought, and only came out of it to say, 'Happily I have signed nothing.' The Prefect tried to continue the conversation, but he fell again into the same state.

All the despatches of the Prefect of Montenotte which we have hitherto quoted were official. In a private letter, addressed to M. Bigot de Préameneu at a moment when he thought, prematurely, that the illness of Pius VII. had come to an end, M. de Chabrol expresses himself more clearly as to the real state of the Pope's health, and uses a word which would never have been formed by our pen, if it had not been read first in the private but authentic correspondence of the Imperial Prefect. 'As this letter is confidential, I think it necessary to make known to your Excellency that it is impossible to treat with the Pope unless he is surrounded by a Council equally cautious and firm, so that he may be kept steady in one resolution. You must have seen by my late letters that the irresolution of the Pope, when wholly shut up in himself, goes so far as to affect his health and his reason. At this moment the mental alienation has gone by, and the physical disorder is less severe, but everything shows that some support is necessary to a weakened intellect and a delicate conscience.'

In these words M. de Chabrol seems to have supposed that he was insulting Pius VII., yet, after all, he can say nothing against him except that he had a delicate conscience, a body subject to human infirmities, and an intellect which in him, as in all other sons of Adam, was liable to be affected by bodily infirmity. But the person upon whom in truth his report puts a brand of never-dying infamy was the heartless tyrant who, for his own selfish purposes, deliberately subjected to a lingering mental torture— more subtle, but no less cruel, than the racks on which the bodies of martyrs have so often been extended—a man whom the very heathen would have regarded with reverence, both for his age and his secular dignity, while to Christians these titles to reverence were as nothing compared with that due to his apostolic office and dignity, as Vicar of Jesus Christ upon earth. It does not appear that Napoleon, one of whose great qualities was, that he insisted on reading for himself all the reports (whether of his generals or his civil ministers), was moved either to tenderness or remorse when he learned from those of M. de Chabrol that both the body and mind of Pius VII. had, for the moment, given way under his unrelenting cruelty. It is some satisfaction to know that the result brought upon him considerable difficulty, perplexity, and embarrassment. The 'National Council' had been convoked for June 9, and he had confidently reckoned on being able to report to it, that the Pope had accepted his proposals, and on obtaining from it a unanimous vote of adhesion to them. He had obtained something like an acceptance of his terms, but he did not dare to make use of it, for the Holy Father had not only retracted it, but declared that, if any use were made of it, he would declare loudly and publicly what his judgment really was. The Council was postponed to the 17th, in hopes of some favourable change at Savona. It met at last, but was far from answering his wishes; and M. D'Haussonville says, 'the lamentable occurrences at Savona which have now, for the first time, been made public, were in fact the principal cause of the failure of the Council of 1811.'

I have detailed the proceedings at Savona both because they so strictly relate to Pius VII. himself and because Napoleon's policy of entire concealment has hitherto been so absolutely successful with regard to them that, as the author shows, M. Jauffret, a man who had special means of obtaining official information, and who published, as late as 1823, a work in several volumes full of very accurate details on the internal affairs of the French Church; and the Abbé Pradt, who was nominated by Napoleon Archbishop of Malines, and who has left numerous works on contemporary history, were wholly ignorant of the real nature of the events at Savona, and in consequence unable to conjecture the real motives of Napoleon's conduct with regard to the Council of 1811. But the real history of these proceedings cannot be too widely known in justice to the memory of Pius VII. Care has been taken by the tyrant, and his adherents, and admirers, to let all the world know he made concessions which he afterwards retracted; but the circumstances under which they were made, the means taken to deceive him into the belief that he was only doing what was judged by all the best and most religious men—cardinals, prelates, priests, and laymen—to be necessary in the interests of the Church, and finally that he did not, even for a moment, give way even to this pressure until his sufferings of mind and body had been so long continued as for the moment to overthrow the balance of his mind and prevent his knowing what he was doing—all this has hitherto been carefully concealed and is most clearly proved by the official correspondence of M. de Chabrol. It throws light, moreover, upon the character of Napoleon as well as upon that of Pius. In his whole history I doubt whether there is anything—even the murder of D'Enghien or the divorce of Josephine—which makes one so deeply feel the utter heartlessness of his selfishness, as does the consideration, that day by day for weeks together, he received and read without compassion, the report of the mental tortures inflicted in cold blood, by his authority and orders, upon a man venerable were it only for his age, his secular dignity, and his misfortunes; who had a special claim upon himself were it only that he had always shown towards him a personal regard and affection more nearly bordering on weakness than anything else in his character; and who added to all this the infinitely higher dignity of being the Vicar of Christ, which there is good reason to believe Napoleon, however irreligious in practice, really recognised with an interior faith.

The next scene described at length by the author is that of the Council of 1811, officially termed 'National,' although, as he shows, it had no claim to that title. Had my object been to select the most interesting parts of the volumes before me, not to confine myself to those which bear most directly on Pius VII., I might perhaps have gone into the details given upon this subject in the forty-eighth, forty-ninth, and fiftieth chapters of M. D'Haussonville's book, even in preference to those which I have already given. Here again he has been fortunate in obtaining several original narratives of all that happened which have not been available to those who wrote before him, and his narrative is most graphic and interesting. What is specially to be observed is that Napoleon, while of course wishing that the proceedings of what he called a National Council should appear free, took especial pains to keep undiminished the terror which he had already imposed on its members by the persecution of the Abbé d'Astros, of the 'Cardinals in black,' and of so many others. Immediately before the assembling of the Council he had broken out with strange and most undignified violence against M. de Bois-Chollet, Bishop of Séez, a man who had done great services in the pacification of La Vendée, and against whom there seems to have been literally no charge even of opposition to the Emperor's policy, but who was complained of by the Mayor, to whom he had given some slight offence. Napoleon, who visited his diocese with Marie Louise, called him before him, and after railing at him in coarse language, ordered all his papers and those of his vicar-general to be seized, and commanded him immediately to resign his see. Then he sent for the chaplains.

These gentlemen found Napoleon kneeling in a chair, the back of which he held in his hands. This was with him an habitual attitude. They began very humbly to intercede on behalf of their bishop, when the Emperor began one of those scenes of premeditated violence in which he seemed to delight more then ever. The victim selected was M. de Gallois, a simple parish priest, made an honorary grand-vicar by M. de Bois-Chollet. He was a priest of great virtue, celebrated for his knowledge of the canons, and who was considered the model ecclesiastic of the diocese. Napoleon, still leaning on his chair, without giving them the least salutation, abruptly addressed the canons the moment they had entered the room, and asked very shortly 'Which of you guides your bishop, who is nothing better than a fool?' One of them pointed to M. de Gallois. 'Ah! is it you? Why did not you advise him to attend at the marriage of the Rosières?'[1] M. de Gallois,

[1] The complaint of the mayor was that some young ladies who bore this title, as having obtained a prize, had been married, and the bishop had not been present at the wedding.

a little disconcerted but much more astonished, first looked at the Emperor, whose eyes seemed to give him a sign to answer without delay. 'Sire, I was not here when those Rosières were married.' 'Why did you make your bishop issue that circular about the suppressed feasts?' 'Sire, I was still absent and, to speak the whole truth, as soon as I knew of it I returned to Séez to advise a circular of a very different nature, which did actually appear.' 'F——,[1] where were you then?' 'With my family.' 'And with such a bishop, who is nothing better than a F—— fool, why are you so often absent? and who governs the diocese then? and why did you become grand-vicar to such a bishop?' 'Sire, I obey my superiors. Every ecclesiastic owes obedience to his superiors.' 'Are you a good Gallican?' 'Yes, Sire, perhaps one of the most decided in your empire.' (Vol. iv. p. 179.)

The result was that M. de Gallois was sent to a dungeon at Vincennes, and was never restored to liberty till the fall of the Empire. The ministers interceded for him, but Napoleon said he was 'too clever.' This case was just before the meeting of the Council.[2]

The proceedings in his own Council provoked the Emperor beyond endurance. He was enraged at the sermon preached to the bishops at their first sitting. He had taken the precaution of requiring that his uncle should see it in manuscript, and certain passages which declared adherence to the See of Rome had been objected to. The preacher, the Bishop of Troyes, promised to omit them, but whether his feelings ran away with him or for some

---

[1] A coarse expression, which the author does not choose to print.

[2] The author, in apologising for quoting the strong 'military' language of Napoleon, relates a most characteristic scene described to him by an official who was present when it took place. Napoleon on some occasion rated M. de Talleyrand in the coarsest language at the Tuileries for half an hour together. Talleyrand listened without answer and without showing the least alteration of countenance. At last, when the Emperor turned away from him, but while he was still within hearing, he remarked to the bystanders—'What a pity, gentlemen, that so great a man should have had so bad an education.'

other reason, he spoke them as they had been written. Then, when each of the bishops was asked, according to custom, whether he consented that the session should be opened, the Archbishop of Bordeaux (who was reputed to be a saint) said, bowing his head, 'Yes, I consent, saving always the obedience due to the Sovereign Pontiff, which I engage and swear to observe.' When the proceedings opened, his uncle, Cardinal Fesch, the president, himself knelt down first of all and took the oath, ending, 'I promise and swear true obedience to the Roman Pontiff, successor of S. Peter, the Prince of the Apostles, and Vicar of Jesus Christ upon earth.' He then called on all the others to take the same oath, one by one, and was observed to be specially scrupulous in requiring the formula should be distinctly pronounced, when it came to the turn of any who had formerly been constitutionalists, or whose fidelity to the Holy See was for any reason suspected.

Napoleon was so little pleased with these proceedings that he gave the most positive orders that the 'Moniteur' should give no account whatever of the opening of the Council, and rated Cardinal Fesch. Extreme precautions were taken to prevent the publication of any account of what had taken place.

I must refer to chapters xlviii., xlix., and l. of the author's work and to the valuable documents given in the appendix to vol. iv. for the details as to the debates and proceedings of the Council. They are most interesting.

The Council was divided into two groups most unequal in number. On one side was the small cabal of bishops who acted as managers on behalf of the Emperor. In addition to the four who had been sent to Savona (that is, MM. de Barral, Duvoisin, de Manny, and the Patriarch of Venice) there were Cardinal Maury and the Abbé de Pradt. With them the Sovereign was free to discuss without mystery or concealment all the resolutions which he wished to be proposed to the Council; for there was perfect confidence on both sides. With them he was perfectly at his ease in concerting without reserve whatever means he thought most proper in order to triumph over the opposition of their colleagues. Alongside of these complacent prelates, whose number as we have seen was so very small, or rather in opposition to them, was almost the whole mass of the bishops collected from the provinces of France and from beyond the Alps. These bishops, utterly strangers to politics and party spirit, were all animated by an immense desire of conciliation ; and had made up their minds to make every sacrifice, not absolutely against their consciences, to procure the peace of the Church. Their admiration for the great man who governed France was so great, their assurance of the wisdom of his plans still so entire, and their faith in the power of his genius so unshaken, that they arrived in Paris with the deepest conviction that everything must have been almost entirely settled beforehand at Savona, and that no concession would be demanded either of the Holy Father or of themselves which would be contrary either to their religion or to their dignity. Such was the *mirage* of happiness which the Minister *des Cultes*, speaking in the name of his master, dispelled at a single blow [on the second day of sitting]. Hardly could the unhappy bishops believe their ears. Not more scared would be a band of pilgrims who heard for the first time the roar of the lion in the desert. What was now to be wished, to be done, or managed? To the guileless security of the first days there succeeded a want of confidence reaching the extreme of terror. What they professed to themselves was that they would be firm in the good cause and accomplish their duty to the end, but they secretly asked themselves whether they had the strength to do it. Midway between the Court prelates prepared to do anything, and the majority of the Council so little satisfied but so much terrified, fluctuated the president of the Council, himself drawn in opposite directions by his ultramontane convictions and his dynastic inclinations, without credit with his nephew, without influence over his colleagues, full of good intentions, agitation, and contradictory views, and with all his impetuosity managing only to embroil matters more by his want of good sense, discretion, and tact. (Vol. iv. p. 232.)

No state of things, as M. D'Haussonville observes, could have been more favourable than this to the wishes of Napoleon, and yet so exorbitant were his demands, that in the end he had to break up this assembly and have recourse to more violence against its members. It was with extreme difficulty that his uncle could prevent the assembled bishops from going in a body to ask for the liberty of the Holy Father; and, what still more enraged him, the committee appointed by the Council to report on the matter voted, that the Council was not competent to settle the question of the institution of bishops. He dissolved the Council, and ordered four of the leading bishops (the Archbishop of Bordeaux, the Bishops of Ghent, Troyes, and Tournai) to be sent to dungeons at Vincennes. The first of the four, who fully expected this sentence, and was prepared for it, was not actually seized, because the Minister of Police, the unscrupulous Savary, remonstrated, saying that he was regarded by all men as a saint, and that the universal feeling would be against such a step. The others remained in imprisonment, more or less severe, until the fall of the Empire.

Napoleon, having thus not only dissolved his Council but taken measures which, even if it had still been sitting, would have deprived it of all plausible pretence of freedom, caused his ministers to deal with each of the bishops severally, and by threats and persuasion to obtain his promise to vote for the resolutions demanded by the Emperor. When this had been done, the Council was again called together and obliged to vote; and that those who had been compelled to promise might be kept to their engagement, the vote was taken, not as before by ballot, but by a public vote. What the Emperor demanded was then carried, but thirteen, or as it seems fourteen, bishops still ventured to vote against it. At this last sitting, on August 5, 1811, a report of what had gone on at Savona, drawn up by the Archbishop of Tours and altered by Napoleon himself, was read. This was the first intimation the Council had had on the subject. The President then put to the vote two questions, after saying that as the majority had already expressed their approval of them, discussion was needless. The first was that 'The National Council is in case of necessity competent to decree as to the institution of bishops.' The Archbishop of Bordeaux publicly protested that he did not admit the competence of the assembly, and the Bishop of Chambéry proposed as an amendment 'in case of extreme necessity'; but the original resolution was carried. The next, carried without the formality of a vote, was 'Should the Pope refuse to confirm the decrees which the Council shall make as to the institution of bishops, that will be a case of necessity.' Then the decree itself was voted and signed by the President and secretaries.

ART. I. Conformably to the spirit of the Holy Canons, archbishoprics and bishoprics cannot remain vacant more than a year in all. During that space of time the nomination, institution, and consecration ought to be completed. (ART. II.) The Emperor shall be petitioned to continue to nominate to vacant sees in conformity to the concordats, and the bishops nominated by the Emperor shall address themselves to our Holy Father the Pope for canonical institution. (ART. III.) Within six months after the notification of such nomination, made to the Pope in the usual way, the Pope shall give canonical institution, in conformity to the concordats. (ART. IV.) Should the six months expire without the Pope having given institution, the metropolitan, or, in default of him, the senior bishop of the ecclesiastical province, shall proceed to the institution of the bishop nominated. If the metropolitan is to be instituted, the senior bishop shall confer institution. (ART. V.) The present decree shall be submitted for the approbation of our Holy Father the Pope, and for this purpose His Majesty shall be petitioned to permit that a deputation of six bishops should wait upon His Holiness to beg him to confirm this decree, which alone can bring to a conclusion the troubles of the Churches of France and Italy. (Vol. iv. p. 368.)

And now he had at least obtained a vote from his so-called Council in favour of all that he wished. Six bishops were to lay it before the Holy Father, and ask his confirmation. The accounts of his bodily and mental health sent by M. de Chabrol had at last become so much improved that it was no longer impossible to negotiate with him. But the same unscrupulous agent had already reported that it was useless to try the old plan of keeping him absolutely without communication with any advisers, and then working upon his feelings until he at last gave way. The result of this he saw would only be (as it had already been) to wear out his strength both of body and mind, and wholly to incapacitate him from making any definite arrangement. What the Holy Father had declared from the beginning was, that he could do nothing without the presence and assistance of his natural counsellors, and M. de Chabrol had now reported the same thing. Napoleon therefore resolved to allow some of the Cardinals to resume their natural post in attendance on the Pope. But who were they to be? As for those who were called the 'Cardinals in black,' whom for their fidelity to their conscience he had already deprived of their revenues, forbidden to wear the dress of their office, and sent to live in different out-of-the-way towns of France under the surveillance of the police, he felt sure that he could not trust them; still less the Pope's former ministers, who had been lying in dungeons at Fenestrella or elsewhere for their fidelity to him. And yet to send none but Frenchmen born would hardly do. Accordingly he selected four, of whom three were Italians—Cardinals Dugnami, Roverella, Ruffo, and De Bayane. They were to go, ostensibly free to counsel the Holy Father on the questions in dispute between him and the Emperor. It is humiliating to find that they submitted to pledge themselves in writing, before they went, to advise whatever Napoleon wished. Cardinal Pacca, in recording this, says:—

I blush and grieve in making up my mind to expose an action of my colleagues which must inflict a real stain on their memory. But the whole world ought to know the base intrigues employed by the French Government to draw from the Pope concessions injurious to the Holy See, in order that in time to come the like may not be successful against Popes. When the Cardinals set out, it was rumoured in Paris that they had left with the Emperor, at his desire, a promise in writing, and signed by each of them, that they would use their influence with the Pope to induce him to give way to the Emperor's desires. The truth of this rumour was at first doubted by good Catholics; they could not believe that cardinals of revered character could forget their solemn oaths and commit an act, I will not say of treachery, but of unpardonable weakness. They went [says the author] as if voluntarily to offer to the suffering Pontiff, a prisoner at Savona, their treacherous assistance and advice, professedly disinterested, but they had concerted every particular of it beforehand with his all-powerful gaoler. It must be added, that this unworthy comedy was to last a long time. Is it credible, those who had undertaken these characters mustered courage to represent them without fear for whole months? (Vol. v. p. 1.)

But the Emperor heard of another person who might, he thought, be useful in the same way—M. Bertalozzi, Archbishop of Edessa *in partibus*. He was in Italy, and had not even been called to the Council. But it came to Napoleon's ears that he had the entire confidence of the Holy Father. He received orders to come immediately to Paris; but had no sooner crossed the frontier than he was arrested and committed to prison. Whether this was done to intimidate him, or whether it was a 'regrettable mistake' of the imperial police, the author doubts. However this may be, 'no one could from that moment be more strongly convinced than he that the great thing for the head of the Catholic Church to do was to put an end to the differences which led to mistakes so unpleasant.'

While Napoleon was thus providing a council of advisers for the Pope, he did not allow the bishops of what he called the National Council at Paris to choose those of their own number who were to go in their name to present what had been voted by them for his acceptance. He chose the Archbishop of Tours, the Archbishop-nominate of Malines (De Pradt), the Patriarch of Venice, and the Bishops of Feltre and Placentia; he afterwards added to their number the Bishops of Trèves, Evreux, and Pavia. They received their instructions not from the Council, but from himself. It was his character, that success always made him raise his terms and make more exorbitant demands, and this was the case now that the bishops of the Empire had ended so ingloriously the Council in which they had at first shown unusual courage. He insisted that the Pope should receive, absolutely and without modification, all the propositions as to the institution of bishops which he had forced on the assembly at Paris. They were to be applied to all the sees in his Empire. At first he contended that they should be applied to the See of Rome, as well as all others. This was too much. Even his own creatures among the bishops complained that the faithful would not hear of it, and his ministers supported their objection. Napoleon, therefore, found out that Rome was not included in the decree; but he still required that the Pope should receive it 'pure and simple,' and that it should include all places which he either had added or might add to his Empire. It is a remarkable proof of the utterly unlimited extent of his voracity for annexation, that he expressly says, the decree includes 'whatever he may hereafter annex on the side of Spain'; showing that his brother Joseph, the puppet King of Spain, whom he had set up, was already destined to be removed in due time, and his kingdom annexed to the Empire, as that of Louis Bonaparte in Holland had already been. When all instructions had been given, the Cardinals, the Pope's faithful advisers, and the prelates, who came to treat with him nominally on behalf of the Council, set off almost at the same moment; but by different routes, lest Pius VII. should see that their plans had been arranged together.

The Holy Father had been again in absolute solitude since the bishops had left Savona on May 20. 'One hopes,' says the author (though nothing shows it) 'that his common books of devotion, paper, pens and ink, and the "Office of the B. Virgin," which had been seized, had been restored to him. But certainly none of his old servants had been allowed to return to him.' All access to him was watched as closely as ever. All the Italians who had left Rome with him were scattered, some in the State prison of Fenestrella, some in other imperial fortresses. Dr. Porta alone was left to him, not without good cause, as his daily visits were more serviceable to the clever Prefect of Montenotte than to the Pontiff himself. M. de Chabrol, exactly informed of the state of health and disposition of his prisoner, was the only person who came from time to time to interrupt the melancholy monotony of his existence by bringing him such news from Paris as he thought it expedient he should hear. His chief subject was to enlarge on anything which had fallen from the Emperor.

M. de Chabrol could hardly think the Pope in his right mind, because when he exhorted him to secure the triumph of the Church by uniting himself to Napoleon, the Pope suggested that possibly 'constraint and persecution might be advantageous to the Church. There might be fewer Christians, perhaps, but better, and more zealous.' 'I left the Pope,' he said, 'amazed to see the class of facts and ideas in which he seeks examples for his conduct and support for his views. I assure you, however, it is the exact truth.' Meanwhile his reports, especially of what he learns through Dr. Porta, are sent in continually. On the 29th of August arrived the Cardinal de Bayane and M. Bertalozzi; a few days later the other cardinals. The absolute prohibition of all news except what M. de Chabrol had found it convenient to communicate (the quantity of which was less remarkable than its falsehood) made him wholly dependent on them for all knowledge of what had really taken place in the Council at Paris. They had offered themselves as his advisers. Certainly their first duty as honest men, not to say as members of the Sacred College solemnly sworn as the Pope's counsellors, was to undeceive him as to the false accounts given by Napoleon and his agents with regard to the opinions entertained by the Catholic bishops, clergy, and laity. But unhappily they had made engagements to Napoleon inconsistent with the honest discharge of their duties to the Holy Father. They left him under the impression that the Council had been wholly favourable to Napoleon's demands; communicating only the votes ultimately passed, but wholly concealing the opposition made to the Emperor's demands — the demand for the liberty of the Holy Father—the vote carried that the Council was not competent to settle the question of episcopal institution—the arrest of the three bishops who were actually in the dungeons of Vincennes—and, lastly, the means by which the votes which they communicated had been obtained. This great breach of honour and fidelity was but a sample of all their proceedings. There were at Savona two sets of ecclesiastics — the bishops sent ostensibly by the Council, really by Napoleon, and the Cardinals, with his old confessor, the Archbishop of Edessa, who had come to be his advisers. These two bodies really concerted together all that was to be said or done, while the Pope was made to believe that there was no communication between them. Nay, care was taken that his Council should talk over affairs with him one by one, in order that the impression might be produced on his mind, that the opinion and advice which each of them expressed to him was not concerted even by themselves in common, but was the spontaneous judgment of each one of them, arrived at separately as his judgment upon the questions which the Holy Father put to him. M. de Chabrol wrote to the minister, after the two first had arrived, 'The opinion of two men worthy of confidence could not be insignificant, given, as it was, at once, and when they were still isolated, so that their advice could not be attributed to any preconcerted deliberation, but must have its full moral weight.' No man, surely, who reads these proceedings, can restrain his indignation, when he remembers that every word spoken by the Pope's advisers had been settled beforehand with his oppressor. The Archbishop of Tours writes in the same way to the minister, how important it is that they should each have private conversations with the Holy Father, instead of going to him together. With the same object, the Cardinals were most careful to have no communication with the bishops sent by Napoleon; they privately communicated the state of his mind and purposes to his gaoler, by whom all they said was repeated to the bishops.

Before long it appeared that the Pope had not been merely alleging a fallacious excuse, when he said that he could not meet the Emperor's wishes unless he had the presence and advice of his natural counsellors, and that if they were restored to him a settlement might perhaps be made. We have seen that M. de Chabrol expected important effects from the presence of the cardinals, and the result confirmed his expectations. It seems as if Pius VII. had before been really uncertain in his own mind whether or not he could, without betraying his trust, concede what Napoleon demanded with regard to the institution of bishops; and felt that if he could it was evidently important to do so, in order to obtain peace for the Church. But the change was so momentous that, when he thought of conceding it by his own unaided judgment and in entire ignorance how the matter would be viewed by other men of learning, sanctity, and high office in the Church, his conscience refused to take on it such a burden, and he could not make up his mind to the responsibility. This responsibility he no longer felt when he was acting, not merely on the advice of the cardinals and of his old confessor, the Archbishop of Edessa, but on what they assured him was the deliberate judgment, not only of all the bishops of France and Italy assembled at Paris, but of all good and sober-minded Catholics, both clerical and lay, throughout the civilised world. The fraud, concerted by Napoleon and carried out by these cardinals, produced its full effect. The result was, that before the cardinals had been a month at Savona, he drew up a Brief addressed to the archbishops and bishops assembled at Paris, in which he recited and confirmed the resolutions which had been passed on the 7th of August; thus conceding the whole of Napoleon's demands about the institution of bishops. The French bishops asked for some changes, chiefly verbal, in the drawing up of the Brief, and to most of these the Pope consented. M. de Chabrol then begged him to write to the Emperor. To this he willingly assented, and wrote, with his own hand, a letter of most fatherly kindness. Nothing could exceed the satisfaction and joy both of the cardinals and the bishops. M. de Chabrol felt quite as much. That Napoleon, a man who well knew his own mind, and who had obtained all that he had demanded, should be otherwise than satisfied, never occurred to any of them. The bishops asked Cardinal Fesch to obtain for them, as the reward of their own services, the restoration of the Pope to liberty; nor did they doubt that they should obtain it. The Pope himself considered the change completed, and although he felt it to be momentous, evidently hoped for the best. In fact, if the Brief had been accepted by Napoleon, as no one doubted it would, and put into immediate operation, it is difficult to imagine that the new system introduced by it would ever have been abolished except by the express command of Pius VII. or one of his successors : for even when the time of Napoleon's fall arrived, those who came in his place would hardly have ventured, whatever might have been their individual wishes, to deprive the civil government of the immense accession of powers he had obtained for it.

But the good Providence of God, once more taking as its instrument the evil passions of the oppressor himself, averted from the Church this danger. Napoleon had, somewhat suddenly, become unwilling to make up his quarrel with the Church, even upon the terms which he had himself dictated. He was on the eve of the Russian war. That he must be victorious in it was a matter of course; and when the time came that he should return to Paris, after conceding peace on his own terms at Moscow or St. Petersburg, what was there to hinder him from making himself far more absolutely master of the Church than he would be, if he now carried out on his side the terms which he had proposed, and which Pius VII. had accepted?

x

He was no longer content that the Pope should reside, as he had himself proposed, either at Rome or at Avignon, in a sort of quasi-independence. He had made up his mind that for the future the Head of the Catholic Church should reside in Paris, and be as completely a tool in his hands as the Russian prelates already were in those of the Czar. He delighted to feel, that he should thus make himself really master of the consciences as well as the bodies and properties of all Catholics, not merely on the European Continent (which he regarded as already his own), but of the millions in Great Britain and Ireland, in America, in Asia, and throughout the world. The first fruits he would reap, by employing the whole authority of the Church against the English and Spanish opponents of his brother Joseph, and against the English in Sicily and Naples. But what might be the future uses for which he might employ such a vassal, who could say? And against hopes like these what was there to set on the other side? —merely the welfare of the Church, the glory of God, the souls of men, and his own honour and good faith. Such things were of course less than dust in the balance. Accordingly he resolved, on some pretext or other, to pick a new quarrel with the Pope, to retain him in captivity, and leave matters unsettled until his triumphant return from Russia, when he would take the settlement of them into his own hands. His first ground of quarrel was, that the Bulls for the institution of those whom he called 'his bishops' had not arrived, although the Pope in the terms of his Brief had engaged to send them. In fact there was a little delay; but M. de Chabrol explained how it arose, by pointing out that all the secretaries and other officials accustomed to draw up such documents had been separated from the Pope, and that the Bulls were being prepared as speedily as was possible under the circumstances. But the wolf had no difficulty in finding a new ground of quarrel with the lamb. The next was about the application of the terms of the Brief to the episcopal sees immediately about Rome. They had always been in the immediate nomination of the Holy Father. The Emperor, having seized the temporal dominions of the Holy See, had taken this nomination to himself. Now it had been well understood, and expressly agreed to by Napoleon himself, that Pius VII. should not be required in any way to sanction the annexation of the States of the Church to the Empire. The Pope had declared that to himself personally nothing could be more grateful, but that he felt precluded from giving any sanction to it, by the oath which he had taken on his election to the Holy See. The matter therefore had been arranged, by adopting in the Brief such general terms as provided for the nomination by the Emperor to the episcopal sees in all districts annexed to the Empire, without mention of the States of the Church in particular. Thus Napoleon practically secured his object, as he was in actual possession; but Pius did no act recognising his possession. The Emperor therefore now demanded that it should be expressly stated that the settlement applied to all the Sees of the Empire, 'of which the Roman States form a part.' This was selected as a ground of quarrel, because it was well understood that it was the one thing to which Pius could not in conscience agree; and Napoleon's present object was to demand something, which he would be, however reluctantly, obliged to refuse. A little later he objected to the terms of the Brief, because it provided that a metropolitan, if he gave institution to a bishopric, should do it 'by the Pope's authority,' and because it spoke of the Roman Church as the 'Mother of all Churches.' In a word, if the Holy Father was willing at once to enter voluntarily into the condition of entire vassalage which he designed for him, things might be so arranged at once, and he might be left during the Emperor's absence as the most dignified of his slaves; if not, (and Napoleon neither expected nor altogether wished it) then the matter must stand over, until he could finally arrange it himself after his great Russian triumph. Anyhow it must be done by himself, and himself alone; for he had, not without good grounds, the most absolute confidence in the ascendancy which he always gained over every man with whom he came into personal contact, and he felt the matter to be both too difficult and too important to be trusted to any subordinate agent.

With these views the Emperor, as much to the disappointment and astonishment of the able Prefect of Montenotte as of the cardinals and bishops, professed to be wholly dissatisfied with the Brief. The Pope's private and conciliatory letter he refused to answer. When he received it he was at Flushing, on a journey through the northern provinces of his empire, undertaken to prepare matters for the Russian campaign. He wrote instructions to his Minister *des Cultes* at Paris to keep the Brief absolutely secret, not allowing anyone to know that it had been sent; immediately to break up the Council, and send every one of the bishops out of Paris, not allowing any exception to this except in the case of those who were members of his 'Commission.' As for the Pope, the bishops and cardinals already at Savona were to announce to him the demands of the Emperor. Grievously as they were disappointed at the manner in which their past services had been received, they obeyed. They had an audience on December 13th, but found the Pope inflexible. He was specially displeased with the cardinals. They had come to him professing to act as his own advisers; they had suggested the concessions which he could possibly make, and he had followed their advice; and now in a moment, because it so pleased the tyrant, they came to demand from him further concessions, which they had not only not asked before, but had (either explicitly or implicitly) declared he could not make. They were therefore self-convicted of playing false with him. M. de Chabrol he hardly blamed; he was avowedly the agent of Napoleon. That agent wrote that further concession was, at present, not to be hoped for. 'The Pope has refused it in terms which showed that his resolution was fixed; indeed it was founded upon what the Holy Father termed " an inspiration in his prayers."' He had found that he had been betrayed by his counsellors, and had resolved to act on his own judgment. The most indecent threats, both from the bishops and even more from the Prefect, produced no effect on him. He was calm as ever, but quite unmoved. He resolved, however, to write again to Napoleon himself, and M. D'Haussonville gives his letter. It was in his usual spirit of gentleness; it ended—

'We have most seriously reflected, and God knows how much meditation and anxiety this matter has cost us. We are in the greatest distress of mind, and cannot refrain from once more representing to your Majesty that it is essential to us to have a greater number of counsellors, and especially free communication with the faithful. When once we are in this situation we assure your Majesty that, with aid from Heaven, we will do, in order to satisfy you, everything that can possibly be made compatible with our Apostolic Ministry. We live in the confidence that by His help who is the supreme disposer of good things in this world, we shall then be able to arrange everything to our mutual satisfaction. Whatever tends to the spiritual advantage of the Church will at the same time restore tranquillity to our own mind ; a tranquillity the more necessary to us because our advanced age brings every day more forcibly before our mind the strict account which we are on the point of giving to God of our own awful duties. With overflowing heart we pray the Lord to pour out upon your Majesty the abundance of His benedictions.'

What answer could Napoleon give to this touching supplication of the Holy Father? He dictated it himself to his Minister *des Cultes*. Reproaches, recriminations, threats—this was all that the Emperor returned to Pius VII. for his advances and his benedictions. (Vol. v. p. 127.)

This insulting answer fills more than four pages of the volume before me. It is hardly possible to give any idea of it by extracts. What Pius VII. seems to have felt most when it was read to him by M. de Chabrol (for the cardinals and bishops to whom it was addressed in the name of the minister, though dictated by Napoleon himself, had left Savona before it arrived) was—first, that it accused him of 'hoping to excite public troubles;' then that it called on him to resign his office, if he was so ignorant as not to know what every seminarist knows. On hearing the first of these propositions, he protested, 'Never.' When the letter was read, 'He listened with profound emotion. I saw him so much overcome and agitated that his hand trembled greatly.' When M. de Chabrol pressed the advice, he said that, 'Come what might, he would never resign.' What seemed most queer to M. de Chabrol he shall tell in his own words :—' He is always fortifying himself with the idea that God will interfere in the decision of his affairs.' M. de Chabrol was by no means the first, and I fear he will not be the last, who thinks that he cannot more strongly describe the infatuation of his victim, than by saying, 'He trusted in God that He would deliver him. Let Him now deliver him if He will have him.'

The mere rudeness and impertinence of Napoleon's language does not seem to have affected the Holy Father; as for instance, 'His Majesty pities the ignorance of the Pope, and feels compassion when he sees a Pontiff who might have discharged so grand and glorious a part become the calamity of the Church;' 'His Majesty is better acquainted with these [ecclesiastical] matters than the Pope, and too well, ever to be turned aside from the course he has marked out for himself;' and much more of the same kind.

Negotiation was now at an end. Napoleon gave express orders that the imprisonment of the Holy Father should be made as severe as ever; i.e., that no person should on any ground have access to him; that he should be deprived of all books, pen, ink, paper, &c. And M. de Chabrol announces that the order was fulfilled. He gave positive orders that the very existence of the Pope's Brief, and also the fact that he had sent the Bulls for the institution of Napoleon's bishops, should be kept an inviolable secret. And thus it happened that those bishops never were canonically instituted into their sees, although there was no longer any reason why they might not have been so. Thus Cardinal Maury never really was Archbishop of Paris, or Mgr. de Pradt Archbishop of Mechlin; and the result was that at the fall of the Empire they lost their possession of those sees.

All this part of the history has been till now entirely unpublished. The only authorities for it are to be found in the secret correspondence and reports of Napoleon, his ministers, and his agents, and these have hitherto been strictly concealed. Not one of the important letters given by M. D'Haussonville has been admitted into the official publication of the 'Correspondence of Napoleon I.,' and, he adds, nothing can be more curious than the absolute contradiction which is to be seen throughout, in the manifestoes, letters, &c. of Napoleon intended for the public, and those which he designed only for his ministers. He is perhaps the only man in history who was invariably, universally, and deliberately false in all his statements and dealings with others, and who yet retained such clear perspicuity of mind as never in any instance to allow himself to be the dupe even of one of his own most favourite lies. At this very time, for instance, his boast both to the Pope and to the world at large was that the clergy of his Empire were to a man with him and against the Holy Father. His private correspondence proves that he never for one moment allowed himself to be deluded upon this subject; he well understood and ever remembered that, whenever he had to do with a Catholic, he had to do with one who regarded him only as the early Christians regarded Nero and Domitian. He could never take precautions enough against them. This was his reason for chasing every bishop from Paris. At this time he writes to his minister to remove the Sulpicians from every seminary in France; to allow the immunity from military service, which had been given to the Seminarists, to be extended only to the dioceses of those bishops who had given him complete satisfaction. He at once excepted the dioceses of Saint Brieux, Ghent, Tournai, Troyes, and the Maritime Alps (the last was held by Mgr. Miollis, the original of the bishop whose portrait is drawn in 'Les Misérables'), and adds, 'report to me which dioceses it will be well to strike with this interdiction. But this manner of acting must be kept most secret.' Then he wrote to break up all houses of Sisters of Charity, who adhered to their rule by continuing to obey their superiors whom he had displaced. He was by no means insensible to their services to his sick and wounded soldiers; but he felt that the better Catholic anyone was, the more sure it was that the influence of that person would be thrown into the scale against his plans.

Napoleon set out for Russia. He stopped some days at Dresden, where he was surrounded by the princes of Germany. Some years before he had declared that he was compelled by his 'conscience' to interfere with the Pope because he was suzerain of Germany. He was now really exhibiting himself in that capacity. He was attended by the Emperor and Empress of Austria, by the Kings of Saxony, Bavaria, Wurtemburg, and by almost countless princes and nobles; the unfortunate and oppressed King of Prussia following him more like a captive than an ally. There, on the same day, he wrote two letters on ecclesiastical subjects; the one ordered new severities against the Sisters of Charity, the other ordered the removal of the Pope from Savona to Fontainebleau. No person was too humble, none too high, for his ever-wakeful wrath.

He laid down every detail of the Pope's journey. He was to be dressed as a simple priest, to pass through Turin, Chambéry, and Lyons by night. His companions were to be Dr. Porta and the Archbishop of Edessa, sent for on purpose. The real reason for this last measure seems to have been that he would have his prisoner within his own reach on his triumphant return home, as he had resolved to take the matter into his own hands. Characteristically he invented a false one in writing to his brother-in-law, Prince Borghese, to whom he gave his orders. The Pope nearly died on his journey; and a surgeon was sent for while he lay at the Hospital of Mont Cenis, and told, 'You will see a sick man, for whose relief you are to do all you can. I do not say who he is. You will no doubt recognise him; but if you make it known, farewell to your liberty, perhaps to your life.' Such was the liberty of private subjects under the First Empire.

At Fontainebleau the Pope was intended to have lived in state, and the Emperor's plans for him were in some degree allowed to appear; for the Archbishop's palace at Paris was gorgeously furnished for his use and received a new name—'The Papal Palace, formerly archiepiscopal.' He, however, declined everything of the kind. The carriages and horses provided for him he would not use, nor celebrate Mass pontifically, or even walk in the public gardens. He said he was still a prisoner. He had, however, the use of books, and the company of some ecclesiastics. Months passed rapidly away; and Napoleon returned, not in triumph, but as a fugitive. Not a year ago he had refused to answer the most touching letters from the Holy Father, and had sent in return only one loaded with insults, written nominally by his minister. On January 1st, 1813, he volunteered a letter, for which, as monarchs seldom write such productions, it is difficult to find a royal name. It was what schoolboys would call 'sneaking'; assuring the Holy Father of his distress last summer when he had heard that he was unwell, and that in spite of all that had happened, his own affection to the person of the Holy Father had never varied, and that he 'prayed God that he might have the glory of settling the government of the Church, and might long enjoy and profit by his work.'

This was followed by negotiations. But Napoleon treated the Pope as he did the allied powers; his demands were as large as they had been even in the hour of his proudest success. The

Bishop of Nantes and all the actors on the scene at Savona were now collected in the palace of Fontainebleau, and the Bishop had his instructions from Napoleon.

The Pope and his successors shall swear before their coronation not to do or order anything contrary to the four propositions of the Gallican clergy. The Pope and his successors shall in future have the right to nominate only one-third of the Sacred College, the other two-thirds shall be nominated by the Catholic sovereigns. The Pope shall disapprove and condemn by a solemn Brief the conduct of those cardinals who were not present at the ceremony of the religious marriage of the Emperor; who, however, will restore to them his good graces, on condition of their consenting to sign the said Brief. Cardinals Pietro and Pacca are excepted from this amnesty, and they are never to be allowed to return to the Holy Father. (Vol. v. p. 216.)

Then the Pope was to reside at Paris, and to receive 80,000*l.* sterling annually out of his alienated dominions. The institution of bishops, including those of the Roman States, was to be according to the decree of the Council. These terms were pressed upon him, as more moderate terms had been pressed at Savona. The result was the same. He said he could not act without counsellors, and the stress upon his mind already seriously affected his health. The Bishop of Nantes reported this to the minister. Two days later, January 18th, 1813, the night had set in, the Pope had taken his *siesta* and was sitting in conversation with the cardinals and bishops who resided in the palace, when the door suddenly opened, and the Emperor came in. The party hastened to leave the room; but ' Napoleon,' says Cardinal Pacca, ' ran towards the Pope, seized him in his arms, kissed him, and loaded him with demonstrations of affection.' No discussion took place till the next day. Several succeeding days were spent by the two *tête-à-tête*. What passed in these secret conferences has never been known. The accounts published under the Restoration were quite without foundation. The stories of personal violence to the Pope, M. D'Haussonville declares are 'false.'

Pius VII., whom his most intimate servants hesitated to question, and who was always loth to explain the particulars of this interview at Fontainebleau, always denied that any violence had taken place, but gave it to be understood that the 'Emperor had spoken to him, says Cardinal Pacca, with hauteur and contempt, and had even treated him as ignorant of ecclesiastical matters.' On the other hand, Napoleon, in the notes dictated at St. Helena, says absolutely nothing on the subject of the interviews at Fontainebleau. He contents himself with saying that he exercised more patience on this occasion than suited his situation or his character. For our part we have found nothing in any of the numerous documents we have examined to contradict the testimony, unfortunately contradictory, either of Pius VII. or of Napoleon. But if we know nothing of the details of the conferences of Fontainebleau, their result at least is certain. At first sight of the text of the new Concordat it appears that the Emperor did not hesitate to withdraw much of his original pretensions. All the clauses which, according to the Bishop of Nantes, had at first sight so greatly shocked the Holy Father, were totally left out. It contains nothing about the four propositions of the Gallican Church, nor of the interference of the Catholic powers in the composition of the Sacred College. Residence at Paris is not distinctly imposed upon the Holy Father; it is only implied in vague terms that he will fix himself in France or in the kingdom of Italy, (Avignon seems to have been the city preferred by Pius VII.). The Emperor no longer demanded that the 'Cardinals in black' should be censured, nor does he impose upon the Sovereign Pontiff the obligation of banishing from his presence for ever Cardinals de Pietro and Pacca. Moreover, if he maintains the fatal limit of six months for the canonical institution of bishops, he makes in return certain concessions, upon which the Pope set great value, and which he had ruthlessly refused at Savona. The six bishoprics suburban to Rome were re-established and restored to the nomination of the Holy Father. Moreover he was to have the right of nominating to ten bishoprics to be hereafter named, either in France or in Italy. With regard to the bishops of the Roman States absent, owing to circumstances, from their dioceses, the Pope might name them to sees *in partibus* until they were replaced in vacant sees either in the Empire or the kingdom of Italy. Finally, His Majesty engaged to restore to his favour the cardinals, bishops, priests, and laymen, who had incurred his displeasure during the last few years.

These clauses, some more favourable to the Church than those which had been presented to him at Savona, others especially favourable to the persons who had most warmly embraced his cause, no doubt influenced Pius VII. in his assent. It is known that he insisted on its being stated in the preamble to the Concordat that the articles composing it 'were to serve as the basis of a definitive settlement.' He insisted no less stoutly on laying down in the last article, that he 'had been led to this arrangement in consideration of the actual state of the Church and in the confidence with which His Majesty had inspired him, that he would give his powerful protection to many things so necessary to religion.' (Vol. v. p. 227.)

The same evening Napoleon dictated to the Bishop of Nantes a letter, addressed to the Pope, declaring that he did not consider the articles of the Concordat as implying any surrender on the Pope's part of the States of the Church. I cannot doubt, although the author does not so view it, that this letter had been demanded by the Pope, and was virtually part of the Concordat.

My readers cannot fail to observe that at this point of the history the novelty of M. D'Haussonville's narrative fails us. The reason is plain. As to all that went on at Savona, his history is founded on the original documents, the written orders given by the master to his agents, and their reports to him of their proceedings. From the moment at which Napoleon begins to act himself, these documents of course fail; for of the two who discussed the Concordat of Fontainebleau, neither owned any master on earth whose orders he could receive, or to whom he could report his fulfilment of them; and hence it is that the details of those interviews can never be known until that day when the Master in Heaven shall reveal the secrets of all hearts. I have thought it necessary to enlarge on the facts which were first made known by the author; but the narrative which follows, deeply interesting as it is, I am induced by want of space to cut short, especially as it is chiefly founded on the well-known memoirs of Cardinal Pacca. It must be remarked, that before Napoleon came personally on the scene, the Bishop of Nantes had already reported to the minister that the Pope was in a state of bodily health in which 'he could not bear any discussion.' When in that state he had been kept five long days in perpetual discussion with the terrible monarch of the European world. The result naturally was, that before the Concordat was signed, his whole strength, both of body and mind, had totally broken down. He was again in the state of total prostration to which he had before been reduced at Savona. When the paper was ready for signature, the cardinals resident in the palace, and the Empress Maria Louisa were admitted. The Pope, utterly broken down, hesitated at the last moment; and looked to the cardinals. It is believed that a look from one of them would have decided him to refuse, but he saw none; and the cardinal nearest to him 'inclined his head as if in assent.' Then Pius VII. put his signature to the paper.

Napoleon, (no doubt anxious to prevent his retracting) gave orders that the Concordat should immediately be carried out; and then laid it before the Senate, contrary to agreement, as what had been drawn up was not a Concordat, but only preliminary articles. He also at once ordered the singing of a *Te Deum* throughout France for the restoration of peace between the Church and the Empire. The imprisoned and banished cardinals returned from their several dungeons or places of exile, and found the Holy Father in a state which made them fear for his life. The moment Cardinal Pacca congratulated him upon the courage with which he had borne so long a captivity, he answered, 'Alas, at the end of it we have fallen into the mud.'

Deeply interesting as is the narrative of the discussions which led to the solemn retractation of the Concordat and the precautions which were necessarily taken to keep what was going on from the knowledge of Napoleon's spies, I must refer my readers for all this to M. D'Haussonville. These difficulties long delayed the sending of the touching and beautiful letter to the Emperor, in which the Pope declared, with expressions of hearty sorrow and humility, that he had done wrong, and that his conscience would not allow him to abide by some of the articles of the paper signed on January 25th as a basis of a definitive agreement; expressing also his sorrow and surprise, that it had been published contrary to agreement. It was characteristic of Napoleon, that after an outbreak of rage he sent this letter to his Minister *des Cultes* with orders to keep it strictly private, 'in order that he might be free hereafter to declare that he had, or that he had not received it, as might be most expedient.'

My space will not allow me to follow the changes of Napoleon's conduct towards the Holy Father, as the changing fortunes of the campaign of 1813 made him less or more reasonable. M. D'Haussonville throws much light upon it, from the letters addressed by him to his Minister *des Cultes*. At one time, while renewing his orders that the protest of the Pope against the Concordat should be kept a profound secret, he directs the minister to order the archbishops and bishops before returning to their dioceses, to visit the Pope and deliver to him, as from themselves, an address, which the Emperor was so good as to write for them, and which speaks of the Concordat of Fontainebleau as 'an inspiration of the Holy Spirit,' and expresses regret that he delays to put it in execution. There could hardly be a greater sign that men felt Napoleon's power was departing, than the fact that this letter seems never to have been obeyed. Then he orders that the Pope should not be allowed to see anyone but the cardinals, and that Cardinal di Pietro should be again arrested and banished to some remote town. Then he fills up by his own authority the vacant sees, and orders measures of persecution against the Seminarists and others who refuse to recognise his new bishops. His minister writes a letter to the bishops to ask prayers for France, now invaded, but Napoleon suppresses it, feeling that the French clergy could not but feel the triumph of the invaders as their deliverance. His too faithful tool, the Bishop of Nantes, dies suddenly, and has only time to write to entreat him to restore the Pope to liberty. The allies come on, and Murat, his puppet King of Naples, turns against him and tries to seize the States of the Church for himself. Then Napoleon proposes a peace with the Pope, and the restoration of all his dominions. At last Fontainebleau became no longer safe, and the august prisoner was once more sent away for security, under the custody of M. Lagorse, who had long been his gaoler (under M. de Chabrol) at Savona, by a circuitous route, once more to that place. His journey was, as before, a triumphant progress wherever he passed. Italy was now in the hands of Napoleon's enemies, and both parties agreed to the restoration of the Pope. Napoleon wrote, on March 10th, 1814, to order that he should be escorted by Asti, Placentia, and Parma, and given up to the advanced posts of the allies under the command of General Count Nugent. Pius VII., before leaving Savona, gratified the long-disappointed desire of the people by celebrating Mass in their cathedral church, on the feast of Notre Dame de Délivrance, March 19. He stayed a few days on his way at his native town, Cezena, and was restored to Rome amid the rapturous thanksgivings of his people, March 24th, 1814.

The author concludes by contrasting the false and malignant mention made of Pius VII., in the notes dictated by Napoleon at St. Helena, with the noble and generous disposition with which Pius interceded for him with the British Government when it was reported that his exile was affecting his health.

I had hoped to make some remarks on the lessons of this remarkable history, and their bearing especially on our own day, but my space does not admit it, nor is it necessary. One consideration, which will surely force itself upon every reader, is that the spiritual interests of the Church were always in extreme danger from the very day on which the exercise of temporal sovereignty was wrested from Pius VII.

LONDON: PRINTED BY
SPOTTISWOODE AND CO., NEW-STREET SQUARE
AND PARLIAMENT STREET

www.ingramcontent.com/pod-product-compliance
Lightning Source LLC
Chambersburg PA
CBHW030743230426
43667CB00007B/829